T0330351

Face Value

Face Value

The Entwined Histories of
Money and Race in America

MICHAEL O'MALLEY

THE UNIVERSITY OF CHICAGO PRESS   CHICAGO AND LONDON

MICHAEL O'MALLEY is associate professor of history at George Mason University. He is the author of *Keeping Watch: A History of American Time* and coeditor of *The Cultural Turn in US History.*

The University of Chicago Press, Chicago 60637
The University of Chicago Press, Ltd., London
© 2012 by The University of Chicago
All rights reserved. Published 2012.
Printed in the United States of America

21 20 19 18 17 16 15 14 13 12   1 2 3 4 5

ISBN-13: 978-0-226-62937-7 (cloth)
ISBN-10: 0-226-62937-6 (cloth)
ISBN-13: 978-0-226-62938-4 (paper)
ISBN-10: 0-226-62938-4 (paper)

Library of Congress Cataloging-in-Publication Data

O'Malley, Michael.
    Face value : the entwined histories of money and race in America / Michael O'Malley.
        p. cm.
    Includes bibliographical references and index.
    ISBN-13: 978-0-226-62937-7 (hardcover : alkaline paper)
    ISBN-10: 0-226-62937-6 (hardcover : alkaline paper)   1. African Americans—Public opinion—History.   2. Equality—Economic aspects—United States—History.
3. African Americans—Economic conditions.   4. Monetary policy—Social aspects—United States—History.   5. Money—United States—Psychological aspects—History.   6. Money—Social aspects—United States—History.   7. United States—Race relations—Economic aspects—History.   8. United States—Economic conditions.
9. Public opinion—United States—History.   I. Title.
    E185.044 2012
    332.4′97308996073—dc23

                                                                                        2011038982

♾ This paper meets the requirements of ANSI/NISO Z39.48-1992 (Permanence of Paper).

TO KATHLEEN

Contents

Acknowledgments

This book grew out of ideas I was first exposed to, many years ago, in undergraduate classes at Temple University with Miles Orvell and Carolyn Karcher. For comments on this work in progress I would like to thank Michael Bottoms, Robert Devens, Charles McGovern, Mark Meigs, Stephen Mihm, Adam Rothman, and Rosemarie Zagarri. Jim O'Brien did an extraordinary job indexing the book. Early versions of this book appeared in *The American Historical Review* and the online journal *Common-place*. Portions of chapter 3 appear in James Cook, Lawrence Glickman, and Michael O'Malley, eds., *The Cultural Turn in U.S. History: Past, Present, and Future*. I am especially grateful to the late Roy Rosenzweig, for a great deal more than I can fit in this small space.

Introduction

"The securities and coins of all nations should be held sacred. People should not seek to transform them into objects of curiosity." — U.S. Secret Service agent Andrew Drummond in 1886[1]

Agent Drummond took his job seriously indeed. In 1881 he began investigating the manufacture of toy money, the investigation culminating when he confiscated 160 boxes of play money from R.H. Macy's Department store. The Secret Service, founded during the Civil War largely to police the money supply, humorlessly suppressed any imitation of American money, however outlandish. They arrested men who printed laundry tickets or discount coupons that looked like money; they seized the molds of a confectioner who pressed chocolate bars in the form of a dollar and a Philadelphia baker who, in 1891, baked cookie dough into coins; in 1924 they nabbed a six-foot-long hooked rug in the form of a dollar bill and hurried it away to their vaults.[2] Clearly, no one thought a rug or dry goods circular or a cookie could "pass" as money. Secret Service men did their part to make money unremarkable and unthinkable. Thinking about money's nature leads to questions about the nature of value, and of profit. It seems much easier to agree with Secret Service agent Drummond, quoted above: people should not seek to transform money into an object of curiosity.

This book tries to do the opposite, and recapture money as a curiosity. It does so largely by closely analyzing the language people used when they talked about money: the metaphors and analogies and comparisons they used to try to make this puzzling subject sensible. For most of our history, both ordinary Americans and elites passionately, even violently, debated the nature and character of money. They painted it and drew it, sang songs about it, organized political parties around it: they printed their own when they thought it necessary and winked as they passed counterfeits. Nineteenth-century Americans sacrificed acres of trees to books, pamphlets, newspaper, and magazine articles on "the money question." They fought bitterly about banking, interest, commerce, and profit itself. We have a long history of more or less distinguished money theorists (or, if you like, "cranks") ranging from Benjamin Franklin through Andrew Jackson through William "Coin" Harvey to Ezra Pound. Why did the subject generate so much heat?

When they argued about the nature of money Americans also argued about the character of American society—its relative openness, its degree of opportunities, its democratic potential, and its commitment to equality. Historically, debates about money's character inevitably turned into arguments about the character of the nation and, on further examination, about the individual character of its citizens themselves. Was wealth and social position something substantial, something natural, or just luck? Could anyone succeed, or did success come only to the naturally gifted? In a society of men and women "on the make," how could you tell the genuine from the fake? Did the nation's wealth represent an intrinsic greatness, a difference from other nations, the "genius" of the Anglo-Saxon race? Or could any nation achieve the same thing?

The booming American marketplace encouraged what we often call "the American Dream": the idea that with hard work and vision "anyone can become anything they want," that no one need be confined by the circumstances of their birth. The dazzling possibility of freedom in "self-making" may be the single most attractive thing about American culture, and who among Americans today would not endorse the right to "self-making" as a sacred principle?[3] In the marketplace, theoretically least, we can all remodel ourselves, transform ourselves, shed the past and become someone new.

As a result, in the United States the social order has always been notably open to negotiation. Immigrants could Americanize, the poor become rich; the children of the plains could transform themselves into slick city dwellers; the urban family could recreate themselves in the pastoral suburbs. Ralph Lifschitz, second-generation immigrant, could transform himself into "Ralph Lauren," high-WASP fashion oracle.[4] The transformations continue today at the same giddy pace. The homely can cosmetically alter their bodies; we can even change our genders. The dream of freedom includes the capacity to rewrite ourselves with new characters, new identities. All we need is money.

But these fantastic possibilities are also frightening. Prices rose and dropped, markets boomed and collapsed and took thousands of people's savings with them. Any merchant might fail and wind up among the army of unemployed. An artisan could lose his job to mass production, the speculator see his empire fall. Ambition alone offered no guarantees of success—in practice, what really made the difference between the monied and trustworthy man of business and his failed competitors? Maybe nothing more than the next cycle of boom or bust. How could you tell laudable ambition from sleazy resume padding, entrepreneurial vision from hucksterism and fraud? The market's fantastic, terrifying possibilities made Americans hunger for verities, for stable facts, for standards of judgment that transcended market whims. In a society where everyone is on the way to being someone else, how can you ever know who anyone really is?

American individualism has combined, not always successfully, an idea of plasticity in character, freedom in self-making, with an idea of the individual as something fundamental and concrete, the solid building block of society. Does "individualism" mean the indissoluble rugged fixity of individual character, or does it mean the right to change? One is never more individualized than when in the grip of authority—fingerprints, DNA records, Social Security numbers, retinal scans—these things individualize in the most profound sense, by making us unique and identifiable. But these things are not what most us think of when we imagine "individualism." We tend to imagine individualism as freedom from authority or as nonconformity, as boundless choice. Americans experience individualism as both freedom to be whatever we like, and as a fixed, "natural," essential self.

We see this most clearly in the persistent bugaboo of race. In a society committed to the idea that anyone can be whatever he (or she, maybe) wants, "race" should be a repulsive idea, unthinkable. But for most of our history, while a white man could be whatever he wanted, no amount of "self-making" could make a black man equal. A society confronted with the boundlessness, the sheer fantastic range of possibilities market society endlessly offered, protected itself by elaborating theories of intrinsic, biological, and non-negotiable difference. The contrast repeats itself again and again in American history: genuine freedom of opportunity for some, unyielding and bitter denial for others. How is it, Samuel Johnson asked of the American Revolution he opposed, "that we hear the loudest yelps for liberty among the drivers of negroes?"[5]

This book argues that the freer American market society became, the more Americans demanded or established categories that resisted freedom, that resisted change and the market's power. The famous American paradox—the simultaneous claim to universal freedom and to the right to own slaves, to beautiful equal rights and to institutionalized, "natural" inequality, stems from the conflicting ways liberal, free market philosophy imagined individualism itself: as both endless negotiable potential and fixed natural value. The logic of racism is deeply rooted in the logic of the free market itself, in its contrast of the real and the false, the solid and the speculative, genuine and counterfeit. Americans imagined money in the same way: as both a thing with essential, "natural" value and as a thing of endless negotiability.

For two hundred years American debates over money took place between two basic camps. One camp insisted that money could only be something with "intrinsic value," like gold or maybe silver. Anything else was a fake and a fraud and a cheat. "Specie" money, based on gold or silver, could measure value because it *had* value; derived from nature, it produced "natural" values. The other camp argued that anything could serve as money if all agreed to use it—paper, for example—and that money was a mere symbol of labor. Reliance on gold or silver, they argued, amounted to a superstitious fetish and an artificial monopoly. "Hard money" partisans wanted an intrinsic or "essential" value to regulate speculation and growth, and imagined gold or silver's "natural" value as a check on *all* values, something above human tampering which would anchor economic cycles and make social hierarchies "real" as well. The "soft money" camp treated value as purely social, purely "conventional," and looked for ways to stimulate growth and engineer social equality by increasing or decreasing the amount of money available.

American debates about money follow the same basic lines as American thinking about individual character and individual potential. When they argued for gold, Americans tended to use the same terms and metaphors and strategies they used to argue for white supremacy. When they pushed for paper money, they usually rooted value and identity in society rather than in nature. In the United States, debates about money have always *also* been debates about the problem of racial difference in a free democratic society. What are the limits of racial difference? Is it fixed by nature, or is the meaning of racial difference negotiable?

This thesis depends on a simple assumption—that money is our primary sign of what the differences between things or between people *mean*, a shorthand way of assigning a value to difference. Imagine two virtually identical white cotton shirts, one selling for forty dollars and the other for twenty. Money gives a meaning, a "value," to the difference between them. Money is a sign of what the difference between the two shirts means. Spotted apples once cost less than smooth apples—their blemishes suggested dirt and pollution. Today, spotted apples might suggest freedom from chemicals, and with the right label they might cost more. The difference in price expresses, in a simple way, what we think that difference means. Faced with two nearly identical sedans, we look to the price to make some sense of the tiny difference between them, to give that difference meaning. Money elaborates the difference between skilled and unskilled workers, between men and women working the same jobs, between established citizens and new immigrants. It illuminates social hierarchy, social difference. Of course, money does many other things, fills many other functions, and we have many other ways of making sense of difference. A house with two bathrooms costs more than a house with one bathroom, because two bathrooms offer some added convenience. But money is a shorthand sign for what we think the difference between one and two bathrooms means.

But money only works as a sign of what difference means (and what sameness means as well) when it seems stable. Otherwise the system of making sense of difference trembles and falters.

We might consider this idea in terms of the relationship between "value," in the sense of "economic value," and "value" in the sense of moral value, the relationship between "price" and "value." If a sober, honest, hardworking person prospers, the relationship between economic and moral value seems good and just, but if "loose money" enables a scheming, shifty man on the make to also prosper, the relationship between price and value seems less secure. It is almost impossible to disentangle money from questions of moral value, because money symbolizes what we think differences of "value" in both senses mean. We make money a sign not just of economic value but of the meaning of individual and group character: of a person's social as well as financial worth.

Those who argued for paper money wanted to see both economic value and social worth as socially created things, derived from agreement rather than natural fact. They tended to see "equality" as an idea, an agreement society made with its members. By this logic, society could simply declare African Americans equal and it would be so. "Hard money" partisans yearned instead for a world in which there was no difference between value and price, between social worth and economic worth. Equality (or inequality) was a natural fact, not a social construct. In fantasizing about natural law in money, "goldbugs" also imagined "natural" moral and social hierarchies, a world in which money indicated differences in essential being.

It is that phenomenon this book will describe. Capitalism unleashed staggering transformative energies. Facing those transformations, Americans looked for stability in gold and silver, in "real money," but also in renewed ideas about essential character, about race or ethnicity. The more turbulent social life appeared, the more pressing the desire for certainty became. American society always stressed the possibility of self-transformation, of assuming new identities as they bought new clothes, but at the same time Americans have devoted enormous energies to pinning character down in genetic tags or psychiatric profiles or chemical signals, to lock men and women in the place supposedly assigned them "by nature." In the first version, identity is socially fluid, free-floating, and endlessly potential. In the other, identity is discrete, fixed, and indestructible. These are incompatible approaches to individualism, on the surface at least. But their interrelation, their tense duality, gives capitalism its energy as a pendulum drives a clock.

*   *   *

Face Value broadly surveys the history of American thinking about money, from the colonial period to the present. Not a history or analysis of monetary policy per se, the book examines the various ways people thought about money. It focuses on the problem of "race," but readers will see many places where the analysis might extend to the way gender is negotiated and essentialized. The book amounts to a critique of the ways the market both undermines essentialism and produces it.

Chapter 1 reviews the colonial Atlantic economy and the special conditions that affected the English colonies in North America. This chapter looks at how, in the origins of modern economics, the meaning of "specie" and "species" blurred. It compares paper money, which made value from nothing, with slavery, and argues that Americans were drawn to racial slavery partly because they lacked a stable referent or authority for value.

Chapter 2 extends that argument into the antebellum years, when the Treasury Department estimated that at times more than 40 percent of the money in circulation was counterfeit. In that environment, having rejected central banking, Americans "banked on slavery," and on the fantasy of a non-negotiable racial identity. Slaves served as the real and the psychic capital behind the antebellum economy: their commoditized racial difference enabled Americans to use an astonishingly chaotic variety of money forms. Chapter 2 suggests that had Americans established a central bank like the Bank of England, they might have abolished slavery as England did, by compensating slaveowners.

During the Civil War the United States abandoned slavery and gold in favor of "greenbacks," pure legal tender paper money. The Union also enlisted African Americans in the Army, where they served with distinction. The greenbacks financed an unpopular war, while African American soldiers helped the Union prevail. Political satirists routinely compared negro soldiers to inflated paper money: both lacked "natural" value. Chapter 3 explores the controversy over the greenbacks by looking at their appearance in minstrel shows and popular political rhetoric. It demonstrates how paper money became associated with racial equality and "inflated value," gold with natural superiority and economic "law."

Chapter 4 follows the money question into the Gilded Age. Starting with the problems and pleasures of mass production, it looks at the career of Emanuel Ninger, an immigrant counterfeiter, to explore symptoms of a "crisis in subjectivity." It charts how the language of economics, and the gold standard, moved away from "the negro" to settle on the backs of immigrants, who economists saw as members of "low-wage races." The triumph of the gold standard in 1896 marked the triumph of a white supremacist consensus, and a new emphasis on eugenic solutions to social problems.

The money question began to fade from political view with the establishment of the Federal Reserve System in 1913. The Federal Reserve took money out of the hands of politicians and made it "scientific," the domain of experts. Chapter 5 looks at the origins of the Fed, and then moves to discussing Roosevelt's gold policies, and particularly the establishment of Fort Knox, which FDR used to suggest the idea of a gold standard even as he moved away from gold as money. As the United

States left the gold standard it also began to erode the ferocious white supremacist consensus established at the end of the nineteenth century. Considering the civil rights movement, the chapter moves into the 1960s to speculate about the relationship between a managed, fiat currency and racial equality.

The Epilogue reviews some of the accounts of Wall Street in the 1980s, after the end of the international gold standard, and looks at the renewed enthusiasm, in the wake of Barack Obama's election to the presidency, for gold and the gold standard on the political right. It suggests that our unease with the promises of market freedom remains, and tends still to express itself in terms of "natural," racialized difference.

History tends to unsettle assumptions. It often reveals that attitudes and ideas we take for granted—about freedom, individualism, property, equality, childhood, sexuality; about public and private—simply did not exist in the past, or existed in very different forms, with very different meanings. "Freedom," for example, made perfect sense in a society where millions of people labored in legal unfreedom, as slaves or indentured servants: their lack of freedom dramatized and clarified the meaning of freedom itself, in the way that "black" clarifies the meaning of white. But without its opposite—legal, tangible unfreedom—"freedom" becomes a very different concept, harder to explain or quantify, subject to different arguments and meanings. By the mid-twentieth century, in most industrial nations, "money" had become standardized, regularized, and removed from popular discussion, rendered simply a "given": something desirable and ubiquitous, but unthought; a bottom line of meaning made all the more powerful for being unexamined. Historians tend to look back at economic debates and take money as an ahistorical fact, when in practice the idea of money was as hotly contested as the idea of freedom or the idea of equality, and with just as much or more at stake in the debate's outcome.

In terms of what historians usually call, somewhat euphemistically, "economic interest," histories of money typically pit those who want loose, easy credit and rapid speculative growth against those who want stable returns and secure values for that they already have. It complicates that history to realize that just about everyone involved always wants both things at the same time. It complicates the history of economic interest even further to confront the fact that the historical people shouting from each camp are not only simultaneously in the other camp, but also that they have no real sense of agreement about the nature of "money," the thing around which their supposed economic interest is founded and through which it is expressed. Indeed, it complicates to the point of incoherence the entire idea of people having some kind of static "economic interest" that they can rationally know at all beyond the very local and the very short term. The idea of economic interest as a cause in history, like the entire discipline of economics itself, works best if a set of formal assumptions are taken for granted: that is, if you listen to Agent Drummond, quoted above, and don't render money an object of curiosity. This book will try to unpack some of those assumptions and ideally restore some of the "curiosity" money lost when it became purely a tool.

This is a cultural history, and in that sense it emphasizes language, and linguistic affinities, over material cause. Many of the central moments in other histories of money, like Jackson's war with Biddle, the Panic of 1893, the election of 1896, receive scant notice. *Face Value* assumes that while we experience economic forces as real—real scarcities, real pressures—these forces are social constructs, manifestations of ideas. Water is scarce in northern Mexico because it is a desert, but also because the United States drains the Colorado river. The scarcity is real, but also a real product of social forces. Even the most brutal acts of nature, things like droughts, floods, or plagues, come to us as a system of ideas about meaning: "God's wrath," "global warming," the epidemiology of disease. We negotiate constantly over what these real material events mean.

In that sense, every financial market is also a marketplace of ideas: the things we buy are themselves both real things and also ideas about scarcity and abundance, about joy and pain, duty and pleasure; about what is pretty and what is ugly, what is good to eat and what is not. There is much to celebrate in the idea of a free market: its generative creativity, its capacity for renegotiation, the possibilities of freedom in self-transformation it offers, the ambiguities it makes available: the play of ideas and possibilities.[6] But this book grows from a deep revulsion about the way the idea of "the natural" is used to stop exchange and arrest the circulation of ideas; about the way Americans resort to "race" or biology or human nature when they want to close off possibility and keep someone else from experiencing the full potential of the American dream.

Face Value argues that American history and culture are to some extent distinct. Lacking a central regulating authority and a source of gold or silver, strongly inflected with individualism, Americans from their origins embraced financial innovation and led the world in financial experiments. But the promise of self-transformation also made them uneasy, and they turned for refuge to theories of intrinsic value or intrinsic racial difference. Our emphasis on market freedom paradoxically produced its opposite.

This is not a strict cause-and-effect argument: it does not argue that economics causes racism or racism caused the gold standard. Rather, it argues that American ideas about money and about race both stem from our ambivalence about free exchange itself. This puts *Face Value* probably most squarely and humbly in what might be called the "ironist" tradition of de Tocqueville, Twain, Mencken, Richard Hofstadter, or even Michel Foucault; it is an argument about ironic and unexpected outcomes. Free market ideologues insist that unregulated markets will erase racism: *Face Value* points out that in the United States market freedom has always given rise to its opposite, fantasies of intrinsic or natural value. A century ago ordinary Americans felt entitled to discuss the question of money. *Face Value* seeks to bring that subject back into the national conversation.

CHAPTER ONE

This New Black Flesh Coin

I was brought on board by one Robertson Mumford, steward of said vessel, for four gallons of rum, and a piece of calico, and called VENTURE, on account of his having purchased me with his own private venture. Thus I came by my name.[1]

Circumstances forced Colonial Americans to rethink money. Trained to regard money as gold or silver, something with a fixed, natural value, they responded to the lack of gold or silver in North America by inventing new forms of money. These new forms depended on social agreement, not natural value: they emphasized the infinite potential of labor rather than the finite stock of material goods, and so paper money upset the idea of "natural" class distinctions. In these same years, Americans adopted racial slavery, a system based on the idea of natural, intrinsic difference but at the same time deeply enmeshed in market exchange and negotiation. Like the idea of gold's intrinsic value, the supposedly non-negotiable racial difference of Africans stabilized value in exchange: as the idea of intrinsic class difference declined, Americans built a financial system in which racial value anchored monetary value. Americans resorted to racial slavery partly because they lacked a "natural" standard of value and character in commerce.

*　*　*

Slave narratives often include a moment when the slave considers buying his or her own freedom. The moment always stands out as pivotal. Sometimes the slave rejects the possibility altogether, because buying oneself legitimizes slavery's principles. Sometimes the moment comes with relief, tempered by necessity; sometimes it comes with elaborate details of the negotiation.

This moment of potential sale dramatizes several interesting problems, most notably the fairly obvious point that if the slave can earn the value of his or her redemption, then the slave must have a value beyond that price—bringing the master cash for one's redemption only advertises one's continuing value as a slave. But if the slave can earn *more* than his or her purchase price, then the slave has no fixed value, which undermines the central premise of racial slavery, the black person's natural, fixed state of inferiority and lesser value. The slave at that moment is in effect worth more than he or she is worth, and in fact the moment of self-purchase implies that this would *always be so*: what if the master doubled the redemption price, and the slave met it? Of course the master must balance the utility of cash in hand against potential future value; the same considerations that would apply with, for example, houses or stocks or cows. Except cows do not come with cash in hand asking to buy themselves; nor are they keenly aware of the ironies of their situation.

Olaudah Equiano had a Quaker master, merchant Robert King, who had promised Equiano he could one day buy his own freedom. In 1766, after much hard work, Equiano took the forty pounds he had earned trading on the side and humbly asked King if he could redeem himself. This speech seemed to confound King, Equiano recalled; "he began to recoil: and my heart that instant sunk within me." His master asks, "Why, where did you get the money? Have you got forty pounds sterling?" "Yes, sir," Equiano answers, with justifiable pride, he had got the money by honest thriving industry. "On which my master replied, I got money much faster than he did; and said he would not have made me the promise he did if he had thought I should have got money so soon."

Confounding indeed—a slave who can so quickly earn his own purchase price is always already more valuable than the price itself; the very act of earning the purchase price demonstrates the price's inadequacy as a mark of value. Equiano's request raised a set of questions about the difference between the slave's value as a good, a commodity, versus the slave's potential to generate value beyond the selling price. The passage initiates what would later become a central part of antislavery debate, the comparative economic value of slave and free labor. Was he worth more as a slave or as a free man?

Equiano had wisely brought a friend with him, who points out to King that "[Olaudah] has earned you more than an hundred a-year, and he will still save you money, as he will not leave you—Come, Robert, take the money." The master relents, to Equiano's joy. In this account the promise of wage labor trumps the value of slave-owning; King will get the pounds sterling now and a promise of continued profits in the future. Equiano's narrative points quite deliberately to the logic of the "free market" and to the way wage labor will eventually replace slavery. It also shows two ways of understanding the self—the self as a fixed quality, an essential value, and the self as a bundle of endless future potential, literally "priceless."[2]

As a slave Equiano had a more or less fixed value, a price, and that price depended on and from his body—its strength and health but also fundamentally, in the slave market, on its blackness, its "race." But he also had the potential to earn more value than his price, a market potential limited only by his own energy and ambition, and in this light his race is irrelevant: indeed, his master sees clearly that Equiano is worth more—"gets money faster"—than King himself. Caught between boundless potential and fixed, essential value, between speculation and the bottom line, Equiano literally embodies both. This contradictory position is crucial to understanding the peculiar character of American racial slavery and its relation to the colonial economy.

* * *

Why slavery? Well before the American Revolution, Europeans could see the economic inefficiencies in slave labor. Widely attributed to Adam Smith, the notion that slaves worked less efficiently "was commonplace in eighteenth century Britain."[3] So "why would Europeans revive slavery [at a time] when the institution had disappeared from large parts of Europe?"[4] They had other forms of unfree labor to choose from—mostly indentured servitude and apprenticeship—which worked quite well. Cheaper than slaves, indentured men or women had some incentive to work hard knowing freedom lay at the end of the indenture term. Colonial North Americans eagerly extracted as much labor as they could from indentured servants, who they often treated quite badly. Up to the moment of the American Revolution, ads for runaway indentured servants filled the *Pennsylvania Gazette*.[5] Why resort to slavery? We do quite well today without it; indeed, the example from Equiano's narrative, quoted above, shows a clear awareness, in 1766, of wage labor's superiority to slavery as a money-making proposition.[6]

And why *racial* slavery? Colonial Americans were more than happy to treat indentured servants badly, as disposable inferiors, because they had entrenched traditions of class and rank to draw on. When advertising for runaway indentured servants in the *Pennsylvania Gazette*, owners often showed little interest in the difference between white and black, so long as they got their labor back. Why did they need the elaborate and creaky intellectual apparatus of race?

For though it worked and still works with pernicious efficiency, "race" was and is a hard idea to maintain. Common sense, in the form of people of mixed race, and in the form of slaves capable, like Equiano, of doing virtually any kind of work, kept pointing out the failures of racism's most basic premises; its boundaries, like sandbanks in a rising current, needed constant shoring up.[7] There was unfree labor available, in reasonably plentiful supply, without the idea of race. And there was work for wages, again with no need for "race" as a justification. Why bother with racial slavery if the whole point is just extracting labor from people?

Presentism obviously informs the question, because slavery went away: not entirely, of course, but the modern reader lives in a world where racial slavery is almost unimaginable. Teachers struggle every semester to help students understand a worldview that made racial slavery not just possible but ubiquitous, because nowhere in the world today is the permanent hereditary enslavement of millions of people ever contemplated. It is now unacceptable on moral grounds, *and* it simply does not pay as well as hiring wage hands. Why resort to it?

Historians have offered many possible answers to these questions. Slavery had existed for centuries—better to ask "why *not* slavery?" Slavery could make the master and his nation a great deal of money. Slavery reinforced a rank-ordered view of the world. Slavery was possibly cheaper than indenture in the long term; racially based, hereditary slavery allowed for increases in wealth in the same way raising cattle did. And as a bonus, racial slavery allowed the ruling class to divide the working class. These are all good answers, but they overlook some of the oddities of slaves as goods, as market objects and market actors.

Historians generally explain racial slavery in the U.S. either with economic arguments, in which slavery appears to have economic advantages to the ruling class, or with ideological arguments, in which a supposed predisposition to racism leads English people to treat Africans as less than human, even in the face of economic rationality.[8] I would like to propose another answer, an answer that combines the economic and the ideological.

Americans resorted to racial slavery, and resorted to it with particular enthusiasm, because racial slavery recapitulated the assumptions and tensions underlying free market exchange itself. The slave had a generative, speculative potential to make wealth, like money loaned on credit, like paper bills circulating on faith, but also a fixed character that could never be negotiated away or altered, like the value embodied in gold bars. Slaves literally embodied the contradictory desires at the heart of capitalism; they were like money, and like money they were founded in irrationality and paradox.

Racial slavery turned people into property by imagining a "bottom line" of identity, a place at which negotiation stopped. "Blackness" served as a non-negotiable difference, the thing that marked Africans as enslavable; it marked them as different, and different in a way set by nature and not subject to human reconsideration. But as a resolutely commercial enterprise slavery put the enslaved at the forefront of commercial negotiation—as objects for sale, as producers of value, and as targets of sexual opportunity and genetic exchange. Racial slavery was a product of capitalism, but not just of capitalism's desire for profit or its need for a tractable labor force. Racial slavery helped ease the transition from mercantilism, with its essentialized notions of wealth, to modern capitalism, with its more subjective, virtualized sense of wealth and value. Racial slavery re-presented the dilemmas and attractions of exchange itself, and particularly it re-presented the problem and potential of money.

In the spring of 1766, Olaudah Equiano journeyed to Charlestown, South Carolina, to earn the money he would use to buy his freedom. Robert King of Monserrat, his master, traded at sea; Equiano had brought sundry goods with him from Monserrat, hoping to find time to trade on his own. He found Charlestown "illuminated" by bonfires, ringing with the sound of weapons fire, cheering, and multiple "other demonstrations of joy shewn."[9] England had just repealed the hated Stamp Act.

The Stamp Act, passed in 1765, required that colonists pay a modest tax on a wide range of goods. Taxed goods would bear the Crown's "stamp." England hoped the tax would recover some of the high cost of quartering troops in North America, especially the costs associated with Indian war.

The measure outraged colonists for two main reasons. First, it marked an example of taxation without representation. Second, it continued a long history of England's attempts to hinder colonial commerce by controlling the money supply. The Crown required payment of "stamp" taxes in "specie," meaning gold or silver coin. Benjamin Franklin, then serving in England as agent for Pennsylvania, argued forcefully that the measure would bleed money from the colonies, bringing commerce to a halt and choking enterprise.[10] The violent opposition the act inspired startled English observers, but the colonial economy had always operated in strange ways.

*   *   *

Had the first colonists found gold in North America events might have turned out very differently. But all the gold lay buried far to the south and west, and so while the Spanish mined or stole mineral wealth from Central and South America, English colonists scratched around looking for ways to make money—literally. The original colonists, north and south, had energy and ambition. They just claimed to have no money to conduct commerce with.

Just as we could call nearly all the European settlers simply "Christian," by ignoring the often-violent differences between their different Christian beliefs, so in economic thinking we might generalize and call the English colonists "mercantilists." The word "mercantilism" could have many shades of meaning. It generally revolved around questions of international trade, and how one nation prospered and another failed. For our purposes we can concentrate on one general assumption: for mercantilists, real wealth was finite.[11]

"Wealth" consisted of tangible physical goods, especially land and precious metals. An industrious people could turn gold or other useful commodities into ships, then use the ships to get more gold or silver or other commodities, and thereby grow wealthier. But it cost real money to build ships, so financing the ships' construction depended ultimately on gold or silver, or on land that could produce other material assets, like timber or wheat, which artisans could turn into a ship or into goods traded for gold. The world contained only so much gold or silver, only so much fertile land; only so much "real wealth," according to mercantilism. The Stamp Act reflected this philosophy—it required colonists to pay taxes and other bills to the English government in specie, so that gold would flow from the colonies to London. Nations prospered, mercantilism argued, only by taking some of this finite material wealth from other nations or regions.

This might seem like simple common sense, but it gradually stopped making sense beginning sometime roughly in the eighteenth century, as the power of money and credit—capitalism—replaced mercantilist notions with new visions of wealth as something less tangible, something more like "standard of living." Who today believes in any natural limit to how rich a corporation can grow, for example? According to the most enthusiastic prophets of capitalism, the world can simply get richer and richer. Industry, making vast quantities of goods amazingly cheaply, complicated the idea of wealth. So did the elaboration of forms of credit complicate what "wealth" means. Today, when we think about it at all, we probably tend to think "wealth" consists more in the fantastic products of human ingenuity, like digital devices or mortgage bonds or private equity firms, than it does in acres of timber or national gold reserves. Acres of timber, or bars of gold, are still good to have, but they are not the only measure of "real" wealth, as they had seemed to Anglo-American traders in 1700; those men had a much more literal notion of "wealth."[12]

England hoped to prosper by getting gold from the New World—the world that had brought Olaudah Equiano, by a complex, tangled path, to Charlestown, South Carolina in 1766. Equiano's autobiography claims he was born in Benin around 1745, fell into African slavery and then, at age eleven, into the hands of English slave traders.[13] He spent most of his life as a sailor; his extraordinary narrative describes a world of constant international mobility, from England to the Caribbean to the North American coast to the Arctic Circle. The ships Equiano served on carried a variety of goods, including slaves, back and forth between England, Africa, the Caribbean islands, and North and South America. Even then, forms of speculative credit were challenging mercantilist orthodoxy. Equiano's narrative gives vivid details of the horrors of slavery and sharp accounts of his own spiritual struggles with Calvinist Christianity. The narrative also, to a surprising extent, describes his economic activity, in one of those classic Protestant accounts in which the author's spiritual and financial progress mingle unembarrassed. Equiano managed, though careful trading, to buy his own freedom and eventually become a wealthy man. Indeed, Equiano's story is largely a story of "free" trade and exchange, its limits and its advantages. He spent his adult life trying to negotiate what marketplace freedom might mean.

Equiano's life had an American context, the context of radical fiscal experiments, "loose" money," and "self-making," and a context rooted in English thinking about money and difference. Before turning to Equiano's life in more detail, we can take a look at the peculiar way trade, value, money, and the character of Africans figured in the writing of an influential economic popularizer, Daniel Defoe.

Defoe frequently wrote on economic topics, especially England's international trade. His bi-weekly *Review*, published in the 1710s, offered a middle-class audience explanations of the dazzling new world of international trade, critiques of international trade policy, and repeated accounts of the nature of money—what money was, if it needed an intrinsic value, or how it "reproduced itself" through credit. Defoe's language in the *Review* is especially intriguing, as he tries to come to terms with money, value, and difference.

Sometimes Defoe offered readers of his *Review* a straightforward, mercantilist explanation of money. In 1706, for example, he argued that money is "something whose value being always intrinsic, would be accepted everywhere."[14] Here he means gold or silver, something with a universally recognized material value, which makes it acceptable regardless of government or society. Gold or silver's value came from its physical properties in the same ways the value of wood came from *its* physical properties; for many mercantilists gold was simply valuable in the same way that it was yellow, valuable by its nature.

But when Defoe looked at England's trade with other nations he noticed that not all peoples valued gold the same way. In a later essay, part of a series on trade, he concluded that no, money need not have an intrinsic value. He wrote:

> nor is it always requisite that this something [money] should have an intrinsick value in itself; we find the money of some countries to be made of the most contemptible trifles . . . as in the case of our traffick with the negroes; this is very obvious, when on the coast of Africa, they willingly barter their gold, as a useless trifle to them, for the much more valuable toy of a cowrie or little shell, fit here only for the use of our children.[15]

Defoe here recognizes money in a different way, as a mere token, a symbol, something all agree to accept—clearly contradicting his earlier claim that money had to have intrinsic value. That he contradicts himself in a discussion of Africans is crucial—Africans' failure to recognize gold's value, their willingness to treat shells as money, complicates not only his sense of what money is or could be but also his sense of what Africans *themselves* are.

At first, Defoe looks at the fact that Africans allegedly prefer cowries to gold and concludes that money is just a social convention—anything can serve as money, he says, as we see in Africa. But Africans seem an exception, because most nations prefer precious metal, and as he goes on to consider the intrinsic properties of gold and silver—their luster, purity, and "incorruptibility"—he concludes that nature itself "seems to prompt mankind to this general agreement" on the worth of gold and silver. In this he returns to the orthodox mercantilist position: gold and silver were presumed to have a universally recognized, intrinsic money quality. This general agreement about gold then establishes an economic hierarchy that, when Defoe discusses Africa, clearly reflects and reveals existing hierarchies in nations and peoples. The italics in what follows are mine. "From hence they [gold and silver] become best qualified to the general medium of trade, and *to fix a value of their own upon all other species*; first being secure in their own intrinsick worth; *and all the worth of the inferior species in the world are measured by them.*"[16]

When Defoe wrote that gold and silver "fix a value of their own upon all other species," did he mean other forms of money, or other cultures, other races? Defoe repeatedly conflated the two terms, "specie" and "species," when he wrote about money three hundred years ago. "As people increased," he wrote in another essay on the origins of trade, "men found it necessary to form one medium, *which being of an intrinsic value to its species*, should be received as an equivalent in all demands from one to another."[17] Later he argued that money "is a species in trade, that supplies all the disproportions of commerce, and brings all matters between man and man to a stated equality."[18] But Africans themselves were also "a species in trade," enslaved because they were different beings, a different "species."

Clearly, the word "species" meant something different to Defoe than it does now. According to the *Oxford English Dictionary*, in 1710 "specie" originally meant "of a kind" and in this sense it might refer to "a kind of money," a "kind of property," or a "kind of animal." Its specifically zoological or biological meaning first appeared in 1608. Its specific usage as "coined money" dates to 1615, and at that time included the final "s", which we now use as the differentiating mark of the two meanings, "specie" and "species." We now see "species" as pertaining to biology, and "specie" to an increasingly obsolete notion of money. That was not the case when Defoe wrote: John Locke sometimes referred to gold and silver as two distinct "species" of money, as in "the raising of one species of your coin"; he could also use the phrase "raising one species of your money."[19] Even into the period of the American Revolution and beyond newspapers would regularly refer to slaves as a "species of property."[20] The word had a less precise meaning in the seventeenth century, which Defoe's essays reflect.

It is exactly that slippage, that imprecision, that matters. "Specie" and "species" in both their modern and archaic meanings concern exchange and its limits. Buffon, for example, the most influential enlightenment theorist on race, defined a "species" as "those organisms which can produce fertile offspring among themselves."[21] "Species" in this sense marks what can and cannot be fruitfully exchanged; it establishes the boundaries and terms of negotiability. So too does "specie" as money: it referees or arbitrates value in exchange; it gives meaning to difference and makes differences comparable. A modern reader notices that in Defoe the Africans' enslavement—the ability to make them a "species" of property—depended on their being a different, inferior "species" or race. And one of the signs of that inferiority, for Defoe, is not using gold.

Defoe's semantic blurring predates the formal development of both racism and economics—he wrote before economics existed as a distinct discipline or field, and before the development of formal scientific or anthropological theories of racial difference. It took several hundred years of intellectual heavy lifting to fully separate "specie" from "species," to give them their modern definitions as parts of two distinct, discrete, and formal bodies of knowledge. The separation of this single word into two made it possible for one to rank the other, for gold to value slaves and for blackness to represent a fixed and non-negotiable value in the free market, an identity that resisted the individual's desire to change his or her self.

But in their respective fields of knowledge "specie" and "species" both pose as the "bottom line," the final division, the foundation of identity. Gold theoretically marks the "real" value or price of goods, while "species" supposedly represents a stable and fundamental difference between different kinds of sparrow or lizard or human being. In the texts presented here, racial explanations of social hierarchy and economic explanations of money's function appear to be emerging at the same time, codeterminate and interdependent.

Defoe argues as follows: gold and silver are the "natural" medium of trade, because of their intrinsic value. This value was discovered over time—"time and experience fix'd" their place as money, he says. Some wretchedly ignorant nations remain backwards; they fail to recognize this superiority, demonstrating their primitive difference from Englishmen and other Europeans.

But Defoe holds out some possibility of change. Like many of his peers, Defoe believed in a natural historic progression, in which primitive societies began commerce with barter, then adopted ordinary materials like shells or wood as money as they advanced. Next they turned first to non-precious metals and then at last to gold and silver, natural medium of the highest nations. But gold or silver, in the hands of Europeans, might elevate even the most primitive peoples; it might civilize and liberate.

Musing further on Europe's trade with other continents, Defoe notes that "even the nations of America, whose ignorance of things was so gross . . . yet the people found out the beauties and excellencies of gold and silver . . . heap'd them up as their treasure, and exchang'd them, as the essential medium of their trade." Eventually they learned to understand gold and silver as money, as Equiano did when he left the world of his village, where money was of no use, and entered into Defoe's world of international trade. Defoe continued by praising "the native dignity of the species, having thus far prevail'd upon the world."

Now again, which "species" does he mean? Gold and silver? Or the prevailing white traders who introduced gold and silver as money and conquered native tribes? Did Englishmen's "native dignity" persuade or "prevail upon" the Amerindians, or did gold and silver's? The reader simply cannot tell. While Defoe hints that use of gold and silver might bring the various nations of the world into some form of rough equality, he also clings to the hierarchy gold both reveals and allows.

Defoe clearly does not know precisely what either money or value might be. He wrote, again, at a time when "specie" and species" still meant nearly the same thing, and at a time when mercantilism was giving way to capitalism. But his inquiry into the nature of specie and species grew from the puzzling difference between African and European societies, and from the problem of making sense of that difference in both economic and social terms—the problem of value and meaning in exchange. "Money," Defoe argued, "is the general *denominating* article in the world," the universal namer of what the difference between things means.[22] Africans' failure to recognize gold's value names them "primitive"; it puts them outside the realm of "mankind," with its "general agreement" on gold; their exchange of gold for shells points, in these passages, not to money as a social convention but to appreciation and use of gold as a mark of essential superiority.

The very questions central to Defoe's essays—what is money, what is value, how is trade established—depend from and upon the problem of difference. What does the difference between Africans or American Indians and Europeans *mean*? Is it stable? How can we negotiate it? Defoe continued: "Gold and silver . . . are now the governours of trade, the umpires and determiners of every value: in our merchant books, the stated columns reduce every article of merchandizes to their *proper value in this species*." The species of gold and silver makes the negotiation possible. It establishes the value of other species; money is the sign of what the difference between people *means*.

Defoe links the language of money and the language of international hierarchy in a final sentence, claiming that "in the language of trade, money [gold] is the alphabet that forms the sound; all labor is valued in it, paid by it, rated, and bargained for under its title. Millions of value are transacted in its name, without *removing its species*; and the respective nations that are *most kin to it* [gold], are by consequence . . . masters of all the trade in the world."[23] "Most kin" to its "species"; kin to gold: Defoe connects English mercantile dominance to the money England covets. He makes Englishmen "kin" to gold itself. This language connects the international hierarchies specie reveals and establishes to natural law, to a presumed basic natural difference between goods and people. Defoe argues that gold marks English people as different, but also that it makes trade possible by rendering difference exchangeable. The complicated play of difference and equivalence shows up in his confused and ambiguous language. Here, at the general moment of their origins, theories of law in political economy and theories of racial difference are merged.

Defoe wants a gold standard in the African slave trade: a gold standard of meaning which will make both finance and human difference sensible and stable. Defoe wants to make gold the basis, the evidence and sign, of genuine intrinsic differences. But he also wants the freedom and negotiability and speculative possibilities the market promises. He wants money as an equalizer. We can see this duality through the life of Equiano, who married himself to the market and its contradictions and who gives good evidence of the particular complexities of the colonial American economy.

*   *   *

After being taken from Africa, he tells us, Equiano served first in the British Navy. He wound up in the West Indies with a relatively kind owner, a merchant with offices in Philadelphia and Montserrat. The merchant taught Equiano how to clerk and judge trade goods, for the African had a talent for business. "There was scarcely any part of his business, or household affairs, in which I was not occasionally employed," Equiano notes proudly, and even his master admits he "saved him more than one hundred pounds a year" and is worth more than any of the other clerks—"tho their wages," Equiano adds, "are from sixty to one hundred pounds current a year."[24] He also allowed Equiano to do some commerce on his own when he sailed on trading voyages. "He commence[d] merchant with three pence," begins one chapter subheading: "on St. Eustatia, a Dutch island," Equiano continues, "I bought a glass tumbler with my half bit, and when we came to Montserrat I sold it for a bit, or sixpence." From this humble beginning the profits build: one glass tumbler became two on the next voyage, then four, then multiple tumblers and a jug of gin; "going all about the islands upwards of four years, ever trading as I went." Equiano diversifies his product line and scale of operations in what looks much like a morally prescriptive tale of self-improvement and thrift.[25]

Equiano clearly relishes the details of his financial success, often re-telling the reader of each trade in each port, keeping the reader informed of his financial progress. His ability to trade marks him, in the pure calculus of the market, with a value independent of his African heritage. Rather than simply embodying a certain limited value as a slave, as we will see, he can actually create value. Eventually his "trading for myself" allows him to transcend slavery and buy his own freedom; he even lends money to the captain of one of the ships he works on. By "trading for himself"—that is, trading to buy himself—he was finally able to trade "for himself" as a free man. He seems to escape the logic of the gold standard Defoe envisioned.

But Equiano consistently notes how his skin color limits his ability to do business, and though the narrative presents many vivid accounts of slavery's injustices, in his account the limits bigotry imposes on market freedom often seem the worst cut of all. His story of trade is also a story of how trade *can't* overcome prejudice, a fable of the market's failings. Equiano continually returns to how whites take advantage of his lack of rights to deprive him of his just profits, as when he steps ashore in Charleston during the celebrations over the end of the Stamp Act.

As usual, Equiano finished his master's business and then set off to sell some of the small goods he had brought with him. "Here I disposed of some goods on my own accounts," he recalls, "the white men buying them with smooth promises and fair words, giving me, however, but very indifferent payment." But one gentleman, Equiano continues, "bought a puncheon of rum from me," then refused to pay. "I lost some time in seeking after this gentleman." Equiano continues; eventually he hires "some black men to help pull a boat across the water to go in search" of the rogue. Confronted by Equiano and the group of "black men," as well as the captain of Equiano's ship, "he at last paid me in dollars."

At this point Equiano runs into some of the problems that made the Stamp Act so intolerable to the white colonists. "Some of the dollars," Equiano says "were copper, and of consequence of no value." Equiano objects to the copper dollars, but "he took advantage of my being a negroman, and obliged me to put up with these or none." How he did this is unclear, but "immediately after, as I was trying to pass them in the market among other white men, I was abused for offering to pass bad coin." He tries to tell the men in the market how he got the money, but it does no good: "I was within one minute of being tied up and flogged without either judge or jury. However, by the help of a pair of good heels, I ran off and so escaped."[26]

The story has several puzzling points, including the whites' seemingly irrational anger. If the coins are worthless, why does the "gentleman" have them in the first place—and, more puzzling, why does Equiano eventually accept them? Why does his attempt to spend the coins enrage the whites, when they could simply refuse to accept them in payment? Possibly Equiano simply did not know about the local money and thought the coins had value. But his story says he already knew about the coins' lack of value before he took them, and besides he was a skilled trader by then, familiar with the coins, paper, and credit relations of many different islands and colonies. Widespread counterfeiting plagued all the colonies, so the coins might have been fakes.[27] Possibly the coins had value somewhere else, but not in Charleston. But then still why would this enrage the whites? Perhaps the mere spectacle of a black man doing business for himself, presuming to act as if race did not matter in setting price and value, set them into violence. Perhaps a black man of ambiguous character—free, a stranger, "not from here"— acting independently and negotiating freely, combined with the sign of ambiguous value in money, was too much for them, and they acted to resolve the ambiguity by attacking Equiano. All these answers may apply: to make sense of Equiano's troubles we need to review the history of colonial money and its relation to ideas about "character."

*   *   *

The North American colonists had acres of timber, cotton, and other staples, but no indigenous money; no gold and silver in the ground. And little gold or silver coin circulated, again partly because England wanted it that way. The Crown, acting according to mercantilist principles, wanted gold and silver, and timber or other goods for that matter, to flow into England, to enrich England. Colonists could trade native goods for other products, but they had to pay their taxes—such as the taxes mandated by the Stamp Act—in gold. When they could get away with it English merchants also always demanded payment in gold or silver, which they regarded as "real money." So typically North American colonists, when they got gold or silver at all, did not have it for very long—it flew from their hands, they claimed, into ships headed for England, to pay for luxury goods or England's taxes. If you found it at all in the colonies you found it in the coastal cities, and even there it tended towards the docks and wharves, leaving the backcountry literally with no money.

Lack of gold made commerce difficult. Barter works for small-scale local transactions, and in ocean trade, where merchants can do business through "book credit."[28] But toting a bushel of wheat to the tavern to pay for drinks makes little sense. Coins could symbolize a bushel of wheat, but money—"real money," meaning gold or silver coins—tended always to head towards England. An enterprising people might clear all the timber they wanted, but eventually they would have to buy things not available locally. Without money, they would soon find the need to produce the real goods in barter slowing things down, clogging exchange. The colonists typically resorted to truly elaborate webs of credit relations, in which each person in town owed dozens of other people various things in exchange for various other things, a dense mental web of reciprocal obligations that sometimes made its way into diaries and account books, but that on any larger scale proved cumbersome.[29] Believing firmly that

England was depriving them of coin, they needed some kind of money. As many historians and economists have pointed out, and as Olaudah Equiano experienced firsthand, from the beginning the North American colonists led the world in monetary experiments.[30]

In Massachusetts, the first English settlers seized on "wampum" as a form of money. For generations, the coastal Narragansett and Pequot Indians had made the shells of certain species of clam into beads. They made two kinds. The more common white beads took much less labor to make than the much rarer purple/black beads, which came from the hinge of the clam shell. William Bradford wrote about wampum in 1627. It revolutionized the local economy, he says in his *History of Plymouth Plantation*, and in 1637 the colonists declared wampum legal tender for smaller transactions. It helped build a bridge between the Indian and white worlds, a bridge across which trade walked briskly. According to law, four white beads or two blue beads equaled an English penny. The Indians quickly seized on the advantages of wampum as money and began producing more of it; so did the white settlers. Inflation set in: in 1641 the colony revalued wampum to six beads a penny, then a few years later placed occasional limits on its acceptance, as inflation worsened. Soon counterfeit wampum appeared, fashioned from wood or bone or white beads dyed blue. Before long wampum became nearly useless, and in 1661 the colonists repealed the law making wampum legal tender.[31]

By then the New England colonists had begun producing other forms of money. The first coins issued in North America were pressed in 1652 from "bullion, plate, or Spanish coin." They gave the government the ability to control prices to some extent—to police the money supply and the price of goods by limiting the number of coins in circulation. The Crown made them illegal in 1665, partly in the belief that metal for coinage should go to England. In 1690, the Massachusetts colonists began their first experiments with paper money on a large scale. By 1755, each colony had printed paper money of various kinds, in various amounts.

Equiano came across some of this paper money in another transaction later in 1766. While in a Georgia port the captain of his ship inexplicably refused to let Equiano board some cattle Equiano had bought. Instead, while loading cattle of his own, the captain repeatedly tried to persuade Equiano to buy some turkeys to bring back to Montserrat for sale. Equiano wanted no part of the troublesome birds but the captain persisted. "This, and not being able to dispose of my paper-money in any other way, induced me at length to take four dozen," Equiano writes.

The paper money, most likely notes produced locally in Georgia, had no value outside the colony, and so Equiano would have little use for it in Montserrat, unless he could hold it for a return trip or find someone from Georgia to trade with. It turned out, Equiano noted with immense Calvinist satisfaction, that on the voyage home, one of the cattle "butted" the captain, who took sick and died, remorseful. All the cattle got sick and died as well, while Equiano's forty-eight turkeys thrived, "and I afterwards gained near three hundred per cent. on the sale of them."[32] Equiano's position as a slave made it hard to refuse the birds, but so too did the pocketful of paper money, which had a value in Georgia it might not have had in the Caribbean isles.

This sort of constant negotiation not just about the price but also about the means of payment took place across the Eastern seaboard. Lacking specie, each colony made do with a profusion of types of money, ranging from various sorts of coin, like the copper dollars Equiano tried to spend in Charleston, to various kinds of paper. Some of this paper came from private "banks," backed by the pooled gold or silver of wealthy men; some from public stocks of land or other goods; and some came from more abstract sources, as we will see shortly. All of it added to the complexity of exchange.

Paper notes, like the career of wampum, demonstrate some of the basic issues of class, value, and identity that would animate American economic debates for the next three centuries. Before examining paper money more carefully, we can look at a simplified example of how paper money, and inflation, can work.

Inflation, and a plentiful money supply, generally helps debtors and the man on the make, while inflation hurts those who already have money, because it decreases the purchasing power of what they have—their money will buy fewer goods. Hypothetically, if I lend lowly Mr. Miller $100 to build his gristmill, I expect to be paid back with interest—say $150 in five years. That would allow me to order a fancy clock to demonstrate my enlightenment to Miller and other less wealthy folk in town. If inflation has occurred in that time, I still get $150, but $150 no longer will buy what it bought five years ago. Prices have gone up; the clock now costs $200. I, the lender, feel I've been robbed, as I haven't gotten the purchasing power I contracted for when I made the loan. To make matters worse, inflation has lowered the interest rate I can charge—with money plentiful, it costs less to borrow. My money, my capital, loses value: it "depreciates," as the colonists put it.

Mr. Miller, on the other hand, started paying me back at perhaps $2.50 a month, one half of his monthly income. But inflation allowed him to charge higher fees for his milling, increasing his income while the monthly loan payment stayed the same. By the fifth year of the loan that $2.50 only equaled one quarter of Miller's monthly income. His *prices*, though, have kept pace with inflation. So his standard of living has stayed the same or actually increased, because the loan payments take less of a monthly bite. Inflation injured me, the lender, but the loan turned out wonderfully for Miller.

Now Miller—the damn'd upstart! —smugly tells me that doing business has its risks as he strolls by in his fancy new clothes. So I act to reduce these risks, or shift them in my favor. I agitate for control of prices, calling for currency reform.

A pamphlet written by "Philopatria" in 1721 captures the flavor of some elite concerns about inflation. "You have seen the wonders, the almost Miracles," Philopatria wrote sarcastically, "which our *paper Bills* have already wrought, & will yet naturally bring forth, if we (the legislatures) will but give them being by our powerful *Fiat.*" The idea that legislative fiat could give "being" to money seemed absurd; even more absurd, he argued, were its effects on society:

> [T]he inferior sort will be clad in as costly Attire as the Rich and Honourable . . . ordinary Tradesmen's Wives . . . dressed in Silks and Sattens . . . Inferiour Apprentices and Servants, having just obtained their Freedom shall be dressed like Lords *of the Mannours*; & in publick Congresses were it not for the different Seats they sit in *one would scarce know* Joan *from* my Lady *by Daylight.*[33]

Philopatria's italics underscore the point: paper money made it hard to tell who was who, because it allowed people to transform themselves. Philopatria's financial interest sits on a bed of social rank and entitlement, a set of assumptions about the elite's intrinsic worthiness. The pamphlet applauded a currency which gives the ability to control the supply of money, and stabilize prices, while at the same time endorsing a "rank ordered" society, in which differences of social station reflect people's basic characters. That hypothetical Mr. Miller above prospered at elite expense is bad enough; his prospering through a paper money economy also erased the real differences between people, or at least confused appearance and reality—lowly "Joan" the tradesman's wife, brazen in broad daylight, looks just like "our Lady."[34]

Most colonial elites, we should note, favored some sort of paper money or other, unlike their English brethren, who generally opposed it in almost any form. The colonists believed they lacked sufficient specie to do business, and they constantly sought new tools for easing exchange and facilitating credit. In the colonies, worry about the stability of social position co-existed with ambition and the desire to stimulate commerce, and as a result, "although mindful of its dangers, men of property accepted it as useful and necessary." The first paper money issues came in response to emergencies, especially Indian wars. Later, they became more customary. Alexander Hamilton estimated that at the time of the Revolution paper made up 75 percent of the money in circulation; other estimates put the figure closer to one half.[35]

The character of paper money issues differed widely from colony to colony. In some cases the paper took the form of a government-issued payment to troops and suppliers, which would circulate as legal tender for all public transactions for a limited term, say six years, and then be "retired" as the bills eventually came back into the government's coffers as payment of taxes or for other services. Such issues took the place of taxes, allowing the colonial authorities to conduct war in the short term, in effect deferring the cost. Sometimes paper money issues took the form of interest-bearing notes—you agreed to take paper money as pay, in return for the promise that at the end of a given term the paper money could be turned in for more gold than its face value. Other paper issues involved "loan offices," through which colonial governments would loan paper to men of property who pledged their land or other goods as security. There were also attempts to fund private banks which would issue their own paper. All of these kinds of paper money might circulate at the same time. Rather than fight over the legitimacy of paper notes, as their peers did in England, North American colonists tended to argue over what kind of paper money to issue.[36]

Philopatria himself favored a limited, public paper-money issue in the form of a loan backed by tangible assets such as land. Such loans worked much like "trickle down" economics—the paper money loaned to men of property would supposedly make its way into the economy as they spent it on goods and services. But he still felt a great deal of nervousness about the "leveling" tendencies of paper, as the quotation indicates. Colonial elites most often favored schemes whereby wealthy men "of substantial character" would pool some of their assets and then issue paper money to represent those assets. They felt less confident of money issued in place of taxes, and probably least confident about paper money issued by the colonial governments as legal tender for private debts. But even this last form enjoyed surprising popularity. Feeling themselves victimized by England's mercantilist policies, colonial elites endorsed forms of paper money they would later, after the revolution, come to detest.[37] Even so, they sometimes expressed uneasiness about the dangerous effects of a plentiful currency.

Paper money put at risk not just wealth but the order of the universe; as Philopatria suggested, it threatened to make meaning itself, the meaning of the differences between people and things, vanish or collapse. "When I heard the first news of the *South-Sea* Stock, rising to such a considerable height," began an anonymous 1721 pamphlet opposing paper money, with "Men of low Degree, being advanced to their Coaches; what could I think but the World is turning upside down?" The author called paper money and its effects an illusion, and insisted: "Had there not been Men of Substance in this Country . . . you might have made Paper Bills till you had been blind, they would never have fed your Bellies, nor have clothed your Backs." He drove the idea of "men of substance" home by asking, "what would an Hundred Thousand Pounds, in Paper-Bills have signified . . . when the *Indians* Inhabited this Country?" The paper would have lacked all value, he continued, "so that it's plain, they [paper notes] have a Credit from some Substance that the People, amongst whom they are, Injoy."[38] Money derives value, he argued, from the "substance" of elites, their character as well as their wealth. In 1779 "Hard-Money" called Continental Currency "that paper-wasted, rag-born, kite-faced fellow," and denounced "the airs that he gave himself, vapouring and effecting an importance, as if he had been equal to the solid coin." Hard-Money continued: "he is of obscure birth, the son of one Lamp-black." But I, Hard-Money boasted, "am descended of the sun-beams; I am related to the family of the pearls and diamonds."[39] These words imply that the "substance" of value is not just gold or silver but some essential, quasi-racial difference between people, a difference of rank or of being.[40]

What would these men have made of Equiano, trading "for himself" and prospering? When Equiano finally got his "free papers," he writes, he bought himself a suit of "Georgia superfine blue clothes" for eight pounds; he gave dances, and some of the "sable females" began to notice him. Had he become one of the "inferiour Apprentices and Servants, having just obtained their Freedom," that Philopatria saw "dressed like

Lords of the Mannours"? Could he ever have the "substance" of real value as a "son of Lampblack?"[41]

But while Philopatria and Hard-Money saw paper money as dangerously formless and chaotic, other colonists saw paper money as the centerpiece of new ways of thinking about value and character. Benjamin Franklin may have made this argument most clearly in 1729, in an influential essay calling for paper-money issues in Pennsylvania. "There is," Franklin declared, "a certain proportionate Quantity of Money requisite to carry on the trade of a Country." Too much money would be no advantage, he continued, and too little "exceedingly detrimental to trade."[42] Too little money caused high interest rates, which Franklin argued hindered new enterprises by making what we would call "start-up costs" high. Barter he called clumsy and inconvenient: and so "men have invented MONEY, properly called a *Medium of Exchange*." "And whatever particular Thing Men have agreed to make this Medium of, whether Gold, Silver, Copper, or Tobacco," Franklin argued, its ultimate value rests on the labor that goes into it, not on any natural attributes or intrinsic properties.[43]

Franklin articulated the "labor theory of value"—the argument that value, rather than simply existing intrinsically in some things "by their nature," rests on human labor. Speaking of silver as money, he wrote: "Silver it self is no certain permanent Value, being worth more or less according to its Scarcity or Plenty, therefore it seems requisite to fix upon Something else, more proper to be made a *Measure of Values*, and this I take to be *Labour*."

In this argument silver has value only because of the labor that goes into digging it out and working it. It has no value sitting underground in a vein of rock; it acquires value when someone makes it into coins or jewelry. Franklin insisted: "The Riches of a Country are to be valued by the Quantity of Labour its inhabitants are able to purchase, and not by the Quantity of Silver and Gold they possess." Trade itself "being nothing else but the exchange of Labour for Labour," Franklin concluded, "the Value of all Things . . . is most justly measured by Labour" itself.[44]

Who opposes paper money, asked Franklin? "[A]ll those, who wanting Courage to venture in Trade, now practise Lending Money on Security for exhorbitant Interest. . . . Possessors of large Sums of Money, . . . Lawyers, and others concerned in Court Business." "On the other Hand," he continued, "Those who are Lovers of Trade, and delight to see Manufactures encouraged, will be for having a large Addition to our Currency."[45] Franklin thought Pennsylvania's colonial government should issue paper backed partly by land and partly by what we might consider its "gross colonial product"—its citizens' labor. Franklin advances the idea that value is socially constructed, not given by nature: a product of skill, energy, and drive, not birth.

"We shall never know why the inflation created by the printing of paper money aroused such extreme anxiety and such deep moral indignation among . . . 'the honest gentry of intrinsic worth,'" wrote Gordon Wood, "until we better appreciate the nature of their proprietary wealth and the social identity and influence that stemmed from that wealth."[46] Wood referred to how the American Revolution eroded the idea of a "rank ordered" society (and "intrinsic worth"), replacing it with a radically egalitarian notion of any man's potential equality to any other, a world in which "worth" became a much more fluid idea. It was this world Equiano hoped to live in—a world where his worth stemmed from his accumulated money and property, not his race or background.

But increasingly, as the eighteenth century drew towards its close, elite social position would come to be defined in racial terms. Paraphrasing Wood, we can never understand debates about money until we understand how closely Americans bound money to questions of identity—identities which came to have, mixed in with class anxieties about the stability of social position, a strong racial component. In the colonial era race became yoked to the notion of money: it came to form a counterbalance to the potential paper money unlocked. Understanding this relationship might help explain how the American society could be both radically egalitarian and deeply racist, both open to "self-making" and dependent on fixed racial difference.

*   *   *

It was exactly this resistance to pure economic calculation that Equiano ran into so often in his narrative—"meeting various scenes of imposition," he says wearily, "as usual."[47] He relates how, at one point, he arrived at Santa Cruz Island with several bags of fruit he knew would earn a tidy profit. But two white men met him on the docks and took the fruit. He followed them, he looked for help, but the men refused to return the goods. "Thus, in the very minute of gaining more by three times than I ever did by any venture in my life before, was I deprived of every farthing I was worth." By his worth he means the goods he has assembled for sale, his savvy, while the whites see his worth as simply the inferior value of a black man. He had the means to prosper, but his substance—his blackness—allowed whites to suspend the rules. And again, though Equiano offers a compelling account of the myriad abuses of slavery, this injustice seems to sting him worst. "I then, in an agony of distress and indignation, wished that the ire of God, in his forked lightening, might transfix these cruel oppressors among the dead."[48] He has reason to be angry, but his particular anger here comes from the market's failure to live up to its word, its determination to have race matter more than money.

Other early slave narratives bear the same message, a keen irony at the sheer negotiability of everything *except* race. Broteer Furro, born in Guinea around 1729, was captured into New World slavery as an eight-year-old boy. Taken onto a boat bound for Rhode Island, he recalled, he was bought "by one Robertson Mumford, steward of said vessel, for four gallons of rum, and a piece of calico, and called VENTURE, on account of his having purchased me with his own private venture. Thus I came by my name."[49] Mumford, who clearly relished irony, made a speculative investment in Furro's potential value in the New World. Mumford ventured a bet that young Broteer/Venture would, over time, be worth more than four gallons of rum and a piece of calico. Named after a speculative enterprise in which he constitutes the main object of speculation, Venture proceeds to live up to his name. Like Equiano, he told his life story as a tale of enterprise and self-making, in the process showing the complexity and ambiguity of colonial commerce and the limits to its market freedom, the ways specie and species intermingled.

In about 1751, in New England, Venture "was sold to a Thomas Stanton. . . . I brought with me from my late master's, two johannes, three old Spanish dollars, and two thousand of coppers, besides five pounds of my wife's money." A typical colonial aggregate, the monies of various nations and kinds had been earned by cleaning shoes, trapping, fishing, and vegetable gardening. "All this money amounting to near twenty-one pounds York currency, my master's brother, Robert Stanton, hired of me, for which he gave me his note."[50] Not just a slave, not just a source of labor, Venture also provides his owner's family with capital, at once in his physical body, his slave price; and in his labor; and in the money he lends. He could be borrowed from and "borrowed against"; he combines the real thing and the symbolic, the speculative.

But Venture, who prides himself on his unusual size, strength, and industry, chafes under Stanton's rule and enters into a plot with a neighbor, "one Hempsted Miner, of Stonington." Miner "requested me to make myself discontented and to appear as unreconciled to my master as I could before that he bargained with him for me; and that in return he would give me a good chance to gain my freedom when I came to live with him." Venture does this, and "Not long after Hempsted Miner purchased me of my master for fifty-six pounds lawful."[51]

By devaluing himself Venture escapes Stanton. Venture hopes to "redeem" himself, buy himself out of slavery, and moreover to stay near his wife and children, so that he might buy their freedom as well. But when Miner reneges on his promise to let Venture buy himself, Venture resists Miner's authority in ways that make him impossible to sell to others and thus destroys Miner's investment. A prospective buyer tells Miner, looking at Venture's truculence, "he would not have [Venture] as a gift."

When a neighbor, "Daniel Edwards, Esq. of Hartford," showed interest, the frustrated Miner "pawned me to him for ten pounds." Venture becomes yet another form of credit and value, pawned like a gold watch. "After some trial of my honesty," Venture continues, "Mr. Edwards placed considerable trust and confidence in me . . . he asked me why my master wished to part with such an honest negro, and why he did not keep me himself. I replied that I could not give him the reason, unless it was to convert me into cash, and speculate with me as with other commodities." In this passage Venture suggests that the money Miner gained in pawning Venture is still "him": when Miner speculates with the money gained in pawn he speculates with Venture. Venture sees his self and the money as the same.

Venture shows a keen awareness of the value of money and credit—he had loaned money to his former master's brother, he recalls, but the disreputable brother had stolen and destroyed the paper which recorded the loan. That he refers to Miner as speculating in him is doubly interesting: Miner had conspired to buy Venture low and sell him high, a financial venture in which Venture himself cooperated but then subverted by further deflating his value to Miner. Miner wishes to convert Venture into cash—presumably the goal of any financial venture. But Venture wishes to do the same—to convert himself into the cash amount that equals his freedom. To put it simply, Venture's narrative depicts competing notions of value and exchange—value as something intrinsic, and value as something speculative, malleable, and fungible.

This complicated and ambiguous situation soon grows more complicated. Venture has been bought by Miner, proven unsellable and then pawned to Edwards. But Miner never shows up to redeem his pawn. When Miner "did not appear to redeem me," Venture goes to see his wife, then a slave of his former master Stanton. But Stanton "appeared much ruffled at my being there," Venture relates, so he leaves, but not before learning that Miner had never actually paid for him—he still owed Stanton money for Venture's purchase. In the meantime Miner negotiated to sell Venture to a Colonel Oliver Smith. Confusing indeed! "These men once met to determine which of them should hold me, and upon my expressing a desire to be owned by Col. Smith, and upon my master's settling the remainder of the money which was due to Stanton for me, it was agreed that I should live with Col. Smith."[52]

A remarkable document, it reveals a great deal about slavery in New England and about financial exchange. Venture can exercise considerable control over his own value, and he can engage in complicated speculations on his own and with local whites. He enters the marketplace at several levels—as a good for sale, as equity for loans, as a source of capital, and as a wage earner. But as those three white men meet to haggle over Venture's value, his race remains the bottom line. His value is both fixed by his blackness, which makes him enslaveable, and fluctuates with his own exertions and the instability of the colonial money market.

Venture stays with Colonel Smith, in fact takes the last name "Smith" for himself. He continues to work towards buying his own freedom, and approaches his master with a sum of money he had saved as a down payment. Venture gives his readers a long and detailed list of the labors he performed, the exact amounts of land cultivated and crops harvested, in order to gain the money for his redemption. Colonel Smith seems to increase the price of Venture's freedom each time Venture completes another Herculean task, but Venture labors on until finally, "My master liberated me, saying that I might pay what was behind if I could ever make it convenient." Venture's freedom cost "seventy-one pounds two shillings." "The reason of my master for asking such an unreasonable price," Venture continued, "was to secure himself in case I should ever come to want." "I had already been sold three different times," Venture says, "made considerable money with seemingly nothing to derive it from . . . and paid an enormous sum for my freedom."[53]

Like Equiano, Venture Smith tells a story of industry, financial savvy, and accumulating value in conflict with a neo-mercantilist idea of fixed value. He takes pains to elaborate the exact price of his redemption— what he was worth—and to suggest that he was both worth more and worth less; Colonel Smith, indeed, recognized his value and kept inflating it to guard against some sickness or injury to Venture's earning power, so Venture describes himself as both undervalued and overpriced. Venture's knowledge of money, his ability to generate value, highlights the contrast between Venture as self-made man and Venture as actual, tangible commodity. Like gold, he is a fixed value, marked as different by race, but like paper money he has the power to make speculation real, to generate value, and to turn an economic venture into a physical reality.

Venture Smith is literally like money. He plays the same role as money in the economy. He has a presumably fixed, "natural" value derived from his race—a purchase price—and he serves, as gold does, as collateral for loans. He also he has a value derived, like the value of paper money in Franklin's account, from his labor. He further has, like money lent on credit, a speculative value, and a purely imaginary "venture" on future outcomes. He is himself like money.

This may seem like "reading too much" into Smith's story. But consider this anonymous satire, published in 1788. The author commented on an advertisement "in a late paper, of a plantation to be sold in Maryland for 'negroes, merchandize, or cash.'" "From this it appears," he continues, "that negroes are to be introduced in that state instead of paper money as a medium of commerce." To save trouble in "counting or calculating the value of this new black flesh coin, I beg leave to furnish the dealers in it with the following table, which I hope, will be current hereafter in the state of Maryland":

	Dollars.
1. A middle aged healthy negro man or woman,	300
2. A negro man or woman above 55 years of age,	100
3. All negro boys and girls between 12 and 18 years of age,	100
4. All negro children between 6 and 12 years of age,	80

As change will be necessary in this species of money, the following mode may be adopted to obtain it.

	Dollars.
A negro's head,	20
A right arm,	16

A left arm,	12
A leg,	8
A hand and foot,	4
A thumb and great toe,	1
A finger and toe of the common size,	2 3-ds of a dollar.
A little finger and toe,	1 3-d of a dollar.

"Should this species of coin be adopted," the Swiftian author went on, "a new mode of determining the value of estates will become necessary. Instead of saying a man is worth ten thousand pounds, it will be common to say, he is worth ten thousand dried hands or feet, or forty thousand dried thumbs or great toes." The satirist signed himself "an enemy to the society for the abolition of slavery." This grim, bitter essay derives its nasty edge from the fact that slaves *had* become a form of money, a store of value, black flesh made coin.[54]

Equiano, throughout his narrative, resists any attempt to value him simply as a commodity—that is, to allow himself to be valued simply for or by his blackness, which he understandably takes as a sign of limited potential and fixed commodity value. Venture Smith does the same—his very name, as his knowing narrative reveals, calls attention to both his fixed nature as a slave, a negro, and his speculative potential as a source of ever-increasing value and money. He can create more value than he represents: he can create value rather than simply *being* a value.

Both men came slowly to abolitionism: both owned slaves themselves once freed. Venture wrote: "After this I purchased a negro man, for no other reason than to oblige him, and gave for him sixty pounds. But in a short time after he run away from me, and I thereby lost all that I gave for him, except twenty pounds which he paid me previous to his absconding." The tragedy in this account is not slavery but the slave's absconding, and Venture drives this home by describing the exact amount lost.[55] Even as a free man Equiano engaged in the slave trade, as an overseer, and not till the end of his life did he come to oppose slavery itself and not just its worst abuses. His repugnance at being treated as a commodity mixes with his love of negotiation, even in his denunciations of slavery. "I have often seen slaves," he writes, "put into scales and weighed, and then sold from three pence to six-pence or nine pence a pound." His careful listing of prices jars the reader: outraged at sale by the pound, he also seems to express as much outrage at the low price range, and he adds that his master preferred to sell slaves "by the lump."[56]

The reduction of the slave to a figure whose value is fixed by and summed up in his appearance or his nature infuriates him as much or more as the practical fact of unfreedom, which was, after all, common in various forms in the Colonies.

In America, unfreedom for whites became offensive because it contrasted so starkly with the speculative market's potential. Indentured servitude had largely vanished by 1800: by then, unfreedom was confined to Africans. In limiting unfreedom to dark-skinned peoples, Americans reproduced the logic of the marketplace, with its simultaneous insistence on negotiability and intrinsic value. Unfreedom became the province of dark-skinned people, who could be imagined, like specie, as a sign of both intrinsic value and intrinsic difference.

If gold promised to stabilize value in "men of Substance," in ways familiar from orthodox mercantilism, so too for white "men of substance" did sale by the pound as Equiano describes, measured in scales in the slave marketplace, express value in the "substance" of racial difference. This substance could be made into a commodity, "negro," and weighed out and priced, but as Equiano finds again and again, in the market run by white people that commodity's nature resisted negotiation as lead resisted turning to gold. The "substance" of blackness served as an economic "bottom line" of value, much as the weight of "men of substance" theoretically provided the real value behind colonial paper money in Philopatria's account. In both cases an idea of intrinsicness, of nonnegotiable essence, serves as an alternative to the market's endless negotiation. But increasingly, a notion of intrinsic racial character is replacing a notion of intrinsic class difference. "Black flesh made coin" anchors value in the way notions of intrinsic class superiority once did: "black flesh made coin" anchors financial exchange in the same way as gold.

Venture Smith filled the last pages of his narrative with the exact amount he earned from various ventures, including farming, clamming, and trading in ships along the coast, and the purchase of two further "negro men," both of whom run off and cheat him. He relates other instances of business deals gone wrong, ending with a story of how he was wrongfully sued and forced to pay ten pounds by a wealthy local merchant: "I applied to several gentlemen for counsel in this affair, and they advised me, as my adversary was rich, . . . to pay the sum and submit to the injury; which I according did. . . . Captain Hart was a *white gentle-*

man, and I a poor African, therefore it was *all right, and good enough for the black dog.*"[57]

Angry at being cheated, as anyone would be, Smith's italics call attention to how racial identity trumps the marketplace's endless negotiation. It marks the final sign of injury in his brief narrative, the worst injustice. He has no real brief with unfreedom per se, no problem with buying other men; what he hates is the market's failure to live up to its promise of freedom in self-fashioning. Despite his reputation for honesty and industry, of having accumulated "more than one hundred acres of land and three habitable dwelling houses," he remains a "black dog." It was crucial that he remain a "black dog," because his blackness stabilized meaning in exchanges of all sorts.

Olaudah Equiano gives a more optimistic account. He returned to England after many remarkable adventures, eventually becoming a hairdresser, arctic explorer, a scientist's assistant, and a missionary. He concludes his last chapter with glowing reports of Africa as a source of resources and a potential market for British goods. "Industry, enterprise and mining," he says, "will have their full scope, proportionally as they civilize." "Supposing the Africans," he continues, "to expend £5 a head in raiment and furniture yearly, when civilized &c. an immensity beyond the reach of imagination!"[58] Any modern capitalist would embrace Equiano's giddy, post-mercantilist vision of the market's transformative power to generate wealth. In his vision exchange, commerce, will civilize Africa, but more importantly it will make race irrelevant, turning "the Africans" into race-neutral consumers each expending £5 a year on British goods.

His last chapter not surprisingly also muses on "a remarkable occurrence relative to African complexion. . . . A white negro woman, that I had formerly seen in London and other parts, had married a white man, by whom she had three boys, and they were every one mulattoes, and yet they had fine light hair."[59] Their golden hair gives Equiano evidence that race *can* be renegotiated, revalued in free exchange. Indeed, he managed to at least partially renegotiate what "black" meant: he lived to see his narrative go through multiple editions, married a white Englishwoman, and became a spokesman for intermarriage as the solution to racial prejudice, advancing a "natural" economy of exchange. To a political critic he spoke favorably of "the mutual commerce of the sexes of both Blacks and Whites, under the restrictions and moderation of law." Nature abhors restraint, he argued: why not "encourage open, free and generous love upon nature's own wide and extensive plan."[60] Having lived his adult life in a world of both volatile mobility, flexible negotiation and trade, and vicious, brutal insistence on the non-negotiability of black "value," he continued to argue for the transforming effects of free markets.

The irony of market freedom, its shortcomings, would come to play a central role in American slave narratives. Again and again, freed persons would find that their "race" transcended the freedom of the marketplace. A number of historians have looked at how, in the Jacksonian period, white workers chose to identify themselves as "white" rather than as simply laborers having something in common with African Americans. As David Roediger has discussed, they came to refer to themselves not as "wage slaves"—persons who had lost independence and autonomy in the wage market—but as "white slaves," unjustly forced to do "nigger work."[61] Frederick Douglass, working as a ship caulker in Baltimore, found that white men violently refused to work even with free African Americans. He describes his joy, as a free, skilled artisan, at the possibility of "being my own master" and contracting for himself, but even after he makes his way to New England, white ship's carpenters will not allow black men on the job.[62] Harriet Jacobs similarly found that freedom in the North meant a continuing experience of small humiliations and restrictions. She took a job as a nurse, and describes how she was forced to sit apart from other, white nurses. They all did the same work, but her blackness transcended the market position "nurse" and relegated her to a separate status.[63]

*   *   *

Historians have often noted that racial slavery and liberal, "free market" economics arose at the same time. The question is why. Why was the market economy, probably the most powerful solvent known to human beings, co-dependent on the "substance" of race? Most frequently, we understand this failure in terms of something called prejudice, or bigotry, and explain it away as lack of education. We assume that this prejudice operates independently of the economy, that it represents some realm separate from the market and its lawful operations. Economists especially like to treat the marketplace as something governed by laws which operate apart from what people may think and believe. Proponents of specie money, as we have seen, frequently touted its resistance to tarnish, to acid, to corruption; its purity. They saw it as a fit basis for all value because it possessed, in its very being, an irremovable value beyond history, beyond politics, beyond culture. Frederick Douglass proudly detailed his value as a wage-earning artisan, but found that his skills could not renegotiate the meaning of his blackness. Facing the promise of market freedom, the ways the market makes it possible to renegotiate our social position and its meaning, we have tended to retreat to fantasies of intrinsic value and difference.

Proponents of the unregulated market described it then and now as a realm of personal freedom, and to a large extent they are right. The free market allows people a wide range of meaningful personal action. But market exchange has also required and constructed new forms of unfreedom, new kinds of limits on freedom, and foremost among them we would have to count the idea of race. Deeply ingrained in our most fundamental economic assumptions lies a desire for stability, and the same impulse to imagine natural stability in gold lies behind the desire to imagine intrinsic and fixed racial difference.

Benjamin Franklin, Venture Smith, and Olaudah Equiano lived in a changing world of rapid, complex international commerce and social mobility; in their lifetime, "mercantilism" gave way to new philosophies rooted in the idea of the economy as a self-regulating, "natural" system best left alone. Nature, Equiano told opponents of intermarriage, "abhors restraint." Prohibiting intermarriage only makes intermarriage more attractive, he argued, and drives people towards "the evils of lasciviousness." Remove the artificial human law, he had argued, and let "nature's plan" bring together those who it will.[64]

Clearly "natural" differences between people exist, physical differences as well as mental differences. What seems so striking is the way the philosophy of market freedom simultaneously promised to liberate people to shape themselves *and* suggested that they had a fundamental identity the market could not change and which they could not reshape.

Both Franklin and Equiano asked readers to consider if the market opened up boundless possibilities for self-fashioning, or only exaggerated a difference already present in an individual's nature but hidden by custom. If anyone can become *anything*—be truly "self-made" in the marketplace—then what people "are" at any given time has no substance, no basis in natural law, and no intrinsic meaning or value. Olaudah Equiano can be Ben Franklin, and so can you or I. But if people can only be what they already are *by nature*, can only be what they are born to be, then no freedom, no possibility of "self-making," can exist.[65]

Here again we can perhaps see one cause of anxiety about paper money—that it confused appearance and reality; that it allowed plain "Jane," the tradesman's wife, to pass for "our Lady." It "turned the world upside down": it looked like an effort to transform the base into the lofty, to make "stones and sticks into gold" by paper fiat. It unsettled the idea that what people were had some basis in natural law. In the Massachusetts of Shays' rebellion, Robert Gross has claimed, "nothing was what it seemed." "The rise of the 'fake' gentleman obsessed social critics," Gross continues, quoting James Warren's distaste at the fact that "fellows who would have shined my shoes five years ago, have amassed fortunes, and are riding in chariots." Warren called it "a world turned topsy turvy."⁶⁶ In Franklin's and Equiano's world too nothing was as it seemed. Fakers abounded, men and women who deceived with a virtuous and genteel exterior. Franklin himself pragmatically appeared as whatever served his purpose, faking the value he hoped to create, and he offered a recipe for self-transformation that served as a model for the idea of the "self-made man." These comments about money and social position, for all their exaggeration, reflect the uneasiness Americans felt about the egalitarian economic philosophy they pursued (and still pursue) so energetically.

Consider again Olaudah Equiano, newly free, as he danced in his "superfine Georgia blue clothes." Equiano lived in this world of shifting negotiation and false appearance. Once he might have shined Warren's shoes. But Equiano's world did *not* turn upside down: he did *not* manage to erase, or even appear to erase, the mark of racial difference. When he finally receives his manumission paper, Equiano says "all within my breast was tumult, wildness and delirium! My feet scarcely touched the ground, for they were winged with joy." He delights that "the fair as well as black people immediately styled me by a new appellation,—to me the most desirable in the world,—which was 'Freeman.'" But his subsequent narrative makes clear—as African American slave narratives would do from then after—the limits on freedom. His world did *not* turn upside down, because the fixed values of racial difference transcended the market's promise of freedom. There were limits to the market's transformative power.

The argument here is ultimately simple—that beneath the enthusiasm for market freedom lies the desire to have value rest on some solid "natural" foundation, to have there be a "bottom line"; and that as enthusiasm for market freedom increases, so too does desire for its opposite.

Americans have drawn that line with race, and African Americans have borne the brunt of that contradictory desire. It seems unsurprising that even today those who talk loudest about the "freedom" of the market place consistently emphasize "natural," fundamental, inexorable laws from which no one can free themselves. Considering what he regards as the foolishness of governments trying to effect economic outcomes, Milton Friedman, that most eloquent twentieth-century spokesman for marketplace freedom, insists "life is not fair," even if "it is tempting to believe that government can rectify what nature has spawned."[67]

Nature "spawned" Equiano and Venture Smith; giving them talents and traits they could test in the market. Friedman and Adam Smith might argue that government kept both down and the marketplace freed them, and they would be partially right. Equiano gives many examples of the law working against him, frustrating his trades and his economic advancement, and in this sense he seems to agree with Friedman and Smith. But he also gives examples in which not government but bigotry—freely chosen, market-derived bigotry—keeps him down. It is precisely this racism that Friedman and Smith cannot explain. It should be unthinkable in a society devoted to the free market, yet the market seems unable to erase it—indeed, as many historians have observed, free market economics and scientific racism—specie and species—arise at roughly the same time. They share a common origin, a fascination with, and fear of, the negotiability of value and identity.

CHAPTER TWO

Banking on Slavery

Does not every whisper of a new issue of paper make men hug their specie the closer?
— *Pennsylvania Gazette*, February 16, 1785

Antebellum Americans used a bizarre and astonishing money system. Lacking a central bank, they made do with literally tens of thousands of types of money: legal, illegal, semi-legal; some counterfeit and all of negotiable value. In the absence of a central bank, slaves served in place of gold. Slaves had value not just because of their labor: they had a value as capital, as money. Imagined as racially inferior, their place fixed by nature, slaves as a store of value allowed Americans to speculate and experiment with money. This made slavery doubly essential: they served as labor but also played some of the role that, in England for example, a central bank with gold reserves played in stabilizing the idea of value.

* * *

In 1821 Congressman Henry Meigs of New York introduced a bill to end slavery painlessly. By "devoting five hundred millions acres of the public lands, next west of the Mississippi," Meigs suggested, the U.S. could accomplish "the gradual emancipation of slaves, by a voluntary exchange of the lands for them."[1] Survey the 500 million acres into the "the usual sections and quarter sections," Meigs argued: number them, and sell every other quarter section for "certificates of the value of slaves." Interested parties would bring their slaves to their local district judge to establish the value of their slave holdings. The judge would draft a certificate of value entitling slaveowners to exchange their slaves for actual western land. They could occupy and farm the land or sell it to others. Meigs thought it an eminently reasonable plan. It would end slavery, encourage the settlement of western lands, and through the conventional sales of the other half of the 500 million acres, generate enough money to fund the colonization of the former slaves to Africa—all at no cost whatsoever to the American taxpayer.

Virginian John Floyd answered with an amendment insisting that slaves so freed "should be distributed in equal proportions" among the various states, beginning with Maine and proceeding "in regular order southward." You in the North must take the freed slaves, he told Meigs. The New Yorker responded with anger at this apparently contemptuous amendment, and Floyd withdrew it, insisting that "some such must be part of any plan of the kind." At that point the House voted to table Meigs's proposal.[2] Floyd's sarcastic amendment made no sense; it failed to answer the economic and moral substance of the plan. But it reminded Meigs and everyone listening how slavery, race, value, and economic exchange were linked.

Plans to compensate slaveowners for emancipation, more or less similar to the Meigs plan, had a long history and appeared as early as 1783. But compensated emancipation schemes proposed by Elbridge Gerry, James Madison, Meigs, Henry Clay, and Abraham Lincoln mostly fell dead to the Capitol floor.[3] In most cases the proposals simply lapsed, or debate was suppressed. For the most part, pro-slavery politicians simply refused to talk about the idea.

David Roediger, following W.E.B. DuBois, described "whiteness" as a psychic wage, a compensatory value Northern workers claimed for themselves as they went from independent artisans to wage workers. Indeed, this mental compensation extended beyond the working classes to white people generally. "Whiteness" constituted a value, a source of stable identity and a bottom line of meaning. If psychic compensation was the "wages of whiteness," blackness was the gold standard against which those wages were drawn. African Americans who could act as economic free agents, who could negotiate their own market value, devalued that standard.[4]

The previous chapter argued that partly because they lacked a stable, standardized money form, a standard of value, Americans turned to racial slavery and to the idea that "black flesh" could be made coin, that racial "species" might be made to act as specie. Americans tended towards racial slavery because slaves could be imagined as a source of stable value, an intrinsic value, derived from their racial character, that in daily exchange played the same role as gold. This chapter extends that analysis by looking at banking, money, and the different experiences of abolition in Britain and the United States.

*   *   *

One of the most interesting of the many historical differences between England and the United States lies in the approach to abolishing slavery. In 1833 the British Parliament passed the "Slavery Abolition Act." Under the Act, Parliament subscribed a fund of twenty million pounds sterling to compensate slaveowners for lost property. In its simplest terms the act freed slaves under six years old immediately; it reclassified other slaves as "apprentices" and provided that all "apprentices," depending on their age and type of work, would be freed by 1840. Their former masters would be paid cash as compensation, cash raised ultimately from British taxpayers.[5] In the British Empire, abolition of slavery appears to have been remarkably swift and remarkably, or at least relatively, painless. Certainly it required nothing like the American Civil War.

For years, following the example of Eric Williams, historians looked at the relative ease of British abolition and saw it as mostly about self-interest—as everyone knows now and knew then, wage labor is cheaper and more efficient than slave labor. Rather than marking a humanitarian triumph, abolition in England marked the triumph of rational, capitalist profit-maximizing. More recently historians have instead emphasized the moral, religiously based aspects of the reform, and termed British abolition as a mass act of "econocide" in which humanitarian antislavery impulses set the British Empire on its heels for a generation.[6]

Even a historian remaining agnostic on this question might wonder why the United States did not take a similar path. The British scheme required people with no direct connection to slavery to fund the cost of compensating slaveowners on distant Caribbean islands. Meigs's plan, by contrast, took advantage of the federal government's access to western land: Indians, not U.S. taxpayers, would bear the cost. And yet it never received a serious hearing. Whether Britons were motivated by economic self-interest and the cheapness of wage labor, or by humanitarian concerns for the injustice of slavery and the moral corruption it entailed, the fact remains that similar arguments advanced by American abolitionists failed to carry the day. To the degree that they persuaded at all, abolitionist arguments in the U.S. often depended more on the idea of a sinister "Slave Power Conspiracy" than they did on concerns for the plight of the slave.[7] It took a massive, bloody Civil War, followed by the military occupation of the conquered territory, to end slavery in the United States.

What accounts for the difference? Why did Americans, co-religionists for the most part, sharing the same language and much the same culture, defend slavery to the point of fratricide while their English brethren struck it down with the pen and the banknote?

Historians offer many excellent and plausible answers. Most Britons had little or no contact with actual slaves, who lived overwhelmingly in the sugar islands of the Caribbean, making slavery a distant and abstract idea. England had advanced farther into the industrial revolution, which made the logic of free market labor more compelling to men in power. England had far, far fewer slaves—less then one million—than the United States, and they were less central to the economy. An effective English network of moral persuasion was, simply, persuasive. Christopher Brown suggests that English abolitionism emerged as both a critique of the hypocrisy of the American colonies *and* as a justification for empire: put simply, abolition granted Englishmen the "moral capital" necessary to make imperial dominion of India palatable.[8] But as David Brion Davis puts it, recent arguments "never really tell us why antislavery, among dozens of competing reforms, won such overwhelming support that [English] abolitionists were virtually unopposed," or how England, "a nation deeply transformed by the world's first industrialization and divided by class struggles," found a way of "uniting a stable leadership with mass appeal."[9]

Here I suggest an additional explanation: England had a central bank: *the* central bank in fact, the Bank of England. The Bank of England gave the British Empire a stable, standardized money form, an index of value in all exchanges. Americans made two similar experiments in central banking before the Civil War: both failed, and neither ever enjoyed near the influence and authority of the Bank of England. Almost precisely as Britain was abolishing slavery, Americas were yet again abolishing central banking, in Andrew Jackson's "war" with Biddle's Bank. In England by 1850 Bank of England notes, backed by gold, were the nation's standard currency. By the 1850s, in contrast, Americans had no central bank, and instead used more than nine thousand different kinds of banknotes, thousands of pieces of "token money," various forms of semi-money issued by private bankers, and an astonishingly persistent range of counterfeits: a chaos of competing money forms. As they used this loose money to promote individual self-making and economic transformation, they clung all the more fiercely to the idea of the Africans' fixed racial value. Indeed: as paper money proliferated, the value of slaves went up. Americans banked on slaves.

The Bank of England stabilized credit relations, both what might be called real credit relations and also the less tangible but perhaps more important psychic sense of value in exchange. In England, the Bank literally embodied political authority's close relationship to the money supply, and in that way it made racial slavery less crucial as the psychic capital, the racial gold standard, that collateralized the wages of whiteness.

Historians rightly avoid monocausal arguments: it would be grossly distorting to name the lack of a central bank as the only reason for slavery's persistence in North America. But surely it might be named as a contributing factor? Examining the antebellum financial system, and its relation to slavery, makes it possible to add this new explanation to the set historians typically offer: had Americans established a central bank and a uniform money system—as well as some of the other features distinguishing British economic life—they might have followed England's path to the abolition of slavery.

*   *   *

If the American Revolution had a conservative side, in which men of property acted to entrench their rights and power, it also had inescapably radical implications. It suggested a level of equality, between white men at least, never before enacted into law. The Revolutionary money system made these radical implications doubly threatening.

The Revolution never enjoyed a broad base of consistent support. Loyalists doubted the wisdom of independence, and even revolutionaries wavered in their commitment. Taxation in part inspired the war, and, as has been often remarked, if Americans hated taxation without representation, they hated taxation *with* representation only slightly less. The Continental Congress had, in fact, not given itself the power to impose a direct tax. To fund the war, the Revolutionary government resorted to the familiar expedient of paper money.

More than 240 million in paper "Continental dollars" came off the presses during the war. Individual states also issued their own paper money totaling about 200 million. The money was made "legal tender" for all debts. It started an economic boom: the sudden infusion of cash, going mostly into the hands of soldiers and those who supplied them, stimulated the economy and tended, as it inflated prices, to redistribute wealth downward. Charles Royster quotes the Deputy Quartermaster of New Jersey: "Our people cry out against the Q. M. for raising prices, and none more willing to get the highest than themselves."[10] "Bad as it is," he wrote of the money "its [*sic*] wanted." In Massachusetts, "continental and state issues, real and counterfeit, were almost the only money circulating."[11] As prices began to climb, people spent the Continental dollars quickly, while they still held their value, often on luxuries.

Continental paper money began depreciating, slowly at first, but by the end of the war the terrifying phenomenon of hyperinflation had appeared, aided considerably by British and Tory counterfeiting, both real and imagined.[12] In conditions of hyperinflation, goods might double in price over a single day: all value seems destabilized and people resort to barter or cast around for an alternative standard of exchange. Recognizing their necessity during the war, conservatives would, for many generations to come, cite the Continental dollars as an example of paper money's danger to public morals.

They linked inflated paper not just to economic instability but to moral instability as well. "The greatest evil of a depreciated paper currency," argued the *Pennsylvania Gazette* in 1786, "remains to be mentioned. It destroys the morals of our citizens—creates extravagance—produces endless disputes and frauds—multiplies law-suits—promotes art and chicanery in business—and thereby prepares us for aristocracy and slavery."[13] Thanks to paper money, went another complaint, "The country swarms with speculators. . . . Not a tavern can we enter, but we meet crowds of these people, who wear their character in their countenances." These complaints, like those cited in the previous chapter, tend to link money of bad character with men of bad character, men "who wear their character in their countenances," whose value is all surface and no substance; "dirty" men of dirty actions. The writer continued: "at the sight of a dirty paper bill think—how many hearts has this worried? What number of dirty actions has it done? . . . Away with all worthless paper money; the source of all daily corruption and misery; let gold and silver restore solid integrity, pure innocence, and splendid honor."[14] Gold would reconcile what people looked like with what they actually were, and end deception.

Gordon Wood, on the other hand, linked Revolutionary-era paper money to a new economy then emerging, an economy with more room for upward mobility, more comfortable with speculation and with representative forms of money, and less committed to rank. During the war paper money made its way into regions where barter had largely prevailed before. By lowering interest rates, it eased borrowing costs.[15] Conservatives, often the ones borrowed from, sought to restore a "sound" gold basis, partly because international trade generally required gold. But the conservative response also suggested some anxiousness about paper money's tendency to make character itself seem less stable. As "ARTEMON" argued in the *Pennsylvania Gazette*, "does not every whisper of a new issue of paper make men hug their specie the closer?"[16] Following the Revolution, colonial elites uniformly enacted measures to return state and national economies to a specie basis, countering the expansionist, inflationary desires the Revolution had fueled. The conflict between entrenched position and economic mobility came into play very clearly during Shays' Rebellion.

By 1786 rural farmers in most states, but particularly in Massachusetts, had become increasingly disgusted with their inability to pay their taxes, and with the high costs of borrowing money. Their situation grew in part from the familiar lack of specie: the law in Massachusetts, and most other states, reflected the bad taste Continental dollars had left in the mouths of the elites who dominated state legislatures. State laws typically required yeoman to pay taxes in gold, but gold, as we have seen, tended to vanish into the coastal strongboxes and then hie itself to England. Come tax time, or when the debt collector knocked, hard-working farmers found themselves required to pay in a material that simply did not exist away from the cities. They had no means to represent their labor. In Massachusetts, angry western farmers, under the desultory leadership of Daniel Shays, marched on the state arsenal at Springfield, demanding issues of paper money to facilitate commerce and ease their debt costs. Similar uprisings took place in nearly all states.[17]

Although the troubles lasted only a short time, Shays' rebellion frightened men of property. Farmers in New Hampshire submitted a "long petition, setting forth their grievances on account of the scarcity of money, and praying for an emission of paper bills of credit, in which there is no single trace of an idea of redemption, or any one attempt to give the currency a foundation." The farmers seemed to believe "that the general court by a mere act of legislation by words and signs, could impress an intrinsic value on paper; which is as fully absurd as it would be to suppose that the legislature had the power of Midas, and could from a single touch, turn stones and sticks into gold."[18] Critics charged the Shays rebels with theft, claiming they were creating something from nothing. "The position of commercial opponents of printed money and their spokesmen was simple. Specie alone had 'intrinsic value'; and no law could make men think 'a piece of paper is a piece of money.'"[19] State militias stopped the insurrections, but anxiety about paper money contributed substantially to the formation of the Constitutional Convention in 1787.

At the convention, hard money partisans managed to include language in Article 1 of the Constitution to the effect that no state could "coin money; emit bills of credit [or] make anything but gold and silver coin a tender in payment of debts." The new Constitution also allowed Congress to "coin money" but said nothing whatsoever about paper. These phrases together would seem to make paper money, and banks, unconstitutional. Indeed, modern libertarian economists, and internet conspiracy theorists, continually reiterate this phrase in order to condemn our present money supply. The clauses (possibly) forbidding paper money would be brazenly ignored over the next fifty years.

Memories of hyperinflation, and fears of paper money, could not stem the entrepreneurial energies also represented at the Convention. Men on the make demanded paper, easy credit, and inflationary expansion, desires always at odds with the desire for stable prices and values. How could the new nation balance the conflicting desires for stability and expansion? How could it have stable value and entrepreneurial possibility?

*   *   *

Alexander Hamilton played perhaps the central role in the early republic's finances, in typically pragmatic, cynical, clear-eyed style. Hamilton persuaded Washington to embrace the national debt, and, against Jefferson's intense objections, to establish a national bank. Hamilton argued for an industrial, commercial, mercantile future, replacing Jeffersonian notions of yeoman equality with a policy frankly aimed at joining the interests of the very wealthy to the new nation's survival. He tried to balance the expansionist, inflationary desires of a market economy against the desire for stable value and specie orthodoxy.[20] His thoughts on money reflect this balancing act.

In his 1791 *Notes on the Establishment of a Mint*, Hamilton advised

Congress that the new nation's money must rest on a metallic basis. Lacking such a standard, he wrote, "defective species" of coin now circulated; these "base currencies" "embarrass the circulation" of individual states: "the mass of those generally current is composed of the newest and most inferior kinds." His words recall the language used to denounce the "inferior men" raised up by paper money, the new men posed against the more ancient and valuable species, driven from public life by paper.

The ever canny Hamilton turned to the question of gold or silver—which of "these two species of coin, of gold or silver, shall have any greater legality in payments?" Though he suggested allowing both silver and copper coin to circulate along with gold, he insisted that the silver coin's value should be based against the gold dollar. Gold, he argued, was "of superior value: less liberties have been taken with it." Hamilton was unsure why gold enjoyed this value, whether from "intrinsic superiority" or from "the prejudices of mankind," but characteristically he did not really care why; he pressed for gold as a standard, concluding: "there is scarcely any point . . . of greater moment than the uniform preservation of the intrinsic value of the money unit."[21]

The phrase shows Hamilton's ambivalence about the whole idea. If the coin's value was truly intrinsic—derived entirely from the substance of the gold itself—then it would need no preserving. For example, could anyone imagine the idea of "preserving" the intrinsic value of a lump of coal? Coal might be burned or lost or smashed into smaller pieces, but no alchemy could change its intrinsic properties. Similarly, if "value" stood among gold's intrinsic properties, then it could not be taken away and needed no preserving. But Hamilton recognized that "intrinsic value" was a matter of perception, not natural fact, and when he argued for a strict regulation of the coins' metallic content, he resorted to metaphors of color and "mixture." He specified alloys of silver and copper for American coins because "the silver counteracts the tendency of the copper to injure the color or beauty of the coin, by giving it too much redness . . . and the copper prevents too great whiteness which silver alone could confer." He also argued for alloying gold coins with silver, for copper would "spoil the appearance of the coin, and give it a base countenance."[22]

Hamilton had a sharp sense of human capacity for self-delusion. "The effects of imagination and prejudice cannot be safely disregarded in anything that relates to money," he argued: more dangerous than actual counterfeits was "the injury which will be done by a change in the appearance of the coin. . . . The intermixture of too much alloy, especially of copper . . . must materially lessen the facility of telling the purer from the baser kind, the genuine from the counterfeit."[23]

In shrugging his shoulders about the origins of gold's value, Hamilton deviated considerably from specie orthodoxy: he treated money's value as at least partly psychological, not "intrinsic," as arising from mental perception as much as physical substance. He argued against mixing gold with copper *not* because the copper coins would be worth less but because he believed that the appearance of purity counted as much as the metallic content. He imagines it will be easier to tell if "whiter" coins have been counterfeited. There is no good reason why this should be true, other than the idea that people will look with less suspicion on "whiter" coins or coins that are not "too white." Hamilton's report mingled a rationalizing, standardizing approach to money with something else, with a sense of value itself as both imaginary and fragile, and of how appearance, and the appearance of mixture, related to value.

It is probably not simply a coincidence that Hamilton disliked slavery and regarded prejudice towards Africans as imaginary. "The contempt we have been taught to entertain for the blacks," he wrote, "makes us fancy many things that are founded neither in reason nor in experience." Hamilton wrote those words in support of a plan for arming African Americans to fight for the rebellion and to "give them their freedom with their muskets." Conferring freedom by fiat, he thought, would "secure their fidelity, animate their courage, and . . . provide a good influence upon those who remain." "Their natural faculties," he wrote, "are probably as good as ours," and "I have not the least doubt that the negroes will make excellent soldiers with the proper management."[24] Hamilton in effect saw racial prejudice as learned, as imaginary, but thought that with opportunity and proper management negroes could dispel it. In his account of both money and racial prejudice, Hamilton foregrounded the effect of perception, of imagination, and of irrational ideas we have been "taught to entertain."

Believing as he did that "the effects of imagination and prejudice cannot be safely disregarded" when it came to money, Hamilton proposed standardizing the new nation's money under the aegis of a central bank. He founded the First Bank of the United States in 1791, hoping it would provide a uniform currency backed by gold and also reconcile public demands for expansive credit, private capital's desire for profits, and the general need for stable symbolic value. He based his short-lived bank on the Bank of England, which was even then grappling with similar issues.

*   *   *

The Bank of England, founded in 1694, is often described as the *ne plus ultra* of a "central bank." "It is to money," John Kenneth Galbraith wrote, "as St. Peter's is to the Faith."[25] The Bank's original 1694 charter granted it the exclusive right to handle the government's money—it was to be the Crown's bank. Money gained by England in taxation or tariff or plunder, through sales of land or settlement of foreign debts— all the government's money was deposited in the Bank, ideally in the form of gold or silver. The Bank could then use this money as a basis for loans to the king or queen, to private individuals, and eventually to other banks, the loans most likely taking the form of Bank of England notes, which were redeemable in gold as long as everyone did not ask at once. The Bank also sold stock, which increased its capital and in effect made stockholders the government's creditors.

The Crown, at the time of the Bank's founding, had a desperate need for cash, and in fact the entire original reason for chartering the Bank was so that the Bank could then loan money to the government. The Bank's loans to the government, once the government repaid, made it profitable but blurred the line between patriotic and pecuniary interest. And this was its genius: as a privately run enterprise, the Bank was supposed to restrain the government's demands for more money, particularly insatiable when wars broke out, while tying the interests of the wealthy to the fate of the nation. Theoretically, the Bank's directors would balk at being asked to loan the government more money as soon as the amount the king requested too greatly exceeded the amount of specie in the vaults—"too greatly" being what we refer to as a "judgment call" on the directors' part. So both the amount of specie in the vaults and the discretion of the Bank's directors would act as a brake on the government's tendency to always want more money.

The Bank's notes, its paper money, became more and more the standard money of England as London became more and more the center of the British Empire. The Bank served, Adam Smith wrote, as "a great engine of state." It was able to shift policy according to political need. In 1791, it temporarily suspended the gold standard to pay for wars with

France. In 1821, the Bank announced that once again its notes would be redeemable in precious metal, once again "as good as gold," placing England back on the gold standard.

Here we might consider what exactly it means to be "on the gold standard." Theoretically, it means that any paper note can be redeemed at any time for gold, which the paper note merely symbolizes. The paper note is just easier to transport than the gold, more convenient: like the tobacco notes used in colonial Virginia, which stood for real bales of tobacco, the paper one-pound note simply said "there is an equal amount of gold sitting in the Bank of England's vaults." In fact, however, there is always more paper money in circulation than there is gold in vaults. The point of a bank, after all, is creating money by lending from its reserves—banks create money in excess of deposits, hoping that the time never comes when all depositors show up and demand the gold at once. This Galbraith calls the "magic of banking," and it explains both why banks so often look like pagan temples and why bankers historically went out of their way to seem impeccably sober and dull. They routinely turned $1,000 in gold into $1,500, $2,000, $10,000 in paper.[26]

But doing this too often—printing too many banknotes—causes their value to decline, relative to gold. How many is too many? That depends on who you ask, and when you ask. Ideally, the increase in circulating paper money matches the rate of economic growth, and, also ideally, the flow of gold into the nation's vaults from overseas. The Bank of England's sober and willfully boring directors would make sure that the amount of money lent—the number and value of paper notes created—did not too greatly exceed the amount of gold in the vaults. At the same time, by lending money to drive economic growth, they would act as Smith's "engine of state." By 1833, Bank of England notes were considered secure enough to be declared legal tender for all debts, and the Bank had emerged as the "governor" on English commerce.[27]

It did occur to Englishman to ask why a group of wealthy private individuals, operating in secret with an exclusive monopoly, got to decide how much money should circulate and therefore how much any private individual should have to pay for a loan or even for basic goods. It also led them to wonder why anyone needed a gold standard, if the Bank was always creating more money than it had in gold. In the U.S. these questions would lead to the undoing of two separate attempts to found a central bank. But in England the Bank managed to stave off that criticism.

It's also important to point out that "being on the gold standard" does not necessarily mean handling actual gold. Gold is extremely heavy and impractical for many applications: hard to conceal, hard to haul, bulky to store. Under a pure gold standard most people would handle not gold itself but some convenient symbol of gold, most likely a paper bill. What matters is not actual gold but the idea that, somewhere, actual gold exists to back this paper note: the *idea* of gold existing, somewhere, rather than the daily reality.

Similarly, it might be fair to say that Englishmen understood money as coming from a fundamentally different place than Americans. In 1805 Robert Banks, Lord of the Treasury, told King George: "There is no doubt that the Sovereigns of most of the kingdoms and states of Europe have enjoyed and exercised from time immemorial the right of declaring at what rate or value the Coins of every denomination . . . shall pass, and become . . . legal tender. In this Your Majesty's kingdom, Your Royal predecessors have always enjoyed and exercised this right." "It is," he continued, "an unquestionable prerogative of the Crown."[28] In fact it was not: even then control of this subject was passing from the hands of royalty and into the hands of parliamentarians and central bankers. But the sense of what money was and where it came from was significantly different in England, different in perhaps the same way that social class exists in both places though Americans and the English experience it differently. Behind each banknote stood the distant, never-glimpsed figure of the king, with all the weight of tradition and history and entitlement that implied.

The Bank of England, with its connection to the Crown, meant that England enjoyed a stable, standard currency and a high degree of central control over the economy. Hardly foolproof, but very different from what developed in the United States. As we have seen, a central part of the history of the American colonies involved American's refusal to accept the idea that money was "an unquestionable prerogative of the Crown" and, after 1776, their rejection of the idea that the Crown had any prerogatives at all. So who did the money then belong to, if not the king?

*   *   *

Hamilton's First Bank of the United States followed the Bank of England in most details. Hamilton designed the Bank as a private corporation which would hold the federal government's deposits. It would be the largest bank in the nation, empowered to open branches in individual states, and it would issue paper money that would, Hamilton hoped, provide a uniform currency and replace the profusion of local and foreign coins and bills then circulating.[29] Hamilton wanted the Bank to play something of the role of a modern central bank: that is, to actively monitor economic conditions and adjust the money supply to suit. The Bank's paper money, backed by federal gold deposits, would be the best, most reliable money available, a standard of value for all transactions. And as the largest Bank in the country, Hamilton's Bank would prevent "excesses." If, for example, Bank managers suspected that a local bank had printed too much paper money, it would send its agents to the bank with a valise full of paper notes and ask for gold or silver in return. This possibility would check the local bank's tendency to over-issue paper money. "Most commercial nations have found it necessary to institute Banks," Hamilton wrote, "and they have proved to be the happiest engines that ever were invented for advancing trade." Like Adam Smith, Hamilton enjoyed a good engine metaphor. Machines generated power and energy, but they regulated force: they "governed" as they worked. But they were happy about it, in the sense of benign and optimistic.[30]

Bray Hammond, author of the most thorough history of American banking and himself an enthusiastic central banker, noted that the First Bank of the United States set off "a rage for banks—a 'bancomania.'" Perhaps recognizing that "banking" and "mania" form an improbable pair, Hammond pointed to numbers. In 1791 there were only four banks in the U.S.: by 1800 there were twenty-nine. By 1811, one hundred seventeen banks served the small nation: by 1815 there were two hundred twelve.[31] The First Bank, and the Constitution, failed to check the enthusiasm for local credit and paper money.

Historians of central banking, a small tribe indeed, come in two basic flavors: those who approve of it and those who do not. The former, epitomized by Hammond, tend to be witty, cynical realists who see a central bank, when staffed by capable men, as the judicious melding of state and private interests. The latter are irritable, idealistic devotees of the free market ever vigilant against threats democracy poses to property. The earliest professional histories of banking dwelt heavily on the menace of paper money and easy credit; they saw a central bank as a bulwark of the gold standard.[32] Histories written after World War II, at the height of Keynesianism, stressed the importance of central banks in balancing inflationary and deflationary political interests: they also fretted about "democratic" attitudes towards credit, but saw expert wise management, not gold, as the solution to balancing expansion and stability. In these accounts, the First and Second Banks of the United States vigilantly checked the enthusiasms of the ignorant and the unscrupulous.[33] But as Milton Friedman displaced Keynes in the 1980s, historians of banking veered towards condemnation: the First and Second Banks, they said, meddled where they had no business meddling and caused more harm than good, as government always does. For these historians antebellum Americans, lacking an effective and permanent central bank, died like Moses within tantalizing sight of the libertarian promised land.[34]

Critics at the time attacked Hamilton's Bank as unconstitutional: they charged it with allowing an "English" influence to control the economy, and they accused it of both choking credit *and* loosing too much credit and paper money. They denounced it as a corporation, an artificial monopoly, "an association of individuals taken from the mass of society, and vested with exemption, and surrounded with immunities." By whom is this immense power wielded, Daniel Webster asked? "By a body who, in derogation of the great principle of our institutions, responsibility to the People, are amenable only to a few Stockholders, and they chiefly foreigners."[35] In 1811, by one vote, the charter of the First Bank was allowed to lapse.

But Congress waited only five years to establish a Second Bank of the United States, organized on almost identical lines and opposed on almost identical lines. "I have ever been the enemy of banks," Jefferson wrote to John Adams in 1814, and of "the tribe of bank-mongers, who were seeking to filch from the public their swindling and barren gains." Sadly he concluded, "the mania is too strong. It has seized, by its delusions and corruptions, all the members of our governments, general, special and individual."[36] If men like Jefferson detested banks and paper money in principle, and dreamed of a specie standard, the proliferation of banks in the early republic testifies to hunger for credit and inflation. When "we wish to get rid of a Bank of the United States," wrote William Gouge in disgust, "we proceed in such a way that in putting down one bank, we put up five hundred."[37] Americans wanted easy credit, but they had mixed feelings about central control.

Historical accounts of the Second Bank of the United States similarly either praise it as a model of equipoise or denounce it as a damaging intrusion into the free market. Economic historians differ on just how much of a restraining or stimulating effect the Second Bank actually ex-

ercised. At no time did either the First or the Second bank manage anything like the authority and control of the Bank of England. In favorable
accounts the Second Bank's president, Nicholas Biddle, managed the
economy judiciously; and the collapse of the bank triggered a disgrace-
ful era of wildcat banking. In critical accounts the Bank either choked
off enterprise and stifled the ambitions of creative men, or encouraged
overprinting of paper by local and state banks and thereby engendered
financial boom and bust cycles. The present study, however, is not a history of banking but a history of attitudes about money.

*   *   *

While the history of the Second Bank of the United States is well known,
the history of money, the actual thing used to pay in antebellum America, has gotten much less attention. Partly this reflects the tendency to
treat money as an historical "given," as a timeless thing. "Everyone wants
money, the bottom line is money": yes, those things are true, but everyone wants food as well—the interesting thing is not the need for food,
which amoebas have in equal measure to people, but rather the elaborate
meanings and complex variations people pile on the act of eating. Who
eats what and when, where it comes from, how is it prepared and by who,
how it gets to market or to table and in what forms: a historian who treats
"food" as simply a biologically necessary mass of digestible calories, like
nutrition in a tube, is missing almost *everything* interesting about the
subject. So too with money—money was never simply one thing, static in
all its functions and permutations.

   Unlike their English forebears, neither the First nor the Second Banks
of the United States ever managed to standardize the currency. In fact
the nation's money, the stuff people used in everyday transactions, was
astonishingly varied; bank issues account for only a very small part of
the overall money in circulation. Although the nature of the money supply varied with the political winds—the economic crisis of 1837 set off a
particularly sharp increase in what might be called "nonbank monies"—
the antebellum money supply was generally and consistently promiscuous. A historian of the U.S. who treats "money" as an objective, static
fact, and views credit only through formally chartered banks, misses all
the most interesting things about the subject.

   Consider as a starting point the remarkable story related by William
Wells Brown in his book *Three Years in Europe; or, Places I Have Seen*

and People I Have Met. Born in Kentucky, the son of a slave mother and a local white man, Brown escaped from slavery and then worked from Buffalo, New York, on Lake Erie steamboats, where he helped other slaves escape. Eventually he became a novelist and abolitionist lecturer in the U.S. and internationally. *Three Years in Europe*, published in 1852, consists of a series of letters mixing accounts of European tourism with anecdotes of Brown's early adult life in his home country. In one episode Brown visits the famous Bank of England.

"I shall sum up my visit to it, by saying that it surpassed my highest idea of a bank," Brown wrote. He described the golden light suffusing the vast building and the "almost countless number of clerks." "But a stroll through this monster building of gold and silver," Brown continued, "brought to my mind an incident that occurred to me a year after my escape from slavery."

In 1835, Brown recalled, he traveled to Monroe, Michigan, on the western shore of Lake Erie, seeking more work on steam ships. Walking through the streets he spied a barbershop, and since he had occasionally cut hair, he asked the barber to hire him. The barber refused multiple times. So Brown secured a room across the street, "purchased an old table, two chairs, got a pole with a red stripe painted around it, and the next day opened, with a sign over the door, 'Fashionable Hair-dresser from New York, Emperor of the West.'" In the grand tradition of Ben Franklin, Brown began denigrating his competitor: "I had to tell all who came in that my neighbor on the opposite side did not keep clean towels, that his razors were dull, and, above all, he had never been to New York to see the fashions. Neither had I. In a few weeks I had the entire business of the town, to the great discomfiture of the other barber."

Brown's fabricated identity gets him more business, but, as he tells it, he had greater ambitions, and the loose state of American banking gave him a unique set of opportunities. "At this time," Brown noted, "any person who could raise a small amount of money was permitted to establish a bank, and allowed to issue notes for four times the sum raised. This being the case, many persons borrowed money merely long enough to exhibit to the bank inspectors, and the borrowed money was returned, and the bank left without a dollar in its vaults, if, indeed, it had a vault about its premises." These were the famous "Wild Cat Banks," says Brown: "banks were started all over the Western States, and the country flooded with worthless paper." The worthless paper included "notes from 6 to 75 cents in value; these were called 'Shinplasters.'"

"Some weeks after I had commenced business on my 'own hook,'" Brown continued, "I was one evening very much crowded with customers; and while they were talking over the events of the day, one of them said to me, 'Emperor, you seem to be doing a thriving business. You should do as other business men, issue your Shinplasters.'" Some in the room laughed, Brown recalled, "but with me it was no laughing matter, for from that moment I began to think seriously of becoming a banker."

We might stop here to consider the world of Monroe, Michigan, as Brown described it: a place where either everyone is black, or there is no race consciousness at all. Nothing prevents Brown from setting himself up as a barber, based on little more than a striped pole and a sense of bravado. Cheerfully unscrupulous, Brown lies about his rival and himself, and thereby prospers. While he clucks his tongue about the sorry state of American banking, lo and behold, in the next sentence he sets about to do exactly as he deplores.

"I accordingly went a few days after to a printer," Brown writes, and chose some designs. It took little time to print them: "the next day my Shinplasters were handed to me," Brown relates, "the whole amount being twenty dollars, and after being duly signed were ready for circulation. Through the assistance of my customers, and a good deal of exertion on my own part, my bills were soon in circulation; and nearly all the money received in return for my notes was spent in fitting up and decorating my shop." So by printing his own money, Brown creates the cash needed to outfit his shop.

This extraordinary story points to the attraction of loose, unregulated money. Brown, who has practically nothing, manages to turn bluster, charm, and printed paper into a thriving shop.

But Brown soon discovers the disadvantages of loose money. "One day," Brown recalled, "as I was sitting at my table, stropping some new razors I had just got with the avails of my 'Shinplasters,'" a stranger entered and said, "Emperor, you will oblige me if you will give me some other money for these notes of yours." Brown has little choice, but he does what anyone of his day would do: "I immediately cashed the notes with the most worthless of the Wild Cat money that I had on hand, but which was a lawful tender." Brown has a cash drawer full of mixed money, of different types from different banks, all of different degrees of stability or value. He quickly pays off the stranger with the worst of what he has on hand. But almost instantly another stranger appears, with a handful of Brown's shinplasters, and asks for cash. "These were cashed, and soon a third came with his roll of notes. I paid these with an air of triumph, although I had but half a dollar left." He begins to think he has perhaps survived this crisis, when he sees a fourth man crossing the street, with a handful of his shinplasters. "I instantaneously shut the door, and looking out of the window, said, 'I have closed business for the day: come to-morrow and I will see you.'" Across the street he sees the rival barber, grinning and clapping his hands. The rival had sent men to redeem Brown's shinplasters and thereby bankrupt him. "I was completely 'done Brown' for the day," says the "Emperor."

Brown sneaks out the back door and goes to find the man who had first suggested printing shinplasters. "He laughed heartily, and then said, 'You must act as all bankers do in this part of the country.'" It was only too simple: "When your notes are brought to you, you must redeem them, and then send them out and get other money for them; and, with the latter, you can keep cashing your own Shinplasters." "I immediately commenced putting in circulation the notes which I had just redeemed," Brown wrote, "and my efforts were crowned with so much success, that before I slept that night my 'Shinplasters' were again in circulation, and my bank once more on a sound basis."

At the end of the chapter he returns to the Bank of England. "As I saw the clerks shoveling out the yellow coin upon the counters of the Bank of England, and men coming in and going out with weighty bags of the precious metal in their hands," he muses, "I could not but think of the great contrast between the monster Institution, within whose walls I was then standing, and the Wild Cat Banks of America!"[38]

But what does he think of the contrast? Brown tells an extraordinary story by any measure. Not only does he have nothing at the beginning of this anecdote: in a real sense, in this story, he is no one. Born of mixed parentage, of uncertain legal status as a runaway, he has no "real name." He took the name "William Wells Brown" in honor of a kindly Quaker man who found him, sick and hungry, in flight from slavery. "William Wells Brown," the author, is born of a happenstance meeting and a stubborn instance on self-control and the right of self-fashioning.[39] His story of Monroe, Michigan, takes place in an odd kind of social vacuum. There are no descriptions of the town or its population, no one has a real name—people call Brown "Emperor." And again the story depicts a world in which money is printed at will, origins are fabricated at will, and race is irrelevant or invisible. There is no "bottom line," no "monster institution" like the Bank of England to prevent the issue of "shinplasters," stabilize value, and limit the ambitions of entrepreneurs. In his anecdote "Emperor" Brown is like his own paper money, perfectly good if all agree to take it.

Possibly Brown exaggerated. The story, like the stories Equiano and Smith told, reflects a desire to have the free market be as free as it pretends, and he never tells how it concluded. Brown's life, again like the lives of Equiano or Venture Smith, reflected quite the opposite, a world where race would *not* stop mattering; where the market would *not* renegotiate what race meant. He lived in a world where the idea, the fantasy, of race stabilized social relations in the same way the idea of gold lying in some vault somewhere stabilized value in paper.

Brown placed his story in 1835—the Second Bank of the United States, though rapidly declining, still existed. Clearly, it did not exert and had not exerted much of a restraining influence on the ambitions, and the credit, of an itinerant runaway slave in the Michigan Territory. In the absence of an effective central bank, Americans printed their own money and negotiated among themselves as to its value. They worked through different kinds of legitimate banks, but also, especially in the South, through private uncharted bankers and semi-bankers, using "unaccounted currency," token notes and coins issued by small businesses and individuals. More likely, Brown did not exaggerate at all.

*   *   *

The antebellum money system seems almost incomprehensible to modern eyes. The United States had a mint and a system of formal coinage, based in silver and gold. The U.S. Mint, by 1838, had four steam-powered facilities issuing "official" U.S. coins. These coins formed the "real money" of the nation. But Americans never deemed them sufficient, and in daily practice continued to use Spanish, French, Brazilian, and other Latin American coins in large number. "The dependence on other people's monies was obviously galling," but political pressure for more currency insured that from 1816 to 1857, foreign gold and silver coins remained legal tender. To complicate matters further, nothing prevented private individuals from founding a mint and striking their own coins, coins made of gold and silver or token coins made of base metal. The Constitution prohibited *states* from minting coins but said nothing about private individuals, and in multiple cases private coiners issued their own gold and silver cash. Between 1830 and 1847, for example, the Wechtler family minted their own gold dollars in South Carolina and Georgia, dollars which circulated alongside—and indeed, sometimes enjoyed a higher value than—products of the U.S. Mint. "Faced with an economy that constantly outstripped the orthodox money supply," writes numismatist Richard Doty, "Americans did as they had done before: they replied with an unorthodox one."[40] These various coins derived their value ostensibly from their metallic content, but they also varied in response to tinkering by political authority. The term "specie" broadly connoted gold and silver, but the forms the specie might take varied greatly. And most important, the federal government lacked any centralized control of the money supply.

Before 1860 individual banks could print their own money. Any person or persons could start a bank, obtain a state charter and some worthy looking engravings, and start issuing currency. Different states exercised differing degrees of regulatory authority over such paper monies, ranging from quite a bit to practically none, but in ordinary life a merchant might encounter not just a profusion of foreign coins but also hundreds of these different state and local banknotes, some issued by marble-pillared and stately institutions, others by backwoods enterprises with more ambition than assets. These legally legitimate banknotes typically circulated at a "discount"—the farther they traveled from their home institution, the less they were worth.

Additionally, our merchant might further encounter pieces of paper which looked like banknotes and operated like banknotes in daily business but which issued from hybrid institutions other than banks. The most well-known example of these *de facto* banknotes, "George Smith's money," circulated in amounts of up to $1.5 million for about twenty years, into the 1850s. Smith, a Scottish immigrant, ran an insurance company and printed "certificates of deposit" drawn on the insurance company in denominations as low as one dollar.[41] These certificates passed as money. The early Mormon Church also established a semi-bank in Kirtland, Ohio, printing at least $150, 000 in paper notes of the "Kirtland Safety Society Anti-Banking Company." Joseph Smith hoped to dodge laws regulating banking by declaring that his organization was not a bank. State authorities disagreed: Smith was fined and the Kirtland semi-bank collapsed.[42] "There were 'unauthorized banks' everywhere," Bray Hammond writes near the end of *Banks and Politics*: "besides partnerships and individuals operating as banks without corporate charter, there were also corporations without the name of banks

FIGURE 2.1. Private bank note of the Mechanic's Bank of Memphis, 1854. Courtesy of the Federal Reserve Bank of San Francisco.

that were engaged in discounting, sale of exchange, and extension of deposit credit."[43]

A merchant would also encounter promissory notes or various forms of commercial paper in which one man endorsed another's debt—in the South especially, cotton factors and "accommodation endorsers" issued paper which served as money. It is extremely difficult to know how much of this "underground banking" went on. In 1856 the Secretary of the Treasury estimated that private bankers accounted for $118,000,000 in capital, about a third of the amount produced by legitimate, chartered banks. But the figure seems highly imprecise.[44]

For smaller transactions, many antebellum businesses issued shinplasters or "token" money of their own. In Washington, D.C., between 1837 and 1841, historian Richard Doty found small denomination notes, typically for six-and-one-quarter or twelve-and-one-half cents, issued by "professions including 'butcher, grocer, singing master, restaurant owner, hotelier, dry goods merchant, printer and druggist.'"[45]

Given the slightest chance, *DeBow's Review* lamented, "the corporations of cities and towns, turnpike companies, bridge companies, railroad companies, and individuals in all the private walks of life immediately commence the issue of notes for dollars and the fractional parts of dollars."[46] In Georgia alone, between 1810 and 1866, " more than fifteen hundred varieties of currency of this type circulated."[47] "Fabulous sums in shinplasters, from five cents to a dollar, were circulated by the people, so that to a considerable extent every man was a banker, and distributed his own notes," recalled traveling magician Antonio Blitz: "In this

FIGURE 2.2. Undated paper money issued by the Delaware Bridge Company. Courtesy of the Federal Reserve Bank of San Francisco.

FIGURE 2.3. Ten cent "Tobacco Currency," 1863. A merchant might give this in change, redeemable in the store and possibly elsewhere, but meanwhile serving as advertising. Prints and Photographs Division, Library of Congress.

manner every State was crowded with all descriptions of worthless paper. Property and merchandise became subject to the influence it produced, creating an artificial value beyond belief."[48]

The broad label "shinplaster" might also have encompassed "token money," privately stamped coins issued in small denominations to serve as change, as advertising, or as political commentary. "A large number of the coins of this period were used as vehicles of political satire and abuse," concludes on early history of token money: "the victim of this abuse is generally Jackson. Thus, one coin of 1834 bears the gaunt figure of the President, carrying in one hand a sword and in the other a money-bag, surrounded by the words, 'A plain system, void of pomp.' On the reverse of the coin is the emblem of a jackass in his most stubborn attitude, with the letters 'LL.D.' on his haunches, in allusion to the degree conferred on Jackson by Harvard University."[49] Such tokens might pass in barter as novelties, accepted because interesting, agreeable, or attractive. *Coin Collector's Journal* of 1876 mentions five thousand varieties of token coins issued by shopkeepers, tradesmen, merchants, and small businesses.

Although evidence of these "unaccounted currencies" is fragmentary, by one estimate more than fifty million pieces of private token money circulated in the antebellum United States.[50] There were, it seems worth noting, less than thirty-five million people in the United States in 1860. "By the time of the Civil War, the American monetary system was, without rival, the most confusing in the long history of commerce and associated cupidity," Galbraith concluded.[51] The forms of money used

FIGURE 2.4. A satirical "shinplaster" from 1837 mocking Jackson's pursuit of the "gold humbug." Such a bill was a cross between a novelty, a souvenir, and actual money. Prints and Photographs Division, Library of Congress.

correlated broadly to variations in class and race. Nearly all preferred specie, the only "real" money around, unless its weight and bulk made the transaction inconvenient. But specie was not always available, either in daily commerce or as credit, while other forms of money abounded. Poor people, and people engaged in small transactions, might use shin-plasters. Travelers contended with banknotes and accepted a "discount" on their value. An established urban merchant might prefer notes of the Bank of the United States, while it existed, and take notes of other banks of necessity. Southern planters and large merchants did business via factors, described below, while most other large-scale trading of staples took place via "bills of exchange," paper promises to pay in the future for goods or services attained.[52] Legally chartered banks only give us a narrow view of what Americans called "money" in the antebellum years.

People typically accepted banknotes, shinplasters, and other token monies only when they knew who ran the bank or issued the tokens. As notes traveled further from the bank that issued them, they usually lost value. Complicating things, antebellum paper notes often shared a visual vocabulary. Travelers expected they would have to change money as they moved from town to town; notes emblazoned with "Bank of Fayetteville" or "Onondaga Savings" gave notice of the insecurity of value across space.[53]

And as they moved from town to town, antebellum travelers ran into counterfeits. It was, one historian claims, "the golden age" of counterfeiting.[54] Anyone doing business with money had to watch out for imitations not only of legitimate bank notes but also for "raised" notes, on which the number "one" might be modified to "ten," or entirely fictitious notes drawn on nonexistent but convincingly far-off banks. Stephen Mihm's marvelous *Nation of Counterfeiters* describes the village of Dunham, Quebec, where "every family in the place was engaged," in the 1820s, "in the production of spurious bank-bills" for the Yankee market.[55] From the village road nicknamed "Cogniac Street" (after the slang word for counterfeit), New York governor DeWitt Clinton claimed, a vast network of engravers, printers, messengers, and "passers" brought counterfeit dollars into the United States. An unscrupulous or enterprising person could travel to "Cogniac street" with real money and choose from a selection of banknotes ready-made for his convenience. "Capitalists and counterfeiters thrived together in the early republic, and for every banknote symbolizing confidence in capitalism, there was a ghostly double born in the village here."[56] Some estimate that at times roughly *40 percent* of the money in circulation was counterfeit.[57]

That figure becomes more plausible considering the lightly regulated nature of banking. A local bank might produce paper money far in excess of any hope of redemption. Was such a note genuine, or counterfeit? "It was a popular remark among men of business," wrote the detective Alan Pinkerton, "that they preferred a good counterfeit on a solid bank to any genuine bill upon the shyster institution." "The handsome counterfeits of the currency put forth by the old time 'Coney men' were not only equal in artistic appearance," he added, but "based upon an almost equivalent in value."[58]And remember also that non-bank monies circulated as well—token monies, paper bills issued by entrepreneurs like George Smith, and forms of semi-money issued by private bankers. Not counterfeit, these were not entirely legitimate either.

To protect themselves, merchants subscribed to "counterfeit detectors," weekly, bi-weekly, or monthly lists of banknotes that gave a description of the bank's paper money and rated the bank's character.

Merchants typically needed more than one: the publishers of counterfeit detectors regularly accused their competitors of "puffing" the reputations of crooked bankers who bribed them, raising the specter of counterfeit counterfeit detectors. Herman Melville satirized the problem in *The Confidence-Man*. When an elderly steamboat passenger receives some unfamiliar bills in change, he rushes to his "counterfeit detector" to examine "a three dollar bill on the Vicksburgh Trust and Insurance Banking Company." His "counterfeit detector," he mutters to himself, "says, among fifty other things, that, if a good bill, it must have, thickened here and there into the substance of the paper, little wavy spots of red; and it says they must have a kind of silky feel, being made by the lint of a red silk handkerchief stirred up in the paper-maker's vat." But "that sign is not always to be relied on," says the old man, "for some good bills get so worn, the red marks get rubbed out. And that's the case with my bill here—see how old it—or else it's a counterfeit, or else—I don't see right—or else—dear, dear me—I don't know what else to think." The passage ends with the old man poring over the bill into the small of the evening.[59] Certainty was scarce: money was not.

In "Emperor" Brown's account, loose paper money, printed at will, enables the ambitious man to rise and renders race irrelevant. Counterfeiting and paper money, just as it destabilized the meaning of both value and legitimacy, might similarly destabilize the meaning of racial

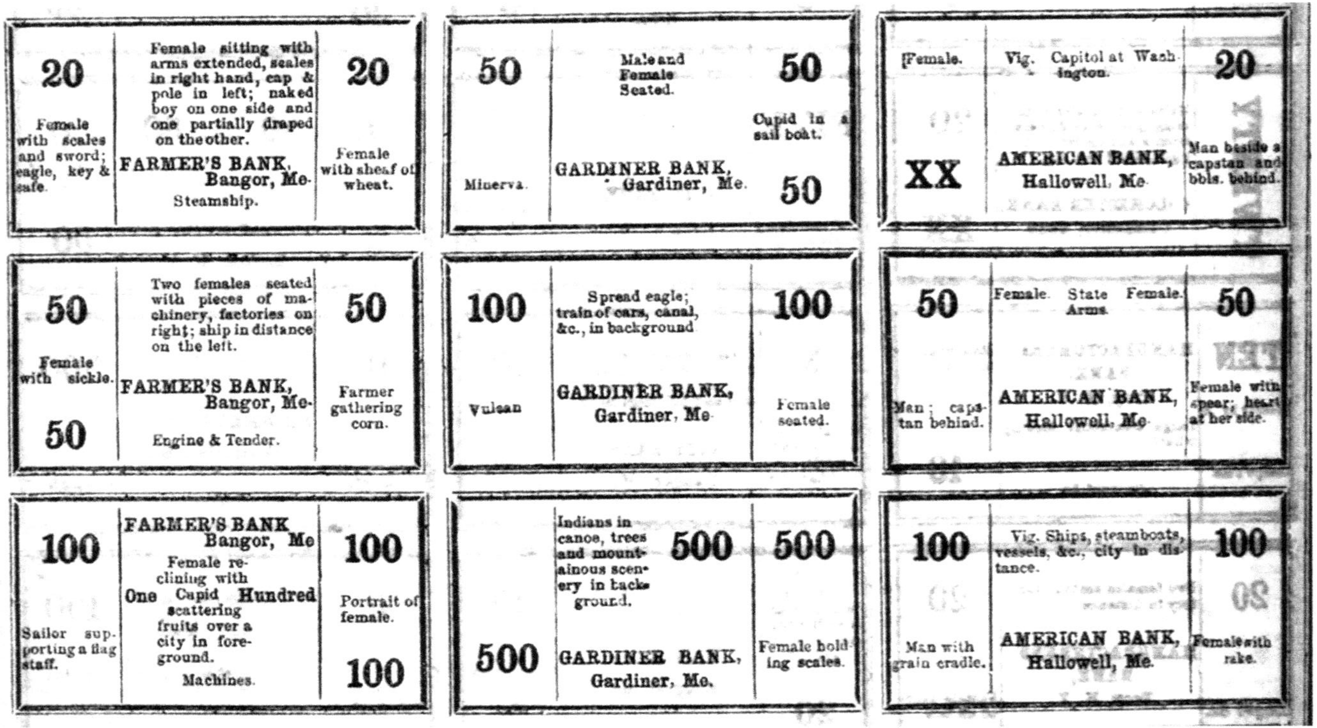

FARMER'S BANK, Bangor, Me. (left column)

20 — Female sitting with arms extended, scales in right hand, cap & pole in left; naked boy on one side and one partially draped on the other. — Female with sheaf of wheat. — 20
Female with scales and sword; eagle, key & safe. — FARMER'S BANK, Bangor, Me. — Steamship.

50 — Two females seated with pieces of machinery, factories on right; ship in distance on the left. — Farmer gathering corn. — 50
Female with sickle. — FARMER'S BANK, Bangor, Me. — Engine & Tender.

100 — FARMER'S BANK, Bangor, Me — Female reclining with One Cupid Hundred scattering fruits over a city in foreground. — Portrait of female. — 100
Sailor supporting a flag staff. — Machines. — 100

GARDINER BANK, Gardiner, Me. (middle column)

50 — Male and Female Seated. — Cupid in sail boat. — 50
Minerva. — GARDINER BANK, Gardiner, Me.

100 — Spread eagle; train of cars, canal, &c., in background — Female seated. — 100
Vulcan. — GARDINER BANK, Gardiner, Me.

500 — Indians in canoe, trees and mountainous scenery in background. — Female holding scales. — 500
500 — GARDINER BANK, Gardiner, Me. — 500

AMERICAN BANK, Hallowell, Me. (right column)

20 — Female. — Vig. Capitol at Washington. — Man beside a captain and bble. behind
XX — AMERICAN BANK, Hallowell, Me.

50 — Female. State Female. Arms — 50
Man; captain behind. — AMERICAN BANK, Hallowell, Me.

100 — Viz. Ships, steamboats, vessels, &c.; city in distance. — Female with anchor; heart at her side. — 100
Man with grain cradle. — AMERICAN BANK, Hallowell, Me. — Female with rake.

FIGURE 2.5. Excerpt from J. Tyler Hodges, Hodges' *New Bank Note Safeguard* (New York, 1859), 134. Digitized by Google.

difference. In Robert Montgomery Bird's satirical novel of 1839, *The Adventures of Robin Day*, loose paper money signifies the collapse of racial hierarchy.

In the novel, country swain Robin ends up a wandering fugitive with but a few paper notes to his name. Arriving in Philadelphia, he is immediately knocked down by "a blow from the wheelbarrow of a black porter; who, counting up from behind, whistling *Yankee Doodle* . . . tumbled me into a lot of pottery arranged along the pavement." Incensed, Robin starts after the porter, but the shopkeeper grabs him and demands payment for the damage to his shop.

Robin hands the shopkeeper a five dollar bill, but the merchant replies that the note was "a New Jersey note [and] like the bills of all New Jersey banks, at a discount;" that is, worth less in Philadelphia than where it originated. He "refused to receive it, unless I allowed him an additional half-dollar by way of premium." Robin is about to pay "when a decent looking man stepped forward, inveighed against the roguery of the fellow," and "swore that New Jersey bank-bills were never at a discount, but always at a par." The stranger gives the merchant a dollar bill "of some Philadelphia bank" and hands Robin "four others as change; which being done, he clapped my Jersey note into his own pocket, and walked off." Robin discovers, "about five minutes afterwards, that the four bills given me by the good-natured stranger were counterfeit, and my liberal gentleman a rascally swindler." In this passage Bird described the complexity of antebellum commerce, even in a major city. Notes of all banks have an uncertain value; the holders of counterfeit money pass them on as quickly as they can.

The misadventures continue: "I had not well got over the anger I had been thrown into by the assault of the porter, when it was my fate to encounter another blackamoor, a strapping tatterdemalion" who blocks his way. "I very naturally expected he would get out of the way," but instead "he stalked against me, as if entirely ignorant of my presence, or quite indifferent to it; and I was, in a twinkling, laid upon my back." Two minutes later, Robin relates, "I encountered a similar accident; a third negro running against me with a violence that pitched me into a cellar." "The coloured gentlemen of Philadelphia," Robin concludes, were "the true aristocracy of the town, or, at least, of the streets thereof." "The insolence of the black republicans" astonishes Robin, as does the submissiveness of whites: within three pages Robin experiences loose money and inverted racial hierarchy simultaneously—in the antebellum North as Bird describes it, bad money equals black people out of place, and instability in both financial and social values.[60]

* * *

Regardless of the presence of a First or Second Bank of the United States, antebellum Americans used an astonishing variety of money forms. Silver coins circulated, both silver coins minted by the U.S. government but also foreign silver coins. After 1849 gold coins started to appear as well, along with copper and other coins. At all times American might use banknotes: by 1860, approximately nine thousand different kinds, issued by banks of vastly different character, circulated promiscuously. They might also discover paper notes issued by non-banks, like the $1.5 million in paper issued by George Smith. They might encounter promissory notes and "accommodation paper" issued by cotton factors and brokers, or bills of exchange drawn on merchants some miles away. They might have a pocketful of shinplasters or private tokens printed by local businesses. And they might find an extraordinary range of artful counterfeits, some more valuable than the things they imitated. Although Americans attempted, twice, to establish central banks patterned on the English model, neither lasted more than twenty years, neither managed to standardize the currency, and no single authority regulated the value or the character of money, other than market exchange itself.

Economic historians of a libertarian cast point to the gold standard and argue that the American economy worked because beneath the improvisational necessities and Barnumesque humbugs of the American money supply lay gold. Gold's natural value regulated currency far more effectively than banks or parliamentary bodies: the idea that somewhere, possibly far away in a place one would never visit, actual gold existed to back the paper money. But Americans banked on other forms of "natural" value than gold. In the South slaves, not gold, formed the capital base of credit. What did the lack of a regulated, standardized money supply mean in the South?

In the antebellum South, writes one historian of Southern banking, "shinplasters became a way of life." Banknotes circulated freely in the South as well. By 1837, the South had ninety-nine chartered banks, all issuing paper notes, along with "numerous railroad companies issuing money in their corporate names, and dozens of private bankers, factors or other financial intermediaries performing a variety of banking services."[61] Frank Alexander Montgomery, in *Reminiscences of a Mississippian*, recalled that in 1855, "All along the river the country was flooded so to speak with bills from Ohio, Illinois, Indiana, Kentucky, Tennessee, and states too numerous to mention. No man could tell not only whether the bills were genuine or not, but whether they were worth a copper if they were genuine."[62] The South embraced paper credit, but in the basic character of its money system, the South differed from the North in a few crucial particulars.

Southern paper money frequently bore images of slaves, many of them chosen from stocks of standardized iconography. In some cases printers simply took standard engravings depicting white people and revised them to make the figures look black. Richard Doty found one instance in which a printer turned an engraving of a white farm worker, produced for a New York Bank, into an image of a happy slave by simply darkening the figure's skin and adding a patch to his shirt. By the 1850s, Southern banks demanded more precise and specific depictions. "Currency from the Deep South can take us through the entire experience of bondsman and that which bonded him," Doty writes, from picking to baling to wagon transport to the Charleston docks. By the eve of the Civil War, Southern paper money tended to feature benign and positive images of healthy slaves toiling in subservience: a proslavery message, Doty concludes, that the circulating money carried with it as it traveled North.[63]

Southern bankers put images of slavery on their notes not simply from sentiment: "slaves were the major component of the wealth structure of the South, " and "slave property was the critical link in antebellum credit relations." "Slaves, not land, made up the collateral of the credit economy," concludes a study of credit in Louisiana.[64] Individual planters typically sold slaves quickly for cash, in the form of banknotes "or good cashable paper."[65] These sales, in all their awfulness, dominate accounts of the experience of slavery. But more than cash, more than gold in vaults, capital in slaves "was integral to a complex financial system amounting to hundreds of millions of dollars" in one Louisiana parish alone.[66] Louisiana classified slaves as "immovables," that is, as real property, not personal property, in transfers of title. Slaves might serve as an "antichresis" in a mortgage—that is, as a pledge of real property, like a pledge of land. When planter Stephen Ball borrowed four hundred dollars from a neighbor, the contract specified a slave as an antichresis and said that if "the said Negro Stephen" should "die before the payment of the said sum of money," then Ball must "furnish another Negro in every respect as good as the said Negro Stephen," and it insisted that "the said last delivered Negro" must be subject to the terms of the loan "in the full manner and in every respect as the said Negro boy Stephen."[67] Slave traders frequently talked of buying and selling slaves "by the pound." Slave speculator Tyre Glen instructed his agent to pay "for plough boys 5 or 6 dollars per pound."[68] Planters lent slaves out, they borrowed against them, they used them to issue forms of paper which were not banknotes yet had some of the functions of money. "Slaves were regularly used as collateral in credit transactions; indeed, rather than giving an IOU when they borrowed money, many slaveholders simply wrote out a bill of sale for a slave who would actually be transferred only if they failed to pay their debt."[69] Slaves did the work of gold in addition to the work they did in the fields.

Although slave traders prided themselves on their expert knowledge of slaves, banks might accept slaves as collateral "simply enumerated as 'Tom,' 'Dick,' Sally,' or 'Mary,' with no further description."[70] Slaves had a specific, tangible individual identity but also an abstracted commodity value that made slave pricing surprisingly resistant to particulars. "Gender alone was not a significant factor in determining a slave's value," concludes Daina Berry; and further, "one cannot make a correlation between the value of slaves and their ages."[71] Planters considered individual characteristics in buying or selling, at the moment of sale or purchase: indeed, they imagined their capacity to judge the value of individual slaves as a key component of mastery. But the central role of slaves in the Southern credit market created a constant pressure to make slaves like gold, saleable "by the pound," an unvarying and uniformly valuable commodity.[72] In 1818 Sam Steers rejected investing in Mississippi bank stock, instead investing in slaves. "For a young man just commencing in life," he wrote, "the best stock in which he can invest capital is, I think, negro stock. . . . Negroes will yield a much larger income than any bank dividends."[73] "Slaves were viewed as an alternative to railroad bonds, agricultural land, textile factories, or other manufactories as an outlet for the investment funds of American capitalists." "In the American South slaves were an alternative to physical capital that could satiate the demand for holding wealth."[74] Slaves took the place of gold.

The Southern economy depended heavily on "factors," also known as commission merchants. The factor played a large and varied role. "He was at once the planter's merchant and his banker," and he could loan money to the planter, purchase supplies in the planter's name, and take a commission on the sale of the planter's cotton crop. "Millions of dollars" might be advanced to Southern planters "upon the mere personal word of the factor." Under the factorage system "a unique basis in agricultural credit was established." "The planter's note, backed by his contract with the factor," "was practically as convertible as the best forms of commercial paper."[75] Factorage introduced yet another form of "money." Factors dealt in cotton and other agricultural commodities. They borrowed and lent against each year's crop. But their calculations of credit-worthiness necessarily included the value of slaves, a commodity more durable than cotton and more stable in the marketplace.[76]

By the 1850s "slave property had become so valuable," concludes Stephen Deyle, "that it was no longer possible to consider eliminating it."[77] By 1860, historians, in an extremely conservative estimate, put the total value of slave property at three billion dollars. A large number indeed: "roughly three times greater than the total amount of all capital, North and South combined, invested in manufacturing, almost three times the amount invested in railroads, and seven times the amount invested in banks."[78] The value of slaves amounted to "seven times the value of all currency in circulation." This latter claim seems hard to substantiate, given the nebulous and varied state of American currency, rife with counterfeits and token moneys and private unaccounted shinplasters. But it gets to the heart of the point: the value of slaves exceeded the value of gold: slaves constituted the bullion which allowed that mass of tokens, shaky banknotes, private paper, and counterfeits to circulate; it grounded the idea that somewhere, perhaps somewhere one might never visit, a set of racially inferior people anchored value. "Our slaves constitute the greatest portion of our wealth," Virginian James Gholson declared, "and by their value, regulate the price of nearly all the property we possess."[79]

To speak of slaves "regulating the price" of other property is to give slaves the same function libertarian economists assign to specie, to gold or silver. This is not some figure of speech, or trick of language: slaves were the foundation of the Southern credit economy, the single largest pool of value—worth more, Deyle concludes, than even land. Slaves, not gold, formed the "real" in the Southern economy. "The entire economy of the antebellum South was constructed upon the idea that the bodies of enslaved people had a measurable monetary value, whether they were actually sold or not," Walter Johnson concludes.[80] Again in the classical gold standard, actual gold might not circulate at all: the *idea* of gold is what matters: a store of natural and non-negotiable value. So too with slaves: even in areas where slavery had ceased to exist, the *idea* of the "negro," naturally and intrinsically inferior, anchored speculations of all sorts. Slaves had a real labor value and a commodity value dependent on the idea of racial difference: that commodity value, again as James Gholson put it, "regulated the value of nearly all the property we possess."

*   *   *

Gholson made his comments in 1832: by that same year the Bank of England enjoyed a near monopoly over the issue of paper money.[81] In 1833 its banknotes became legal tender—not simply another form of money, but money for which the law compelled acceptance. The Bank kept gold in its reserves, but by the 1830s its notes were the standard currency of the British Empire, legal tender for all transactions.[82] Until 1844, local banks in England could print their own notes, but relatively few did, compared to the U.S.

So when England voted to abolish slavery in 1833, by buying the slaves and setting them free, it paid in pounds sterling, the standard money of the British Empire and the ultimate, stable, established standard of value for all commerce.[83] Slaves had value in the British Empire, but their value existed in relation to a stable standard: the Bank of England note. In the U.S., on the other hand, slaves had a value *which itself formed the basis of the Southern credit economy.* "Slave property is the foundation of all property in the South," declared *DeBow's Review*: "When security in this is shaken, all other property partakes of its instability."[84] Abolishing slavery in the United States would abolish the foundation of real credit and the psychic capital that underlay the chaotic money system, the "gold standard" of white supremacy. British emancipation only intensified Southern commitment to unfreedom: Southerners were literally banking on slavery.[85]

Consider this remarkably nasty quotation from Southern humorist George Bagby, about British Emancipation. "The apparently human beings of the British isles," Bagby wrote, "would to this day have remained what they once were, and even now seem to be—a people—but for the Act of Emancipation." Emancipating slaves lowered the British, Bagby thought: "There cannot be a people without niggers, and niggers are not niggers unless they are slaves." He went on: "a free nigger is a monstrosity, a paradox, a hand without muscle, an amputated leg, a glass eye-

ball, and a shinplaster—uncurrent at that."[86] In comparing freed slaves
to shinplasters—valueless shinplasters—Bagby repeated James Gholson's point. Slaves in bondage gave value to everything else: to the mass
of "unaccounted currencies" and token monies; to the banknotes of legitimate banks and the paper of factors and brokers. England had no
shinplasters, but freeing the slaves deprived the English of personhood
itself. Freed slaves destroyed both value and identity. "Feller citizens,"
declared a mock political candidate in William Tappan Thompson's
1844 comic novel *Major Jones's Courtship*, "I am 'posed to counterfit
money and shinplasters; I am 'posed to abolition and free niggers, to the
morus multicaulis and the Florida war, and all manner of shecoonery
whatsumever!"[87] Here again, freed slaves equal counterfeits and valueless money: slaves locked in bondage, fixed in their natural place, on the
contrary regulated value.

When Southern editors and writers addressed currency questions,
they tended to oppose paper money, as men of settled position and
wealth generally did. *DeBow's*, the leading journal of the slave South,
insisted that paper money could only work when founded on unambigu-
ously stable "real" commodities: when so founded "who can doubt that a
bank note will be a species of property as substantial and as enduring as
an acre of land, as a negro, a house, or a mortgage upon any of those?"[88]
Banknotes founded on negroes, banked on slaves, became a species of
property as stable and "natural" as gold or land. *DeBow's* preferred
the gold standard, but it saw the racial character of slaves as fixed exactly as gold: "The inferiority of the negro," *DeBow's Review* concluded,
"has been put to the severest test, by every possible ordeal, in war and in
peace, in times past and times present, and, like gold, seven times tried
in the fire, has proved itself to be genuine."[89] The alleged inferiority of
African Americans enabled them to act as gold and secure paper issues.

But Americans kept issuing forms of money that bore little or no relation to gold. Private and public banknotes, shinplasters, token monies: these monies bore a much more obscure relation to any notion of
fundamental natural value. Putting images of happy slaves on banknotes
implied a reasonable connection to the value of slaves, but no authority managed to regulate the nature and extent of that connection. Paper
money destabilized the economy and the relative values of goods and
people. Following William Gouge, *DeBow's* called paper money a "disease which taints all American blood," a hereditary blood disease, an
"original sin."

Economists frequently used the metaphor of blood to describe money. In this model, money circulated like the blood of the nation. "The currency of a country is to the community," John C. Calhoun wrote in 1837, "what the blood is to the body . . . indispensable to all the functions of life."[90] In these metaphors, paper money "debased" or corrupted the nation's blood. In 1860 *DeBow's Review* called gold money "God's money," and insisted that "all attempts to depreciate it by alloy, or to compel the use of a paper or any other substitute, have resulted in disastrous failure. . . . The surgeon or the anatomist who attempts to invent a substitute for the blood, is not a whit more presumptuous and charlatanic than the statesman who endeavors to force into circulation any other currency in place of the precious metals." "Money is as necessary to the social body as blood to the natural body," the writer continued: gold is "nature's currency."[91]

The language of "blood" in race echoed the language of value. "A community suffering incessant blood-disturbance," wrote a text on "blood admixture," "will exhibit social activity, though, if the disturbing element is very base, a corresponding depreciation of its absolute value will ensue."[92] The linkage of money and blood made particular sense in an economy founded on black slaves as capital. Southern writers used the term "amalgamation" to describe mixed-race children, and not surprisingly they sometimes drew comparisons between racial "amalgamation" and the alloying of gold. But on this point their language and thinking was confused; confused in a way that reflected both the fondness for fixed values and the desire for speculation and loose money.

Southern whites would sometimes insist that "nature has marked, by unerring lines, the distinction between the species, and her tokens cannot be wiped out, by either the sophistry of the negrophilist, or the cant of the fanatic." This writer concluded that "the manifest moral, intellectual, and physical inferiority of the negro issues from the decree of God, which no efforts of man can either alter or abrogate"[93] "Hybridism is heinous," wrote Henry Hughes: "Impurity of races is against the law of nature. Mulattoes are monsters. The law of nature is the law of God."[94] Those who acknowledged the "hybrids'" existence often saw them as inferior and doomed: in 1843 the *American Journal of the Medical Sciences* concluded "the Mulatto or Hybrid is a degenerate, unnatural offspring, doomed by nature to work out its own destruction."[95] "We believe," *DeBow's Review* avowed as late as 1860, ignoring evidence all around it, "that the descendants of mulattoes soon become infertile. . . . The mulatto would seem to fall into that condition of hybrids where they continue to be more or less prolific for a few generations, but with a constant tendency to run out."[96] These writers sought, by rendering mulattoes valueless, to preserve the idea of black Americans as a distinct species, and therefore as a stable ground for credit.

But others looked at the fact of "amalgamation" and drew the opposite conclusion—that the alloy of white blood improved the slaves. Josiah Nott believed "the infusion of even a minute proportion of the blood of one race into another, produces a most decided modification of moral and physical character. A small trace of white blood in the negro improves him in intelligence and morality; and an equally small trace of negro blood, as in the quadroon, will protect such individual against the deadly influence of climates which the pure white-man cannot endure."[97] But it might work the other way: as "the mixture of alloy in gold depreciates the whole mass of purer metal; and so it would be with amalgamation, as is clearly proved by all past experience."[98] White blood might "improve" the slave, but black blood debased the white.

Slave sales generally did not take account of color, except in certain cases: some owners might prefer light-skinned slaves as servants, because they made home life more "high toned," but others might reject light-skinned slaves who could escape by passing for white. Light-skinned female slaves had a high value in the notorious "fancy markets" sensationalized by abolitionists.[99] One would expect the presence of light-skinned slaves to undermine the idea of slaves as fixed capital, as gold—clearly "alloyed," they run against the desire for static racial difference and shout out that standards of racial "value" were arbitrary, contingent, and negotiable. But Americans generally responded by simply pretending the difference did not matter or even did not exist. The child of a slave mother was a slave, end of story, and "hybrids" had no future.[100] Gold alloyed with silver changed its value. "Amalgamated" slaves generally did not. Belief in the fundamental inferiority of African Americans, like belief in the fundamental, "natural" value of gold, depended on and grew from a need to stabilize commerce and identity, and in this sense faith in racial difference exceeded faith in the value of gold.

*　*　*

Historians have recognized for years that slaveowning founded the master's sense of self—that slaveowning—and slave buying and selling—possessed a psychic value. The evidence here suggests that this was more than a psychic value: that it extended into the pocketbook and the purse: that slaves anchored the sense of white superiority while they enabled the expansion of credit and an astonishing variety of regular and irregular forms of money.

Even far from slavery, in the North, the idea of racial inferiority provided a psychic balance to a speculative economy. Just as gold did not need to physically circulate, but merely to exist as an idea, so too the idea of racial inferiority anchored social commerce. Northerners might abolish slavery, but they could regularly redeem their racial character at the minstrel show. The presence of slaves as fixed capital founded the speculative, transformative capitalist economy: ironically, they gave possibility to the profusion of money forms which enabled free blacks like William Wells Brown to prosper.

Historians of money and banking tend to ignore slavery and race altogether. Readers of the seven-hundred-and-forty-two pages of Bray Hammond's magisterial account will find only a few cursory mentions of slavery. "Almost without exception," Walter Johnson wrote in an aside, "antebellum historians treat slavery as a labor system without acknowledging that it was also a system of capital accumulation."[101] Economic historians typically either disregard slavery's central role in the economy or treat slaves as economic units without considering the contested, ambiguous quality of the money they were valued in. Peter Temin's thoroughly researched and otherwise excellent *The Jacksonian Economy* makes no substantive mention of slavery, even though slavery stood at the heart of the American economy, and the value of slaves exceeded the value of all other capital, even in states where slavery had been abolished. Howard Bodenhorn's exhaustive histories of antebellum banking similarly ignore the fact of slaves as capital, or treat "capital" as one of those formal abstractions beloved of economists.[102] Historians write about money as if it had a static, objective, ahistorical existence.

Michael Tadman's *Speculators and Slaves*, quoted above, talks about the cash value of slaves, and how slave traders preferred to deal in cash or "good cashable paper," but gives no consideration of what people used for cash. Was it gold or silver? U.S. coins, or foreign coins? What might the phrase "good cashable paper," idiomatic at the time, actually mean? Banknotes of the Second Bank of the United States? A modern reader thinks of "cash" as Federal Reserve notes, the money we use everyday. The term "cash" might well have meant coins of some kind, or it might have meant "readily accepted paper." That historians typically do not specify the nature of the money shows the extent to which our modern notions of money color our sense of the currency used at the time: we assume it to be like modern money.

It is similarly not possible to divide slavery as an economic structure from slavery as a racial structure. Gavin Wright's *Slavery and American Economic Development* treats slavery, with comprehensive research and incisive intelligence, as a system of capital formation. But it pays no attention to the elaborate and laboriously maintained structure of racial thinking that made slavery work as a source of credit. *What This Cruel War Was Over*, Chandra Manning's beautifully nuanced and deeply researched account of the Civil War's meaning, pays eloquent attention to the psychic value of whiteness and the meanings of liberty for both sides of the conflict. But it makes little or no mention of the economics of slavery.[103] I am not trying to argue that these authors are wrong or misguided—there are no monocausal explanations for any historical event, and no book can include everything. But "money" as an idea must be subject to the same level of scrutiny and analysis as any other aspect of history.

Considering slavery in its relation to debates about currency suggests that slavery played a more crucial role than generally considered—that more than simply labor power, slaves formed a stock of actual capital that supported the issue of paper credit. As the idea of gold, unseen and imagined locked in a distant vault, might allow fantastic forms of paper to circulate, so the idea of African Americans as a stock, a commodity of natural value, allowed them to "regulate" other forms of meaning, other systems of value, in the North as well as the South. The issue here is not simply slavery. Slaves anchored mundane daily values, but "blackness," racial difference, anchored value as well. Northerners who embraced abolition generally embraced "free markets," broadly defined. But they far less generally embraced a notion of racial equality, or the idea markets could renegotiate what race meant. Racial difference offered a store of psychic value, a backing to white supremacy. If Southerners banked on slavery, Americans banked on race.

Considering the money supply as a whole, and not just in terms of banks, illuminates some of the most stubborn peculiarities of American slavery—why did the value of slaves, and the commitment to racial segregation, not change when the slaves bore visible evidence of "amalgamation?" Why did Americans resist the global movement towards abolition? How is that England could end slavery at a stroke, with a compensation scheme, while in the U.S. it took a bloody Civil War? In England the currency rested of kingly prerogatives and the authority of the central bank. In the U.S. the currency rested on a deep commitment not just to slavery but to non-negotiable racial inequality.

"Why is a fifty-cent shinplaster like the war," asks a Yankee character in one of Seba Smith's satirical essays. The Colonel has no answer. "'Wal,' ses I, 'the face is black, which means that we are fightin' to free the nigger, and the back is red—or the blood—the price we are paying for it!'"[104] The next chapter looks and race and money in the Civil War and Reconstruction.

CHAPTER THREE

Rags, Blacking, and Paper Soldiers

Once let the black man get upon his person the brass letter, 'U.S.', let him get an eagle on his button, and a musket on his shoulder and bullets in his pocket, there is no power on earth that can deny that he has earned the right to citizenship. — Frederick Douglass[1]

During the Civil War, Americans conflated the greenbacks—paper declared to be money by legislative enactment—with African American soldiers, enlisted by legislative fiat. For Lincoln's opponents greenbacks and African American soldiers both represented "inflation," unstable and unreliable value. For those who favored racial equality, on the other hand, both greenbacks and African American soldiers represented the way social relations created meaning: both "value" and "equality" came from culture, not nature. During Reconstruction, one political camp wanted to retire the greenbacks: the same side tended to favor rolling back civil rights for the former slaves. Those who favored greenbacks tended to support racial equality and the social legislation required to bring it about. Linking the race debate to the money debate helps explain why Reconstruction failed.

*   *   *

Chapter 2 described the enthusiastic chaos of the antebellum money supply and its relation to the persistence of slavery. A welter of U.S., foreign, and privately minted gold or silver coins circulated alongside thousands of banknotes issued by scrupulous and unscrupulous legally chartered local banks; private notes issued by semi-banks and "underground banks"; multiple forms of commercial paper issued by factors and brokers; "shinplasters" and fractional paper notes ginned up by small businesses and waggish satirists; and base-metal token coins printed by employers and speculative enterprises of all sorts. Adding to this the massive, ongoing, well-organized, semi-formal business of counterfeiting, and the publication of dozens of competing "counterfeit detectors," each of which denounced its rivals as fakes, suggests that slaves, and the notion of fixed racial difference, served to anchor the notion of value both specifically and generally. Slaves, and the idea of race, formed a "bottom line" of value and meaning in exchange. In the absence of an effective central monetary authority, slaves, and the notion of black inferiority, literally secured value in everyday business.

When the Civil War ended slavery, it removed the real foundation of Southern capital, but even more it threatened to undermine the "psychic value" of whiteness in both North and South. During the war the Union took tentative half-steps towards a unified currency and a centralized money supply, while it also experimented with unredeemable "fiat" paper money. The Union, with considerable reluctance, put African Americans in the service of their own liberation. When the war ended, Northerners embarked on a grand experiment to "reconstruct" the South economically *and* socially: that effort demanded loose money and easy credit, and it involved a radical reconsideration of the role African Americans would play in the nation's psychic life. In the face of this renegotiation, Americans retreated to twin forms of essentialism: to a ferocious and unyielding racism and to a fantastic set of opinions about the magic properties of gold. If slavery had enabled loose money and made a centralized authority dispensable, the absence of slavery required the gold standard and a renewed commitment to white supremacy. American notions about race were again deeply intertwined with American notions about money and value.

The etymology of the term "carpetbagger," hurled as a fierce insult after the Civil War, reinforces this claim. When an antebellum banker, particularly an unscrupulous antebellum banker, printed banknotes, he needed to get them into people's hands, or they did no good. He might hire a man to go out and spend them—to "puff" them into circulation, like William Wells Brown with his shinplasters. In those days, Congressman William D. Kelley recalled: "nearly every specie-basis bank had its carpet-bagger—a fellow it sent out with notes by the carpet-bag full into some distant State to get them into circulation there." Carpet bags, cheap and ubiquitous, symbolized vagabondage and low-cost travel. They had an additional, particular connection to money and banking. Kelly used the term "carpetbagger" to describe the agents of a doubtful bank, out to spend the bank's notes as quickly as possible, seeking to inflate something of little or no value.

But in the antebellum decades the term *also* described someone who returned a bank's notes to their birthplace, demanding their equivalent in specie. "No piece of information could be more annoying to the antebellum banker," remembered a North Carolina bank examiner, "than the news that a stranger was in town with a suspicious-looking carpet-bag in his hand; for it generally contained a bag full of notes of his bank for redemption."[2] A carpetbagger in fact might carry a valise filled half with his notes and half with notes from the place he was traveling to. He could then get his own notes into circulation while presenting the other bank's notes for "redemption," and then carry the "redeeming" gold from the competing bank back to build his own bank's reserves—enterprise indeed!

Given enough banks, this relationship of musical chairs could go on for some time, or possibly forever, each bank hoping to avoid being caught short when the tinkling music of circulation stopped at the demand for redemption. Associating "carpetbagger" with banking in this way captured the footloose, improvisational, speculative, and ambiguous character of the American money supply.

Albion W. Tourgée, perhaps the white man most closely associated with Reconstruction, elaborated on the term's history in his novel *A Fool's Errand*. In the days of "wild-cat money," he recalled, notes circulated "by means of agents, who carried the bills about the country in carpet-bags, and were hence denominated, 'Carpet-baggers.'" It is said, Tourgee continued, that one of these veritable "carpet-baggers," a "copperhead" who opposed the war and denounced Lincoln, finding himself "at a loss for some fresh epithet," shouted "Carpet-baggers!" and the term entered general circulation as an insult.[3] The term today famously describes Northerners, presumptively unscrupulous Northerners, who crossed into Dixie to exploit the South's defeat: for a hundred years "carpetbagger" served as a club to beat the agenda of Reconstruction and the effort to promote civil rights for African Americans. Its origins in banking give that usage a different inflection.

"In all history," Tourgée wrote, "there is perhaps no instance of so perfect and complete an epithet." The term signified the pain of Southern defeat, but it also signified a world without standards, a world where monetary and social values were turned upside down. "In those days

strange sights could be witnessed in the streets of Columbia [South Car-
olina] at any time," recalled ex-Confederate James Morgan of Reconstruction. More than once he remembered seeing "a handsome landau
drawn by a spanking pair of high-stepping Kentucky horses and contain-
ing four negro wenches arrayed in low-neck and short-sleeved dresses,
their black bosoms and arms covered with real jewels in the middle of
the day, draw up in front of a barroom on Main Street where the wives
and daughters of the old and impoverished aristocracy did their shopping." What enabled this lavish display? "White carpetbaggers seemed
to have so much money that they did not know what to do with it. I have
seen one of them walk into a drinking saloon by himself and ostentatiously order a quart bottle of champagne, take one glass of it, and care-
lessly throw a ten-dollar bill on the counter and tell the barkeeper to
keep the change; and this in a community where people bred in affluence were suffering for the very necessities of life."[4] The carpetbagger
spends lavishly while those "bred in affluence" suffer: the carpetbagger's
loose money enables slaves "bred" in poverty to flaunt their affluence.

"Carpetbagger" combined the racial history of Reconstruction, and
the effort to promote racial equality, with the monetary policy of greenbacks and paper money. A perfect insult, it made the linkage between
money and race explicit. As the previous chapters have shown, that linkage between race and money appeared much earlier, and it pervaded the
Civil War itself.

*   *   *

As they had during the Revolution, Americans, North and South, financed the Civil War with paper money. Most Northerners, it is safe
to say, disliked slavery, but they generally disliked African Americans
much more, and they liked taxes least of all. Lincoln's administration
tried twice to levy taxes to finance the war, with insufficient results.
Bond sales had also realized less than hoped. Further taxing the Union
to raise money for a war that might free slaves looked like a sure political mistake. Both the federal government and private citizens, antici-
pating crisis, hoarded gold, silver, and copper coins. And when private
citizens began issuing small denomination notes, and even using post-
age stamps as currency, the Union responded by issuing its own "post-
age currency," small notes that looked like stamps but lacked glue. Also
known as "fractional currency," or as "sticking plasters," these notes

would remain in circulation well after the war. But fractional notes of less than a dollar made an inconvenient foundation for a large war.

The Union tried "demand notes," paper money which the bearer might redeem for specie "on demand," the words themselves conveniently printed on the note. By law such demands would only work in five cities, New York, Boston, Philadelphia, Cincinnati, and St. Louis, and no matter what the bearer demanded, only silver would be supplied. Demand notes marked a balancing act between soft money and redeemable paper. Making the sixty million dollars worth of paper inconvenient to redeem was a fairly transparent dodge, and not effective. The Union, it soon became clear, would need a good deal more than sixty million dollars.[5]

So in 1862 the federal government resorted to an old strategy, authorizing the Treasury to print and release "legal tender" paper money. The words "legal tender" meant no one could legally refuse to take the greenbacked bills in payment—if you sold munitions or pickled beef to the government, you took your pay in these new United States Notes, known colloquially as "greenbacks." If you offered a supplier greenbacks in return, he took greenbacks and liked it. Soldiers took their pay in greenbacks as well. By 1865, 450 million dollars worth of "greenbacks" passed for "real money" throughout the North. Putting it over-simply, the greenbacks let Lincoln finance the unpopular war.[6]

But the greenbacks never enjoyed anything like complete acceptance. Immediately upon issue, they mustered into the longstanding war between proponents of loose money and easy credit and those who insisted on a hard-money, specie-based economy. Paper money, critics charged, made value out of nothing, by mere proclamation. It confused the symbol (printed paper) with the real thing it only stood for (gold or other precious metals). For those who loved paper money, one satirist argued, "words are things . . . not only things, but important and valuable things . . . I might even say *better* than things."[7] Advocates of gold argued that no one could simply declare a thing to be money by fiat—only something with real, intrinsic value could serve as money. "I would as soon provide Chinese wooden guns for the army as paper money alone for the army," Vermont Congressman Elbridge Gerry Spaulding declared.[8] "Watered" Greenbacks, with their origins in politics, lacked any real substance, "gold is but a *representative* of values—government bonds are but a *representative* of gold. . . . [T]his new United States Currency is to be but a *representative* of government bonds. These new issues are to be only fourth cousins to a representative, which in fact, is no security at all."[9] Paper money seemed absurd, immoral, like calling good bad or declaring rain was actually snow—or declaring that black was white.

Critics of greenbacks saw a direct connection between the issue of greenbacks and the philosophy of abolition. The *New York Herald* blamed "the abolition radicals," and their "managing agents in the Cabinet and the War Office," "for all the follies, failures and disasters of the war, including a derangement of our financial affairs and a depreciated paper currency."[10] Ohio Congressman Clement Vallandigham, Lincoln's bitter enemy, denounced Lincoln for seizing control of the currency, "the life blood of the nation." Vallandigham called the greenbacks a clever ruse, part of "a fund wherewith to set up the negro trade."[11] Lincoln had long believed in "compensated emancipation" as a way to end slavery, and in 1861 and '62 had floated plans to compensate border-state masters for the end of slavery by issuing government bonds.[12] In plain, "old fashioned English," Vallandigham declared to a laughing and cheering crowd that what Lincoln called "compensated emancipation" amounted to nothing more than "greenback abolition," an ethical system which sought to abolish nature itself by declaring rag paper into money and making negroes the equal of whites.[13]

The argument for paper had waxed and waned in different periods leading up to the Civil War. Calls for paper money, issued by a central bank, appeared theoretically in the work of H. C. Carey, the Whig businessman and later Lincoln advisor. Henry Charles Carey inherited both his Irish immigrant father's business and his objection to England. The Careys ran the leading publishing firm of the day. Henry also invested heavily and successfully in iron smelting, railroads, and mining. People realized their best potential in "association," he argued: in groups voluntarily organized to facilitate mutual prosperity. Carey fully endorsed Adam Smith's arguments about the division of labor, but he balked at the Malthusian implications of unrestrained competition. Like fellow Philadelphian Benjamin Franklin, Carey put productive labor at the root of value, and saw jointly organized community-improvement enterprises as the key to general prosperity. To the irritation of his correspondent Karl Marx, Carey argued for a harmony of interests between employer and employee. To create this harmony, he advocated a "tariff wall" around America, to protect American industries from ruinous English free trade practices. Paper money, issued by a central bank, would demonstrate the virtue of association while sealing the American economy off so that it could develop and thrive.

Historians have often tried to describe this distinctly American form of economic theorizing as "republicanism," a form of private enterprise that emphasized mutuality of interests, the moral superiority of manufacturing and productive physical labor, and the social importance of rough equality between citizens. Neither socialist nor capitalist, this "producerist" or "associationist" vision tried to moralize the emerging industrial order by lifting all boats on the same tide. Marx called Carey America's most original economic thinker, while deriding the emphasis on mutual association as soft headed and naïve, a judgment history would tend to confirm. But Carey's ideas, drawn again from the tradition epitomized by Franklin, would form a crucial part of Whig and later Republican Party philosophy. Carey held weekly salons, the "Carey Vespers," at his Philadelphia home. He invited leading intellectuals, literary figures, politicians, and businessmen, including Thaddeus Stevens, Congressman William D. Kelly, and Joseph Wharton. He also wound up as *de facto* economic editor for Horace Greeley's *New York Tribune*. During the war, he advised Lincoln on banking, the tariff, and the economy.[14]

Some of Carey's arguments appeared in more radical guise in the work of Edward Kellogg, a self-educated businessman appalled by Jackson's war on the Second Bank and the Panic of 1837. Gold money, he thought, stifled enterprise and sheltered the powerful. Kellogg also heavily stressed labor as the source of value, but he went further by insisting on the meaninglessness of gold and silver. "Let the manufacturer cease to toil, commerce be suspended," he wrote, "and gold and silver, however abundant, and however pure and malleable, would cease to be precious to a starving people, compared with food, and with the labor of man, which produces it."[15] Mere commodities, gold and silver enjoyed no magic powers. In his 1849 book *Labor and Other Capital*, Kellogg called for paper money based on generalized social labor, not paper bills representing specie. "If paper money be allowed to pass as representative of specie, there should be a silver dollar for every paper dollar. Otherwise, the paper money cannot represent specie." Banks always issue more paper than they have specie in their vaults, Kellogg argued: paper money cannot function as a direct representation of gold. "A silver dollar cannot be represented by two paper dollars, each of which would be as valuable as itself, more than the owner of one acre of land can give two deeds, each for the one acre, to different individuals, and make both deeds good." What does talk of a specie standard mean, he asked, when banks inevitably issue more value in paper notes than they have specie in their vaults?

Let us cease to pretend: if paper money circulates—and Kellogg argued that indeed it must—"it should not be under the pretence that it represents what it does not and cannot represent."[16] Money Kellogg regarded as a mere social convenience: "it is a matter of indifference by what material the powers or properties of money are expressed," Kellogg insisted; "the material is merely a substance fixed upon by law." Gold and silver contain no natural money power: "The natural powers of any material do not make it money. Its powers and agency as money are delegated to it by law."[17] We should have a "fiat" paper money, backed not by gold or silver but by the productivity of America's workers.

The labor theory of value played a central role in American political philosophy, especially the philosophy of Lincoln's Republican Party. Carey and his circle tended to favor a specie-backed paper money, issued by a central bank, expandable to suit political expediency but controlled by judicious men of conservative temperament. Kellogg and his followers, later to emerge as the Greenback Party, insisted on a purely paper currency backed only by generalized social labor—very much like what we use now. For both men, wealth came from productive labor. Money only symbolized labor and value—it was not value itself. Americans implicitly endorsed Kellogg's arguments, or at least aspects of them, when they resorted to "wildcat" banking and the more than nine thousand different kinds of money that circulated before the Civil War; they created their own money and counted on their own personal persuasiveness, their own potential labor, to carry the day. In economic life a formal desire for fixed value co-existed with a desire for looseness, elasticity, and negotiability. Kellogg's radical view of money as merely a social convenience never enjoyed complete acceptance, but it gained traction during and especially after the war.

*   *   *

As the war continued, and the Northern economy grew, support for paper money rose. By 1863 voters were even writing and singing popular songs about the greenbacks, songs like this one, "How Are You Greenbacks!"

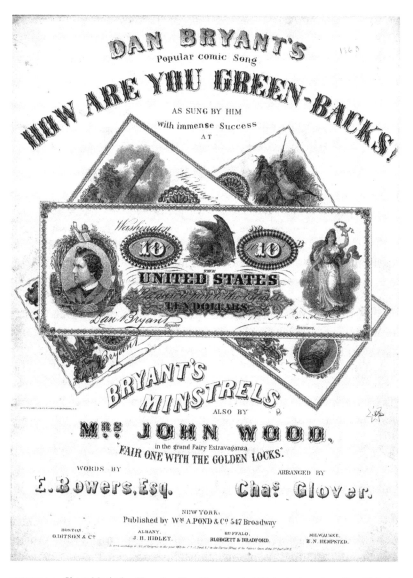

FIGURE 3.1. Sheet Music for *How Are You Greenbacks!* Historic American Sheet Music, Music B-1071, Duke University Rare Book, Manuscript and Special Collections Library.

> We're coming, Father Abram, One hundred thousand more,
> Five hundred presses printing us from morn till night is o'er;
> Like magic, you will see us start and scatter thro' the land
> To pay the soldiers or release the border contraband, . . .[18]

A hundred thousand greenbacks, coming like troops to help the Union cause and release contraband slaves: Bryant's Minstrels, a famous black-face company, performed this song in 1863. The next few pages will follow this song closely, to examine the ways political discourse linked race to money.

"How Are You Green-backs!" was a minstrel show song. Bryant's players would cover their faces with greasepaint or burnt cork, and take their turns on the stage as one of up to a dozen stock characters, all grotesquely styled parodies of African American "types." The minstrel's music—in the hands of gifted composers like Stephen Foster—drew on the songs slaves sang and used many of the same instruments slaves played, especially the banjo. Typically dressed in comically ragged clothes, or the gaudy "flash" clothes of the urban swell, minstrels danced in imitations of slave performances or of the cultural stylings of free blacks in the north. Their accents mocked the accents they might have heard from African Americans on the streets, docks, and in taverns; the canals and wharves and markets where white and black laborers met. This odd spectacle dominated American entertainment and made its leading practitioners rich, at least in the short term. By the time of the Civil War the minstrel show was the most popular form of entertainment in America; it would remain popular well into the twentieth century.

On the one hand clearly a nasty instrument of racial domination, the minstrel shows presented an extraordinarily complex package of attitudes, obsessions, phobias, and desires. Minstrel shows provided a venue for forbidden longings; they fostered political satire; they reflected the creolizing half-impulse, the "love and theft," so pronounced in American popular culture.[19] While the minstrel show helped make ethnically undesirable immigrants into "white" people, it also reflected the market's contradictory tendency to erode meaning and to shore it up at the same time. Minstrel shows would endure well into the twentieth century: by the 1890s, African Americans themselves "blacked up" and performed in minstrel guise. Minstrel shows marked the intersection of possibilities, both a site of fixing racial meanings and a carnivalesque space in which varied meanings circulated.[20]

Minstrel shows typically included patriotic songs and satirical ditties, like the one quoted here, on contemporary politics. In the minstrel context, the song's comment on the money question seems especially pointed. Imitating poverty's rags, the white minstrels "passed" for black. We might think of African Americans, again, as the gold, and the ragged minstrel as paper bills passing current. The idea of the black racial authentic enables the circulation of mass copies which are not the thing they imitate yet which gain their value from that thing's presence: just as banknotes were not gold but gained value from the idea that gold existed somewhere.

"How Are You Green-backs!" continued: "We're coming, Father Abram, One hundred thousand more / And cash was ne'er so easily evok'd from rags before." Printers used rags to make the high quality paper for greenbacks. They turned rags into cash. Critics of paper money frequently called it "rag money" or "bank rags" or "rag currency"; an "accursed load of Rags and Blacking," as one Revolutionary-era critic put it.[21] They used the word to make paper money seem worn, feckless, valueless, like cast-off trash: "a currency no better than unwashed paper rags."[22] The term implied over-circulation, objects or goods used till all value had been wrung from them: it implied that value waned as it strayed too far from the original or moved too promiscuously from person to person. Given the fact that the minstrel himself was a popular fake, a symbol, a ragged counterfeit of an imagined racial authentic, paper money seemed a particularly appropriate and popular subject for minstrel commentary.[23]

Paper money, its enemies repeatedly charged, "evoked cash from rags." Legal tender made valueless rag paper into valuable cash by a sort of magic. "Let the public believe that a smutted rag is money, it is money," scoffed a critic in 1858: "a sort of financial biology, which made, at night, the thing conjured for, the thing that was seen."[24] Those who favored "hard money" saw greenbacks as a violation of natural law, artificial: "paper-money banking," wrote Andrew Jackson's advisor William Gouge, created "an *artificial* inequality of wealth," as men of dubious character puffed themselves up on paper money.[25] The inequalities of wealth produced by a gold economy Gouge saw as "natural" and just: paper money, "miserable, ragged, and loathsome trash," destabilized the social order.[26] "Everything of fixed value will lose [its] value" if "vagabond" paper money circulates, insisted one Ohio Congressman.[27] The *New York Herald* compared those who argued for paper money to real estate brokers who "with a few strokes of the pen convert a rickety old farm house . . . into an elegant villa surrounded by a spacious lawn," or theatrical managers, whose "genius renders a beggarly account of empty boxes into a crowded and fashionable house."[28] An imposter, greenbacks made it hard to know the real from the symbolic. In the mouth of a white performer, dolled up in greasepaint to look black, "How Are You Greenbacks!" took on a double meaning. It described not just how greenbacks symbolized wealth but also how Bryant's minstrels dressed in rags to evoke slavery, and to symbolize black people, and thereby earned cash.

The song also expressed popular ambivalence about greenbacks and more generally about the problem of value itself. The second verse continued: "And cash was n'er so easily evok'd from rags before / To line the fat contractors purse, or purchase transport craft / Whose rotten hulks shall sink before the winds begin to waft." Now the song's initial enthusiasm for greenbacks grows even less sure: "fat contractor's purse" associates greenbacks with men of doubtful character. Or even worse, greenbacks buy shoddy, "counterfeit" supplies, and what looks like a seaworthy craft collapses at the dock. Greenbacks were "a common legalized cheat that promises what he never performs, and lives by palming off counters." Greenbacks, like the minstrels themselves, please the eye; they perform impressive effects, but they are rotten beneath the surface, "counter-feit representative[s] of silver and gold."[29]

Paper money helped the entrepreneur, the man on the make. Having lots of paper money in circulation caused inflation but lowered interest rates and made credit easier to get and repay. In this line of thinking money represented nothing more than our common potential, it symbolized not some fantasy of "natural value" but the work all citizens did: as Kellogg put it, "the value of money perpetually depends upon its power to represent value and not upon its material."[30]

Whig and later Republican Party thinkers argued that paper money would democratize wealth. Dreams, ambitions were themselves a speculation, an imitation—making them come true required faith and vision. An ambitious man imitated the thing he hoped to become, the value he hoped to acquire. If ambitious men and women pooled their resources, founded a bank, and issued paper money, faith in their future partly backed the notes. If they could persuade others to accept their paper money, using the money to buy, say, building materials, they might make their dreams of prosperity into a reality. Thus could people "make themselves" through their own efforts.

Republican editor Horace Greeley wrote: "An extraordinary proportion of our young men aspire to position, consideration, fortune, and expect to achieve these by Trade, or in some department of Productive Industry. Born poor, they seek independence through the use of Credit. . . . To a community thus suffused with the spirit of aspiration, of adventure, of industrial and commercial enterprise, the use of Paper Money is as natural as breathing."[31] An aspiring nation, seeking to turn dreams into reality, needed paper money, itself a representation of possibility and promise. If gold alone served as money, Greeley and others argued, interest rates would rise and individual initiative be strangled. And those who held gold could charge exorbitant interest rates to profit from some one else's work. Instead of imagining a "natural" economy, governed by intrinsic value and natural law, paper money advocates tended to see money, and the economy, as a social creation. In this line of thinking, money, wealth, social position, *even identity itself* were mutable things, not values fixed by nature. They resulted from labor and will, not some accident of birth or creation.

Inevitably, the race question reasserts itself. "How Are You Greenbacks!" mentions Greeley several times: as editor of the *New York Tribune* Greeley linked abundant paper money to the common man's desire for—and right to—self-advancement. The value of the North's paper money, the song continues, depends on the soldier's commitment to the Union cause and the leadership that directs it:

> We're willing, Father Abram, one hundred thousand more
> Should help our Uncle Samuel to prosecute the war,
> But then we want a chieftain true, one who can lead the van,
> Geo. B McClellan, you all know, he is the very man.

McClellan, then enjoying great popularity, would later run for president on a "hard money," specie platform. The song continues:

> We're coming, Father Abram, one hundred thousand more
> To march with gleaming bayonets upon the traitor's shore,
> But you must give us Generals on whom we can depend,
> And not let paper Generals, drive off our faithful men

The subject has shifted: it began as the greenbacks themselves, but the song now refers to Union soldiers. These verses make the greenbacks and the soldiers who take them as pay analogous. Both rush to the aid of Lincoln and the nation, but they need leaders of more than "paper." "How are you greenbacks," the song asks, and the answer seems to be "only as good as our leaders and our willingness to fight": only as good as the Union itself. In the 1870s, the greenback and the scarred veteran would frequently appear as one, as in this 1878 campaign poem:

> O, Greenback, veteran of the years!
> Thou crippled soldier of the war!
> Baptized with blood and wet with tears.
> To-day thou art without a scar.
> Thou stood upon the picket line
> Wherever hissing bullets flew. . . .
>
> Thou stormed the forts; thou sped the ships;
> Thou dealt the gunboat's timely blow;
> Thou forged the cannon angry lips
> That screamed a welcome to the foe.
> Thanks, Greenback! Veteran of the years![32]

In this poem the worn greenback and the weary soldiers who spent it come together. The greenbacks literally embody the citizens—they symbolize the loyal soldiers who fought for the Union cause, wounded as the soldiers they supported, crippled by political opposition. "I stand here" Congressman Benjamin Butler of Massachusetts proclaimed, well after the war, "for inconvertible paper money, the greenback, which has fought our battles and saved our country; which has been held by us as a just equivalent for the blood of our soldiers, the lives of our sons, the widowhood of our daughters, and the orphanage of their children."[33] The greenbacks, then, represented not intrinsic value or natural aristocracy but rather labor, sacrifice, and patriotism. Service to the nation gave both greenbacks and veterans their value. But how much value could service, and individual effort, actually confer?

*   *   *

One of the great questions of the war focused on African American soldiers—what would their service earn them? Bryant's minstrel tune

"How Are You Green-backs!" raised the question itself in its final verses. Again the subject—the "we" that's coming—shifts. It concludes by literally identifying the greenbacks with African American soldiers:

> We're coming, Father Abram, nine hundred thousand strong,
> With nine hundred thousand darkies, sure the traitors can't last long
> With Corporal Cuff, and Sergeant Pomp, to lead us in the melee,
> And at their head, without a red, Our Brigadier General Greely.

In the first verse, greenbacks announced their own coming. Later, white soldiers announce themselves. Finally, the soldiers have become African Americans, newly issued like greenbacks themselves. Mirroring the white public's ambivalence about "colored troops," on one level the song links African Americans in the patriotic celebration of the Union cause. On another, it points again to uneasiness about value and character. Some "inflation" seems to have occurred: "nine hundred thousand darkies" instead of the "one hundred thousand" men and greenbacks of earlier verses. "Cuff" and especially "Pomp" were common, mocking nicknames for African Americans, stock characters used in the minstrel show. Naming "Corporal Cuff" and "Sergeant Pomp" turns the ranks of African American soldiers into a minstrel performance. Is the song praising their service to the Union or mocking it as false, "paper" value?

Although African Americans volunteered for the Union army immediately after Ft. Sumter, Lincoln at first refused their service. Lincoln probably regarded African Americans as inferior, at least initially: he also famously hoped to keep the border states out of the conflict while drawing the Southern states back into the Union. Putting black men in uniform, he thought, would enrage whites and doom reunification. As he stated often, Lincoln saw restoring the Union, not ending slavery, as his first priority. As the war dragged on, necessity and practical facts forced his hand.

As the Union marched into the deep South, African Americans abandoned their plantations, declared themselves free, and sought to make themselves useful to the Union cause. The Union Army at first accepted them as "contraband of war," that is, property seized. But no Northern state allowed slavery, so how could they remain slaves in Union territory? By late 1861 the Army and Navy had set formal rates of pay for "contrabands" who served the Union. By mid 1862 these *de facto* sol-

diers, along with manpower shortages, public pressure from abolitionists, and the deepening crisis of the war, persuaded Lincoln to allow African Americans to enlist in the regular army.

Critics of Lincoln's decision to enlist African Americans in the Union
army claimed that it raised "colored" soldiers to a level of equality with
whites; they argued that blacks lacked the basic qualities of discipline,
courage, and intelligence necessary for battle. They saw the soldiers as
inflated, valueless. An 1862 song attacking Lincoln criticized the "fractional currency"—paper notes for amounts of less than one dollar—that
the North also issued during the war. These "Shin-plasters sure were bad
enough," the song argued:

> That is when Rebels used them;
> And well the Nigger-worshippers,
> In consequence abused them,
> But now to cap the climax, of
> Our manifold disasters,
> We've had to come to one and two
> And three cent *sticking plasters.*
>
> What next I wonder? Nigger troops
> Or some such abomination;
> As Niggers being our equals in
> The states and in the nation.[34]

This poem sees African American soldiers, "an abomination," as the
next logical step after the issue of "cheap" fractional paper currency. The
progression superficially makes little sense—what do "colored troops"
have to do with paper money? But the author clearly saw a connection between purely representational currency, a piece of paper named
"three cents," and the representation of African Americans as equal citizens through the Union uniform.

Other opponents of African American enlistment scorned the appearance of African Americans in uniform, "strutting up and down
Pennsylvania avenue, and aping the port and gait of their illustrious
prototype"[35] in terms that inverted the minstrel show itself. In the minstrel show white minstrels "aped" the "port and gate" of *their* "prototype," African Americans, the whites strutting across the stage in rag-
gedy costume. Their mimicry made them money, turned "rags into

cash," even as it blurred the line between the symbol and the real. Popular commentary on "colored troops," inverting the logic of the minstrel show, focused on the "colored" soldiers as base imitations of the white authentic. Would this "imitation" lead to equality—would they become the things they imitated—or remain a valueless counterfeit?

"The Colored Brigade," another minstrel song written and published shortly after the enlistment of African Americans, reflected this ambivalence:

> O when we meet de enemy I s'pec we make 'em stare,
> I tink he'll catch a tartar when he meets de woolly hair;
> We'll fight while we are able, and in greenbacks we'll be paid,
> And soon I'll be a colonel in de colored brigade.
> Chor.—A colonel, a colonel, in de darkey brigade,
> And soon I'll be a colonel in de colored brigade.

The song's other stanzas refer favorably to African American service in the Revolutionary War and with Andrew Jackson in 1812; it argued: "Now some folks tink de darkey for the fighting wasn't made, / We'll show dem what's de matter in de colored brigade." But it also points— "soon I'll be a colonel"—to inflated rank and argues:

> Some say dey lub de darkey and dey want him to be free,
> I s'pec dey only fooling and dey better let him be;
> For him dey'd break dis Union which de're forefadders had made,
> Worth more dan twenty millions ob de colored brigade.[36]

In this verse the Union is worth more than paper money and colored soldiers. The Union serves as the gold behind the linguistic and social exchange the song initiates. Written in dialect and using terms offensive to modern eyes, the song nevertheless acknowledges African American service in American history, and the force of the Union as a political idea. It mocks "darkey" aspirations in minstrel terms while acknowledging the superiority of African Americans to white secessionists.

Others were less mixed. "Great things are expected from this new principle of military amalgamation," commented the *New York Herald*: "Whether it will change the Ethiop's skin to white or convert the white man's skin to black remains to be tested."[37] The *Herald* wondered, or pretended to wonder, just how much the uniform—the representation of citizenship—might change its wearer's basic character. Would African American soldiers become the things they "imitated"? African American soldiers were like the greenbacks themselves: a counterfeit. "For finance, issue Greenbacks; for war, Blackbacks," one critic of the administration argued.[38] Just as greenbacks could never acquire a value they intrinsically lacked, so African Americans would remain of doubtful value no matter their clothes. "How Are You Greenbacks!" concluded:

> We're coming, Father Abram, Nine hundred thousand more
> With the greatest fighting hero, that lives upon our shore
> He fought in all the battle won, and shed his blood most freely
> But he's fought them all with the Tribune, and his name is Gen'l Greeley

Lampooning Greeley as a paper general, whose battles all take place in the flat world of print, the song also mocks the African American soldier's contribution to the war, or at least devalues it to the level of paper. "How Are You Greenbacks!" begins with an image of printing presses patriotically turning out paper money and, as Bryant's minstrels would have performed it on stage, ends with an image of minstrel characters, dressed as soldiers, comically marching behind their paper general. It makes an explicit link between the possibility of racial equality and the philosophy of paper money.

Other attacks on Lincoln and paper money made the same connection in explicitly racist terms. These attacks came most clearly in material written for the presidential campaign of 1864. "Jokes, Niggers, Greenbacks—all play'd out," mocked the chorus of one song, "Who Will Care for Old Abe Now?" McClellan stood for the return of gold, the song continued. "When 'Little Mac' is in the White House, Greenbacks will vanish—Gold come down!"[39] "We're fighting for the nigger now," went another song:

> I calculate of niggers we soon shall have our fill,
> With Abe's proclamation and the nigger army bill.
> Who would not be a soldier for the Union to fight?
> For, Abe's made the nigger the equal of the white.[40]

This song also claimed that the soldier "must be loyal, and his officers obey, / Though he lives on mouldy biscuit, and fights without his pay. . . . / Though he waits six months for Green-Backs, worth forty-five per cent."

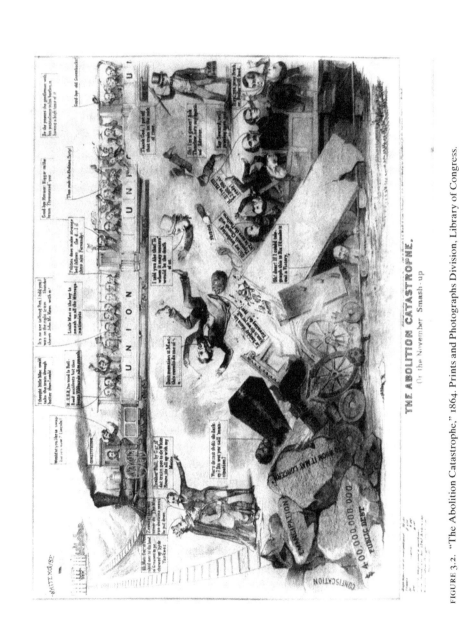

FIGURE 3.2. "The Abolition Catastrophe," 1864. Prints and Photographs Division, Library of Congress.

The song treats greenbacks, elevated to a position of equality with gold they cannot sustain, as part of the same mentality that has elevated African Americans to a counterfeit equality. It stated: "when old Jeff Davis is captured, paid up you may be: / If you do not mind the money, don't you set the nigger free."

"The Abolition Catastrophe," published in 1864 for the election, showed Lincoln's political train crashing into the public debt and exploding. The explosion dismembers several African Americans, who cry out in minstrel dialect: "Is dis wot yer call 'elevatin da nigger'?" and is "dis wot yer call 'mancipation?" Meanwhile, McClellan's campaign express races towards the White House: its passengers comment "Little Mac is the boy to smash up all the Miscegenationists," "Good-bye old Greenbacks," and "Thus ends the Abolition Party." Emancipation and greenbacks explode together.[41]

For Lincoln's opponents the return to gold meant the return to racial hierarchy, while paper money meant freedom for slaves: "Oh! we want no . . . 'Greenbacks,' such as Chase used to utter" went another campaign song: "We want no more rank niggers near the White House frying pan; / Nor to sit at the head of the table!"[42] This song treated greenbacks as part of a general scheme to upset the "natural" order of things, while a third campaign song chided those who "while worshipping the nigger, they'd let the Union slide." It concluded that under McClellan, "we'll *chase* away all greenbacks, and gather in our gold, / And then we will prosper, as in the days of old."[43] All these critics linked paper money to a confusion of the line between thing and symbol, black and white. Paper money had helped depreciate the white man while it inflated the black; it had destabilized not just financial value but the differences between things and people.

The *New York Herald* argued that the issue of greenbacks had served only to further the cause of the "niggerheads" who wanted to make a war for abolition. Referring partly to greenbacks, the *Herald* wrote: "Accursed be that infernal abolition fanaticism which has rendered them necessary; . . . The arts of the niggerheads have made volunteers and money equally scarce. Consequently it was necessary to pass the Conscription bill and issue more paper money."[44] "Negro-worshipers," it argued again, have pushed through a policy of financial inflation. In depreciating the currency they have also depreciated the value of white men.[45] *The Great Paper Bubble*, another Democratic campaign document of 1864, compared paper money to "amalgamation, selection by affinity, polygamy, community of property and all the other disgusting and ruinous theories of depraved minds," and went on to compare those who wanted paper money with "stock jobbers, negro fanatics, bubble blowers, [and] broken-down wildcat [banknote] distributors." These arguments treat the ideal of racial equality, or even just the idea of some modest political considerations for African Americans, as akin to wild financial speculations, to inflation of blacks and depreciation of whites, to miscegenation, and to a general confusion of the symbol for the real thing. *The Great Paper Bubble* went on to compare greenbacks to a bad medical experiment, a transfusion of "cow's blood" into a human, resulting in madness and death.[46]

In the minstrel show, inflated, ragged white imitations of the imagined "black racial authentic" circulated freely, and negotiated multiple meanings. They "made money" by counterfeiting blackness; they enhanced their own whiteness and their own value by imaging racial difference. But for these critics seeing African Americans in uniform, seeing them as counterfeit representations of the *white* racial authentic, made paper money inauthentic and valueless as well.

By the end of the war, African Americans made up 10 percent of the Union Army, nearly 180,000 men. They acquitted themselves extremely well overall in combat and in regular service. African Americans clearly believed that their labor, their service, had earned them equality—they had worn the uniforms, shouldered the weapons; marched in sun and rain and been wounded or killed in the fighting. African Americans marched into conquered Richmond and helped raise the American flag over the Confederate capital. Chandra Manning quotes an African American soldier exulting in the role "the black arm" had played in the struggle, and how its actions were "bringing about a revolution of opinions." Another declared: "the prejudice against color and race is disappearing before liberty and justice, as the mist flees from before the morning sun."[47] The war eliminated slavery, once and for all. Did it also eliminate racial bigotry?

Some of their fellow soldiers came to share these opinions. Manning concludes that "when ordinary northern men" met actual black people, as slaves, as former slaves, and as soldiers, and saw them suffer and fight for their own freedom in a thousand ways, "they found reasons to discard old views." Many did not. One soldier, early in the war, argued

FIGURE 3.3. Unidentified African American soldier in Union artillery shell jacket. Prints and Photographs Division, Library of Congress.

against enlisting African Americans precisely because it would "enable them to Come up and Clame the wright of citizenship." Others reserved a distinct status for soldiers—Manning quotes another who called slaves and free blacks "niggers" but called soldiers "negroes," "soldiers of color," or "citizens of African descent."[48] Overall it may be fair to say that for most Northerners, the experience of seeing slavery firsthand,

and seeing African Americans fight for their freedom and their country, in the blue uniform, changed minds and perhaps hearts.[49]

*   *   *

To what extent, and how deeply, would form the political subject of the next decade. In the 1860s and 1870s two central questions preoccupied voters: the debate over civil equality and the meaning of freedom, and the debate over currency and the greenback dollars. If the Civil War changed ideas about slavery and race, it also changed ideas about money and the federal government's relation to money. In the North the war forced the Union to make major changes in the nation's finance system. Greenbacks depreciated—caused inflation—but they also led to remarkable economic growth. And the war encouraged central control over the money supply.

In 1863 the Lincoln administration oversaw the passage of the National Bank Act. The act, also known as the National Currency Act, established a new office in the Treasury Department, the Comptroller of the Currency, and granted that worthy the power to charter a number of "National Banks." To qualify for a charter, National Banks in large cities had to keep a 25 percent specie reserve. The newly formed National Bank would then buy Treasury bonds, deposit them with the comptroller of the currency, and in return for buying the bonds, receive "National Bank Notes" in amounts of up to 90 percent of the value of the bonds. The Treasury bonds would thus back the paper money issues. But Congress set a limit: the comptroller of the currency could not release more than 300 million dollars in National Bank Notes. These new notes all looked roughly the same, and all National Banks were required to accept the notes of other National Banks at face value. A National Bank charter granted prestige to the chartee, and also made the bank eligible to hold federal deposits. In theory, the National Bank Notes would establish a uniform national currency based on gold and restricted in extent. And the comptroller of the currency would adjust regional money flows by controlling the sale of bonds to banks.

In practice, not enough private banks joined the National Bank system, and so the Union introduced a tax on the issue of state bank-notes—2 percent in 1863, inflated to 10 percent by 1865. The taxes encouraged membership in the National Bank system, and more importantly they brought the gaudy and colorful era of private banknotes to an end. By 1865 the Union had approximately sixteen hundred National Banks, and basically two forms of paper money: National Bank Notes and the "greenbacks" issued during the war.

Predictably, one faction of American politics detested the greenbacks just as much after the war as they did at its start: they wanted the greenbacks "contracted" as soon as possible. "Contraction" literally meant destruction. Hugh McCulloch of Maine, the first comptroller of the currency and later treasury secretary under Lincoln and Andrew Johnson, wanted any greenbacks that crossed a National Bank's counters thrust *poste haste* into the Treasury's furnaces. "Resumption," the return of specie payments, with every paper dollar redeemable for a dollar worth of gold, would then follow.[50]

Arguments for "contraction" and "resumption" stressed the magic properties of gold. "Gold and silver," McCulloch insisted in 1865, "are the only true measure of value." "I myself have no more doubt that these metals were prepared by the Almighty for this purpose, than I have that iron and coal were prepared for the purposes for which they are being used."[51] Only nature, not government or society, could create value and identity. According to economist Amasa Walker, "the true standard of value exists in nature . . . governments have rightfully nothing to do with it."[52] Theorists of intrinsic value cited nature's law, unaltered by legal enactment. Deploring greenbacks, Henry Adams called "the law of legal tender . . . an attempt by artificial legislation to make something true which was false."[53]

McCulloch similarly argued, regarding the former slaves, "it is very evident to me that at the time of their enfranchisement they were not, are not yet, and probably never will be, qualified to properly control the government."[54] Just as no legal enactment could create value, no government could affect the negro's nature—"no legislation of Congress can elevate or improve the physical, moral or intellectual condition of the negro," insisted Senator George Vickers of Maryland in 1869: "we cannot legislate into them any fitness or qualifications which they do not now possess."[55] The debate over race and equality in Reconstruction used the same language, and the same logic, as the debate over money.

As McCulloch imagined natural mineral hierarchies, the most extreme opponents of racial equality imagined natural social hierarchies, insisting that "it is by the standards of nature that we are to determine whether the radical task of negro equality is practicable."[56] The white race rules "by virtue of its intrinsic strength," insisted James Pike, while the newly freed negroes rule South Carolina "by means of an alien and borrowed authority . . . it is not the rule of intrinsic strength; it is the compulsive power of federal authority in Washington." Under this rule, Pike insisted, political identity and economic value collapsed into each other, until "the vote of any Negro in the State is worth as much as a South Carolina bond." Pike equated the ex-slave, inflated to citizenship, to inflated bonds.[57]

Against "bullionist" arguments about the intrinsic value of precious metal, Americans reiterated the "soft-money," producerist philosophy of Henry Carey and his circle. Careyite political economy, again, envisioned a harmony between producers and consumers in which value emerged from their mutual enterprise. Instead of a limited specie money, liable to collect in foreign vaults, Careyites advocated a flexible, "nonexportable" legal tender currency. While no explicit link between Careyite economics and racial equality exists—Careyite Republicans also formed exclusionary associations based on race and gender—the Whig Party, and Republican Party that rose from its ashes, always tended towards abolition. When a historian finds calls for racial equality in Reconstruction, which is much less often than he or she might like, they generally emerge from the Republican side of the political aisle. The idea of value created in social cooperation, in labor rather than in "nature," often lent itself to the ideals of civil rights. Many of the most radical Republicans—Wendell Phillips, Thaddeus Stevens, William D. Kelley, and Benjamin Butler, for example, also supported greenbacks.

Widely disdained by brahmins like Henry Adams—he was, Ulysses Grant observed, "a man fashionable to abuse"[58]—Butler had a fascinating career. As a lawyer and Democratic politician he agitated for the ten-hour workday and for labor generally. When the Civil War broke out he joined the Massachusetts Militia as a lieutenant. Thanks to his political connections and some degree of talent, he quickly rose to the rank of Brigadier General—a "political general," common in those days. Lincoln eventually appointed Butler Major General of Volunteers, in which capacity he oversaw Fort Monroe in Virginia. There Butler introduced the idea of treating escaped slaves as "contraband of war": captured property, not slaves yet not free.[59]

When the Union captured New Orleans in 1862, Butler administered the occupation. From that position he wrote to Secretary of War Edwin Stanton regarding the status of escaped slaves:

> The question now pressing me is the state of negro property here and the con-
> dition of the negroes as men. It has a gravity as regards both white and black
> appalling as the mind follows out the logical necessities of different lines of
> action. Ethnological in its proportions and demands for investigation, it re-
> quires active administrative operations immediately upon the individual in
> his daily life, his social, political, and religious status as a human being, while
> some of the larger deductions of political economy are to be at once worked
> out by any given course of conduct. It cannot be solved, therefore, without
> thought, or discussed by a phrase or a paragraph.[60]

This remarkably garbled, circuitous paragraph reflects Butler's efforts to make sense of the plight of the former slave without laying down any permanent markers. Clearly aware of deep racial antagonisms, he both calls for "ethnological" investigations and "active administrative operations," or what we might call "government action." He insists that the problem of the former slave—the "condition of the negroes as men"—be seen in terms of "his social, political and religious status as a human being." The passage doubtless reflects a politician's reflexive fondness for ambiguity, but it also suggests that, in his mind, the meaning of "negro" remained negotiable; not a subject fixed by nature and immutable but a subject amenable to social action.

In his autobiography Butler strongly denounced those who argued against African American soldiers, and the "folly, injustice, and stupid-ity of this class of prejudice." Of "negro" soldiers, he wrote, "after I left New Orleans General Banks enlisted many more of them, but was weak enough to take away from them the great object of their ambition, under the spur of which they were ready to fight to the death, namely, equal-ity with the white soldiers." Butler recalled that "in spite of his [Banks's] unwisdom, they did equal service and laid down their lives at Port Hud-son in equal numbers comparatively with their white brothers in arms."[61] Butler's experiences in war convinced him that the Union needed to re-consider the status of African Americans.

Butler lives in memory mostly for his notorious "General Order No. 28," declaring that any New Orleans women found insulting or showing contempt for a Union soldier would henceforth be regarded as a "woman of the town plying her avocation," and liable to arrest. The law outraged Southerners and many Northerners; it deprived respectable middle-class women of the privilege of class and deprived all women of the alleged privileges of female gender.

By his order Butler asserted the law's power to define meanings: declaring a rebel woman a "prostitute" made her so. "Prostitution" might be regarded as an act, a timeless act outside of a specific set of national laws, "the oldest profession," everywhere the same regardless of local law. But at the same time the word only makes sense in relation to a body of law: what is formally prostitution and what is not? The answer differs from place to place and time to time. In a very real sense the law makes "prostitution" out of a range of acts it singles out for its attention.[62] When Butler used the power of print and the power of law to declare truculent New Orleans women to be prostitutes, he pointed to the way words may call into being the things they describe. His logic in General Order 28 mirrors his support for both racial equality and greenbacks: value and meaning are socially derived, not natural facts.

Butler's opponents always scented an element of cynical expediency and self-promotion in his conduct and his views. But he thinks very differently from McCulloch, or Pike, who wanted laws written by nature, not by men, and who imagined racial hierarchy and value as intrinsic and immutable.

Butler, who created soldiers from slaves by fiat, who created prostitutes by fiat, regarded fiat paper money as his crowning achievement. "In my congressional career," Butler concluded, "my proudest boast is that through my advocacy and efforts, the legal tender greenback was made the constitutional money of the United States."[63]

From the greenback perspective, legally declaring equality could bring equality about just as a Congressional declaration of paper money's value could give the paper value. "After all, being a citizen and a voter has more than anything else made the negro a man," recalled Samuel Chapman Armstrong: "the recognition of his manhood has done much to create it."[64] "All that is necessary for a government to do to create money," insisted a "soft money" congressman, "is to stamp upon what it would change into money 'its image and superscription,' and it will be money."[65] The Fourteenth Amendment, declared Mississippi Republican James Alcorn, "created the being whom you now call a citizen of the United States" with one stroke of the pen. As governor Alcorn established a public school system in Mississippi, with funding "distributed about equally between white and colored schools."[66] To pay for the schools, Alcorn issued "certificates of indebtedness" to supplement the currency. "The teachers' salaries were paid with warrants or 'Alcorn money.'" This "Alcorn money," like the declaration of citizenship his government was based on, derived its value from political authority alone.[67] "Soft money," money declared valuable by law, funded the project of making citizens by law.

Opponents of both soft money and racial equality recognized the link. Linton Stephens, brother of Confederate Vice President Alexander Stephens, called the Fifteenth Amendment "exactly analogous to the prohibition on the States in the original Constitution—that no State shall coin money; emit bills of credit; make anything but gold or silver coin a legal tender." "Who ever dreamed," he continued, "that these prohibitions on the States gave *Congress* the power to control the whole subject of money?" By overstepping Constitutional limits, the Fifteenth Amendment thus "coined" counterfeit citizens.[68] The bullionist *Nation*, under editor E. L. Godkin, initially supported the project of racial equality. But by the 1870s it ferociously attacked both African American equality and greenbacks. Godkin deplored Wendell Phillips's proposal that the Republicans nominate an African American for vice president. Mr. Phillips believes, sneered Godkin, "that as soon as people saw a negro foisted into the Vice Presidency by political maneuvering, the whites would begin to respect the colored population more than they had previously." Phillips "might as well talk about regulating the temperature by forcing the mercury up and down in a thermometrical tube." Election, he insisted, stemmed from popular recognition of character—it did not call that character into being. Godkin and Phillips repeated the terms of the money debate, asking if character inhered in certain objects and certain people, or value and character derived from social or cultural authority.[69]

In his first act as treasury secretary, starting in 1865, Hugh McCulloch insisted on returning the country's money to a specie basis, and he asked Congress for expanded authority to contract the greenbacks. In 1866 Congress passed the "Contraction Act," which in simple form gave the secretary the power to destroy four million in greenbacks per month. But even McCulloch hesitated to use this power: "resumption" smacked of favoritism. During the war, the Union sold bonds and took greenbacks in payment. Greenbacks "depreciated" in wartime inflation. If the U.S. returned to a specie basis, those who bought bonds with greenbacks would take their compensation in gold—a windfall for bondholders. Those who fought the war and took their pay in greenbacks understandably found the prospect of a windfall for wealthy men who stayed home loathsome. The constituency for soft money remained powerful. In 1868, after $44 million in greenbacks had undergone combustion, Congress repealed the law.

The financial crash and depression of 1873–74 highlighted the political tension between hard and soft money. As the crisis worsened, Congress engaged in a long and windy exploration of the nature of money and value. Had a shortage of specie, fostered by Eastern bankers and their European allies, caused the depression? Or had an uncertain, inflated economy, its morals degraded by irredeemable legal tender, collapsed under the weight of its own paper? At the same time, both House and Senate discussed Charles Sumner's Civil Rights Bill, which abolished most formal racial segregation; they had only recently completed a long series of hearings on the murderous depredations of the Ku Klux Klan in the South. A review of Congressional debate during this crisis offers another example of the congruence of money and race.

Resumptionists loved gold dearly: "preciousness, cohesiveness and divisibility belong to gold as to no other element," New York Senator Jacob Cox rhapsodized: "God has hardened it in the millions of years in which the mountains come and go like the rainbow. It is as true as its burnished source, the sun. Its silent power, like that of the dial, measures our height of prosperity or our depth of adversity."[70] Cox also favored a return to white rule: "the South," he wrote to James Garfield, "can only be governed through the part of the community that *embodies* the intelligence and the *capital*" [my italics].[71] Under slavery African Americans constituted the South's capital, but in Reconstruction, according to Cox, whiteness literally embodied capital. Most gold bugs insisted that without a common standard difference lost all meaning: "Money is the universal medium or common standard, by a comparison of which the value of all merchandise may be ascertained, or, it is a sign which represents the respective value of all commodities."[72] Samuel Chase argued in the second of the legal tender cases before the Supreme Court that without such a standard exchange "would become impossible" and we would lapse into barbarism. Because of their special intrinsic value, "the selection . . . of gold and silver as the standard of value was natural, or more correctly speaking, inevitable" in advanced societies.[73]

James A. Garfield warned of "immutable laws of nature which no Congress can safely ignore and which no legislation can safely overturn." Exchange, he claimed, requires "extension, weight and value." The Constitution lets Congress fix these standards, "but Congress cannot create extension, nor weight, nor value. It can measure what exists, but it cannot make length of that which has no length, it cannot make weight of that which has no weight, it cannot make value of that which has no value." Since all civilized nations of the world recognized gold, "let us restore and preserve our standard of value, which must be applied to every exchange of property between man and man." Congress could not legislate value or substance into being, nor could it derange the natural standard that gave meaning to difference.[74]

In his inaugural address Garfield spoke volubly about the importance of civic equality for African Americans. But he backed away from the idea when it took practical form. Mark Elliot's recent biography describes how Albion Tourgée, who had counted Garfield a friend and ally, lobbied Garfield to appoint an eminently qualified African American to a federal judgeship. When he mentioned the African American candidate, "there was an impressive silence," Tourgée reported, and then Garfield asked, "do you think I would appoint a *negro* to the bench?" Tourgée said yes, and Garfield responded that he himself could never practice law before a black judge, "any more than I would invite him to my table." Though he talked a good game on civic equality, Garfield's private beliefs about racial difference looked much more like his public beliefs about money.[75]

August Merrimon of North Carolina felt that "money implies essential value. It is of the essence that money shall have essential value in it; and the experience of the world from the earliest periods down to the present time is that nothing constitutes the medium of exchange like gold and silver. . . . It would seem that the Almighty had provided these substances to answer for this very purpose." Congress could pass a law tomorrow outlawing gold as money, he continued, and "it would still have value in spite of the statute."[76] Similarly, no one could legislate away racial difference. "Why did God make our skins white?" Merrimon asked in a speech on civil rights a few months later. "Why did He make the negro's skin black?" These natural differences give evidence of God's design, he insisted, and "I ask Senators, where do they get the authority to change the color God has blessed us with? Where can any authority be found to make my skin black and corrupt my blood?"[77]

The instability of both race and money that Merrimon wanted to escape appears in one of David Locke's distasteful "Petroleum V. Nasby" satires of 1867. The story described a projected "Southern University." Among the exam questions proposed for the college was the following:

"A high toned, shivilrous Virginian, twenty years ago, hed a female slave which wuz ez black ez a crow, and worth only $800. Her progeny wuz only half ez black ez a crow, and her female grandchildren wuz sufficiently bleached to sell in Noo Orleans for $2500 per female offspring. Required. 1st.: The length of time necessary to pay off the Nashnel debt by this means. 2nd.: The length of time required to bleach the cuss of color out of the niggers of the United States."[78]

The story's "humor" came from linking race and money in ways that pointed to the negotiability of each. It suggested first that race tended to disappear in commercial intercourse—the term being chosen deliberately—and second that the erasure of racial difference might change the nation's stock of value and money. It echoed Merrimon's fear that intermarriage equaled inflation and the collapse of value.

Proponents of greenbacks countered that "an act of Congress declares what is money. It stamps the money quality, the representative value, upon a piece of gold or silver just as it does upon paper."[79] Greenbackers echoed Justice William Strong in the legal tender cases: "it is hardly correct to speak of a standard of value . . . value is an ideal thing."[80] Congressman David Mellish found "an inconsistency in attempting to make a standard of value" which itself has value all over the world. "The conundrum not yet solved," he suggested, "is how to measure the value of the measure of values. I venture to predict that this difficulty will never be cured until something of no intrinsic value shall be adopted, and its value fixed conventionally or arbitrarily by a competent authority."[81]

Greenbackers formulated a theory of value and identity drawn from nationalism and patriotic labor. "As surely as our flag represents . . . the unity of these States," declared a Michigan greenbacker, "just so surely, sir, do the United States Treasury notes represent the cost of life and blood and treasure, the priceless value of that unity of States." The notes' value came from cooperative work and sacrifice. Just as each citizen required political representation, each citizen required a physical representation of his value. Massachusetts Republican George Boutwell, for example, suggested that the presence of four million new citizens, each anxious to work, spend, and own property, required more currency—otherwise a shortage of money might deprive the freedmen of the building blocks of citizenship.[82]

New Yorker Clinton Merriam praised the republican greenbacks that won the war. Greenbacks had made citizens of the ex-slaves. "The greenback was the first thing they ever earned that they could call their own, the first thing, save our flag, that stood before them, a symbol of their freedom." Greenbacks symbolized government's power to overturn the natural law arguments that justified slavery. "With it they soon learned a power to gather together long-broken families into a common home," Merriam continued. "To the colored men the greenback rose above the dignity of language; to them it almost bore the dignity of religion." Greenbacks made it possible for slaves to own property and establish families, the two bulwarks of republican citizenship. It also taught them the religion of saving and self-advancement.[83]

But could citizens created with the help of valueless currency ever acquire any genuine value of their own? Could they ever measure up to the standard of *Homo economicus*? George Fitzhugh doubted it. "Political economy stands perplexed and baffled in the presence of the negro. Capital can get no hold on him" because the negro lacked the natural attributes. *DeBow's Review* asserted "we must quite expel nature before we can make the negroes the equals of the whites."[84]

Thomas Nast's caricature of inflation and paper money as "the rag baby" admirably expresses this point of view. A Nast cartoon of 1876 depicted a rag doll slumped before a printed handbill. "This is not a rag baby but a real baby, by act of Congress," insisted the note, while a disembodied hand offered the rag doll a slip of paper reading: "this is MILK by act of Con." Nearby a stick drawing of a cow captioned "this is a cow by the act of the artist," and a crudely fashioned bill labeled "this is money by act of Congress" further insisted on the intrinsic reality and value of things and people. By 1876, Nast had abandoned his earlier depictions of the freedmen as noble, deserving citizens and instead drew them as degraded, ape-like semi-savages. Northern sentiment likewise began moving away from racial equality and towards notions of intrinsic racial hierarchy. Nast's characterization of paper money as a wishful fantasy became more persuasive as his depictions of intrinsic racial difference grew more pronounced.[85]

The cartoon instantly dramatizes the hard money position: soft money amounted to a silly, childish delusion, a denial of reality. But look closer at the image and much of Nast's argument collapses. For example, a piece of paper saying "this is a house and lot": clearly preposterous on the one hand. But in the eyes of the law a deed to property *was* the property—it entirely and thoroughly represented the property. An owner might buy

MILK-TICKETS FOR BABIES, IN PLACE OF MILK.

FIGURE 3.4. Thomas Nast, "Milk Tickets for Babies, Instead of Milk," 1876. Digitized by Google.

and sell a house and never live in it or even see it: the paper deed would serve as the house in all transactions. Even more, consider the drawing of a cow: "this is a cow, by the act of the artist." Paper cows don't give milk. But in Chicago, even as Nast worked, traders speculated in the futures market, in which hypothetical beeves and nonexistent bushels of wheat represented only by pieces of paper daily made and lost fortunes.

"This is money, by act of the cannibals," says a card: those who want pa-per money are primitive and uncivilized. But Americans continually did business with paper money, and, increasingly, with checks. As Edward Kellogg pointed out, even under a gold standard those pieces of paper represented not actual gold, but hypothetical gold, gold which the paper money itself, spent in enterprise, might someday cause to arrive. Nast's drawing reflects a yearning for literalness that the actual capitalist econ-omy, based in gold or not, consistently undermined. His drawing itself, nothing more than lines on paper, creates value and embodies concrete arguments: "this is the gold bug position, by act of the artist." Added to a book on money, it increased the book's value.

It is doubly interesting that an artist as capable and effective as Nast should deny the power of marks on paper. Historians widely credit Nast with creating the public image of the gross and swollen "Boss Tweed"; ask many Americans about Tweed and little more than a Nast cartoon, recalled from some textbook, springs to mind. Even more, Nast often gets credit for inventing Santa Claus: his paper imaginings of the jolly, bearded elf-master now undergird an industry that annually generates billions of dollars: an entirely fictitious person generating real economic effects. Ben Franklin, in his *Autobiography* and in his writings on paper money, recognized that representations could become reality—that print representations of ideas might become concrete ideas; that print repre-sentations of labor might generate labor themselves; that print represen-tations of value would in turn generate value. Nast here wants to deny that, and insist on the concrete, bounded nature of things. But his car-toon amounts to a classic "self-subverting text."

Nast's rag-baby cartoon appeared in *Robinson Crusoe's Money*, a gold standard fable by economist David A. Wells based on that hoary staple, the Robinson Crusoe example.[86] Like many of his contempo-raries—social Darwinist William Graham Sumner, for example, was a fierce gold bug—Wells connected political economy to evolution. Reject-ing gold as the standard of value, he thought, "makes warfare upon the beneficence of the Almighty," violates "the natural laws of supply and demand," and attempts "to provide for survival of the unfittest."[87] Nast's cartoon for the cover of *Robinson Crusoe's Money* depicted a gold coin with the head, feet, and tail of a rooster, crowing atop a rubbish heap composed of law books, legal filings ("bluebacks"), acts of Congress, and decisions of the Supreme Court. The caption proclaimed "survival of the fittest."[88]

THE SURVIVAL OF THE FITTEST.

FIGURE 3.5. Thomas Nast, "Survival of the Fittest." Digitized by Google.

The cartoon joins Wells's text in linking arguments for gold to a social Darwinist account of social hierarchy. Political economy texts of the
time routinely imagined a progression in money, in which primitive peoples used wood, or shells, more advanced societies used base metals, till
finally gold emerged as the common standard of the Anglo-Saxon and
Teutonic peoples. Gold bugs dreamed of certainty, natural law, and stable meanings: as we will see in the next chapter, connections of specie to

progress occur again and again, always linking primitive "races" to valueless money and gold to the most advanced.[89]

*   *   *

Despite the close affinities between the gold bug position and racism,
it would be as much a mistake to uniformly charge the gold bugs with
racism as it would to automatically equate the greenback position with
equality. A hard-money man like Charles Sumner could easily support
racial equality—Sumner believed there were intrinsic qualities necessary to citizenship, and African Americans possessed them. Albion
Tourgée, perhaps the white man most closely associated with the idea of
racial equality, counted himself a "hard money" Republican. Humanity
itself, a shared nature, could appear as a "gold standard" which linked
all men and women.

Certainly African Americans struggling for equality found this "intrinsic value" position more useful than the claim that equality came
from legislative enactment alone. African Americans in Reconstruction
clearly believed that their claim to equality came from both the possession of intrinsic rights *and* the value created by their labor. Congressman
Robert B. Elliot insisted in debate over Sumner's civil rights bill that African Americans enjoyed the God-given "natural rights" common to all
men. He further recalled how his people's toil, in the fields and armies of
the Republic, had earned them a place as equal citizens. African Americans served in the Revolutionary War, and with Jackson in New Orleans:
they "flew willingly and gallantly to the support of the national Government" during the Civil War. "Their sufferings, assistance, privations,
and trials in the swamps and in the rice fields, their valor on the land
and on the sea, is a part of the ever-glorious record which makes up the
history of a nation preserved."[90] African Americans in Congress recognized that the greenback position offered no sureties.

Nor did soft money politics preclude racism. Facing an at times
chronic shortage of specie, many Southern Democrats endorsed greenbacks while holding firmly to racial hierarchy. "Throughout the 1870s it
was generally agreed in the South that the region's supply of money was
desperately deficient. . . . [A]s a result, southern congressmen pressed
unceasingly for an increase in the money supply, and they voted solidly
against contraction and specie resumption."[91]

It seems perfectly reasonable, from the logic of the argument presented here and in chapter 2, to conclude that *greenbackism*, not the gold standard, might look more plausible in a society committed to racial inequality—the presence of persons clearly and non-negotiably different could make a certain degree of economic indeterminacy tolerable. This is effectively what happened under slavery—the presence of African Americans *as slaves*, persons with a fixed and non-negotiable identity, enabled the loose antebellum money supply.

But take away slavery, and things become more complicated. Now black Americans could act as free agents: they could negotiate for themselves instead of being negotiated over. They could renegotiate the meanings of their very persons, and for a time Reconstruction attempted that renegotiation on a grand scale. The response, as we see here and will see in the next chapter, was both to intensify and harden the notion of race, *and* to insist with equal ferocity on the gold standard, and the idea of a natural, Darwinian law of value. Most gold bugs argued that gold money enabled a "natural law" economy, in which men's true merit revealed itself, and most had no doubt that in that hierarchy, African Americans would remain on the bottom.

* * *

Greenbackers often tended to be more sanguine about racial equality, given their origins in Carey's producerist, small-capitalist version of the labor theory of value. Greenback philosophy suggested that African Americans could earn their place in a society of producers, while gold bug essentialism either granted them this status or denied it. In general, the greenback position may have offered a more optimistic model of racial coexistence—as the Greenback-Labor Party suggested when it unsuccessfully reconnected racial equality and greenback dollars in the 1870s and 80s.

A remarkable, and remarkably understudied, organization, the Greenback-Labor Party, like many third parties, sheltered a wide range of practical and impractical reforms, including the eight hour workday, graduated income tax, and women's suffrage. The party formed in 1874 over the money question. In 1873 Congress had passed the Coinage Act, later made notorious as "the crime of '73." The 1873 act declared gold to be the *de facto* basis for American money and eliminated the use of silver coins—although not for long. It marked the growing power of "contractionist" forces, who a year later passed the Specie Resumption Act, which insisted that beginning in 1879, greenback dollars could be re-deemed for gold at face value and thereby finally retired. The Green-back Party saw this as a disaster: it would only exacerbate the power of capitalists.

Greenbackers worried, rightly, about what had then just begun, a worldwide phenomenon economists call "the great deflation." From 1870 to 1890 prices for basic commodities in industrial nations steadily dropped, partly because of the insistence on gold money, partly because of the steady increase in industrial productivity. If inflation aids the bor-rower and the man on the make, deflation does the opposite: it acceler-ates the process of concentrating wealth at the top. And it makes farm-ing and small manufacturing particularly difficult. Generally, deflation equals stagnation, but in the U.S. the "great deflation" came along with remarkable economic growth. The Greenback Party sheltered reform-ers who wanted to manage inflation, growth, and their impact on Amer-ican society.

Informed by both the Republican/Whig tradition and by the more radical theories of Edward Kellogg and his disciple, Illinois Congress-man Alexander Campbell, the Greenback Party called for inflation and the issue of legal tender paper.[92] Abolition, and the possibility of racial equality, played a major role in the thinking of its leaders—Peter Cooper, James B. Weaver, and our old friend Benjamin Butler all ran for presi-dent from the Greenback Party. All had deep roots in abolition, in the Union cause, and in the optimistic aims of Reconstruction. The party actively sought to peel African American votes from the Republicans, who more and more favored the gold standard as they backed away from Reconstruction. Greenbackers frequently invited "all classes of people, of men and women too," including former slaves, to their meetings.[93] Af-rican Americans in the South formed a key part of the Greenback con-stituency.[94] But as with their heirs, the Populist Party in the 1890s, the Greenbackers were unable to sustain a commitment to genuine racial equality, and greenbackism as an economic philosophy never managed to carry a majority. As it became clear that African Americans wanted more than a permanent place on the bottom rail of the free market, the greenback position became increasingly unsettling and untenable.[95]

When Charles Francis Adams saw that many white Southerners sup-ported greenbacks, he connected it to the decline in their morals brought about by Reconstruction misrule. "Crushed under negro legislation," he bitterly declared, why should the South "care to maintain those standards of value which represent only ruin to themselves?" Their moral economy deranged by African American equality, white Southerners' political economy collapsed as well.[96] By the end of the 1870s, hard money Southern Democrats had come to share Adams's view.

In the North, Liberal Republicans like Adams led the flight from racial equality, often linking inflated bills to inflated citizens. "The inflation ring," *The Nation* charged, always disguises its economic corruption "with some philanthropic work, such as the care of the poor or the elevation of the black man." Commenting on political corruption and deficit spending in South Carolina, Godkin called the greenback position a disease, "the same disease [that] has been rotting away the fibre of the South Carolina government," producing "a swarm of little Tweeds and little Butlers, some black and some white."[97] He connected Tweed's corruption of immigrants with inflated dollars to Butler's advocacy of greenbacks and racial equality. Only a hard money standard could restore moral and racial order.

It is surely no mere coincidence that when ex–Confederates began overturning carpetbag rule, they called themselves "redeemers"—the same word used to describe the process of turning paper money in for gold, or "redeeming" the greenbacks. There is a certain consistency between the two meanings of "redeem," especially given the origins of "carpetbagger" in paper money and wildcat banking. If carpetbaggers circulated irredeemable paper notes, "redeemers" restored the notes' proper relation to specie. When "redeemers" overturned carpetbag rule, they reversed expansionist and inflationary policies. As early as 1868, *DeBow's Review* complained that, under Reconstruction, "all laws prohibiting intermarriages between whites and blacks are repealed, and all distinctions between the races abolished so far as the impious efforts of man can abolish the natural distinctions which God created." The *Review* called on Southern men to "redeem your pledge to the dead . . . redeem the country from the selfish thrall" of the Republican Party.[98] The Klan, Benjamin Wade reported, aimed to "redeem the State of Louisiana from negro and Radical rule."[99] Southern poverty, according to Senator Richard Coke of Texas, "had been brought about by the war and by the infamous carpet-bag governments." Coke continued: "The people of the south were now striving in every State to make an honourable payment." They would, he insisted, "redeem the South; they would place her where the blood and lineage of her people, where her glorious climate and fertile soil deserved that she should be placed."[100]

The clearest link between inflated value and racial equality appears in the novel that gave the period its name, Mark Twain and Charles Dudley Warner's *The Gilded Age*. The novel's plot centers around Colonel Beriah Sellers's attempt to fund a Southern "Industrial University"—not unlike the Southern College satirized above by Petroleum V. Nasby— "open to all persons without distinction of sex, color or religion." The novel takes place during Reconstruction, and the "Tennessee Knobs Industrial University" echoes Republican attempts to reform Southern education. Sellers represents the inflationist position, the cultural creation of value. Eternally, wildly optimistic, Sellers wants a currency based on everything, including pork: "What we want is more money . . . base it on everything!" Echoing the Congressional declarations in Nast's cartoon, Sellers tries to transmute reality with mere words. "The Colonel's tongue was a magician's wand that turned apples into figs and water into wine as easily as it could change a hovel into a palace and present poverty into imminent future riches." Sellers had a long career beyond the novel, as a stage character and as a symbol of the absurd excesses of "puffery." But the novel established Seller's absurdity by having him campaign for open, unsegregated schooling. By connecting Sellers's puffery to the Industrial University—making the ideal of integrated education the heart of their novel—Twain and Warner connected the enterprise of racial equality to inflated value. In Reconstruction "the Negro," Jean Baker concluded, "stood for immutability."[101]

*   *   *

Today the entire world uses legal tender paper money issued by the United States, a situation beyond the Greenbackers' wildest imaginings. And we live in a world where racism, while very far from vanished, has fallen out of fashion in polite society: today we overwhelmingly hold the notion of a racial equality as an ideal, even if we do not always practice it. It is probably safe to say that the number of Americans today who openly profess to being racists is about equal to the number of Americans who, in 1860, professed to favor racial equality—a complete reversal. So modern readers look at the era of Reconstruction with some puzzlement—why does the idea of racial equality flare so briefly and then gutter out? And why the *Sturm und Drang* about gold, or silver, or gold and silver? Why does Reconstruction crash in such a spectacular and irrational way?

As with slavery and emancipation, historians have many excellent answers, but here again, this chapter seeks to add a new answer to the list. Reconstruction failed because it presented Americans with the negotiability of meanings—with the radical implications of the American dream. The Civil War was conducted, successfully, with "fiat" currency, money backed by the labor, the sacrifice, the courage, and of course the coercive legal power of the Union it represented. The war and its aftermath also saw the elevation, by legislative fiat, of African Americans to full social equality; with the potential of renegotiating what race meant. The two issues cannot be considered separately—the money debate recapitulated the terms and assumptions of the race debate. The combination proved to be too much. When white Americans looked hard at the possibility of renegotiating what "race" meant, they doubled their bet on gold.

CHAPTER FOUR

Gold Money and the Constitution of Man

Congress can no more regulate the relative intensities of human desire than it can regulate the length of day or night. — Frederick Perry Powers, "A Financial Catechism"[1]

In the decades after the Civil War, American society saw an explosive increase in mass-produced commodities. Mass production made millions of identical copies available for the first time in human history. These commodities democratized taste and made social mobility, or at least its appearance, easier than ever to accomplish. In the 1890s, while radical racism gained a stronger grip on American life through Jim Crow and disfranchisement, the money debate shifted its terms, focusing now on white ethnic immigrants and drawing on Darwinian evolution to imagine "low wage" races, people who simply could not understand economic exchange. The triumph of the gold standard also marked the rise of social Darwinism and eugenics.

* * *

Francis A. Walker remembered the greenback era, and "the social effects of a paper money inflation," with the greatest disgust:

> I need not recall the wanton bravery of apparel and equipage; the creation of a countless host of artificial necessities in the family beyond the power of the husband and Father to supply without a resort to questionable devices or reckless speculations . . . the humiliating imitations of foreign habits of living . . . the loss of that fit and natural leadership of taste and fashion which is the best protection society can have against sordid material aims, and man-

ners at once gross and effeminate, against democracy without equality or fraternity, and exclusiveness without pride or character.[2]

This wide spectrum of diverse ills is startling. Paper money threatened patriarchy by "creating artificial necessities in the family"; these
"false needs" drove otherwise respectable men to immoral or dangerous speculations. Little slips of green paper challenged established gender norms, miraculously producing both "effeminacy" and coarseness.
They encouraged foreign habits; they threatened society's "fit and natural" cultural and aesthetic leadership. Paper money caused exclusiveness
without character, destabilizing democratic virtue. It even brought about
loud clothing and bad taste—"wanton bravery of apparel and equipage."
How did paper money manage this cultural crime spree? Not by raising
prices—in this passage Walker never mentions higher prices. Instead,
by removing society from a basis in what Walker imagined as "real" or
"natural" values, paper money overturned natural laws and natural social hierarchies. It decentered the self.

Walker talks of paper money not in what we would call "economic"
terms, but rather as the instrument of moral and aesthetic chaos. A thoroughly "sound" man, a spokesman for orthodoxy and property, Walker
was probably America's leading labor economist in the 1890s. At different points in his career Walker supervised the census and served as
president of MIT. He wrote influential texts on political economy. Henry
Adams collaborated with him in *Chapters of Erie* and in essays on the
duplicity and evil of legal tender: he was, Adams wrote in the *Education*, "one of the types of his generation."[3] Like most of his peers he
imagined steady global progress marching directly towards the United
States of America and its "fit and natural leadership of taste and opinion." To reinforce that notion, he founded his economics, and his view of
money, in natural law. "Money," Walker declared 1895, "is a product of
evolution, a result of the ages." In political economy as in society, in the
markets and cultural capitals of the world, "the better [gold] has gradually crowded the worse out of existence."[4] Like other "hard money"
economists, Walker championed gold as the natural money of the superior races. Paper money reflected human law, not natural law: the desires it created were artificial desires, the goods it bought were counterfeit and shoddy, the habits it encouraged were "foreign." Walker saw
money as a symbolic system on which the meaning of nearly everything
depended.

A close look at these latter two quotations from Walker points only to the incoherence, the contradictions, at the heart of the Gilded Age's formulation of natural, economic laws. In the first quotation, on paper money, Walker draws implicitly on what economists call "Gresham's Law," the premise that "bad money drives out good." Gresham, an Elizabethan merchant, stated that if two forms of money circulate—gold and greenbacks, for example—people will always hoard the better form and spend the worse wherever they can. Anyone's first impulse, on recognizing money of inferior quality, is to pass it on to someone else while saving the better money for emergencies. All parties in a contract will strive to pay others in the worse form of money and to be paid in the better, which they will hoard. Soon no gold will circulate at all: the worst drives out the best. In Walker's first account paper money drove not just gold but taste, culture, and character from the market.

But the second quote, an argument for why we should use gold, draws on the theory of evolution, imagining gold as the fittest in a struggle for economic survival. In this instance, the good—gold—naturally "crowds out" out the bad, surviving because fittest, and Gresham's law lies forgotten. By treating gold as the biological equivalent of superior genes, Walker tried to fuse an elitist notion of taste and class with a Darwinian account of economic competition.

Walker argued consistently for gold money, a material with natural, intrinsic value. As Supervisor of the Census, he also called Eastern and Southern European workers racially inferior and argued vehemently that American society had no place for them. The two positions are directly linked—the gold standard to his belief in the Anglo-Saxon's superiority in worldwide struggle, and the anti-immigrant nativism to his fear of bad blood, bad money, bad culture, driving out good.

This chapter focuses not on Walker's contradictions alone, or on his nativist bigotry, but rather his fear of a destabilized self, and the generalized anxiety about the stability of taste, value, culture, and identity that led Walker and men like him to identify paper money with racially inferior peoples and the collapse of civilization, and gold with the Anglo-Saxon race and its salvation. It explores the relationship between the political battle over money, the mass production of commodities, and the rise of radical racism and nativism in the 1890s.

*   *   *

Among the many differences between the United States before the Civil War and the United States in the 1890s, no observer could miss the flood of mass-produced goods. By 1895, Americans were awash in mass-produced commodities to a degree exponentially beyond anything imagined in 1845. Those who visited the 1876 Centennial Exposition in Philadelphia saw commodities in staggering abundance, magical in production and nearly infinite in extent; heaped up in grand pyramids, formed into mosaics and busts, arranged into long receding ranks. Shopping in department stores, or by the 1890s leafing through the Sears catalog, one found goods of all imaginable kinds for sale, each an identical perfect copy of some distant unknown original. Watches, clocks, musical instruments, toys, tools, housewares, furniture, clothes of all degrees of intimacy and publicity; sporting goods, medical supplies, decorative knickknacks, farm implements, buttons, jewelry: nearly the entire range and extent of human desire made concrete in multiple copies, each identical, each available on easy terms.[5]

Money might count as the first human attempt to mass produce perfectly identical copies. Coins began as a precisely measured amount of metal, a measurement as careful and accurate as technically possible at the time. At the mint, the lumps of metal were stamped on both sides using a metal die or punch. The results came as close to perfectly identical copies as ever attained. Each coin, stamped typically with the image of the king or queen, promised an identity of function and value and character with each of its brethren. Coins theoretically took uncertainty out of the marketplace and sped commerce by standardizing. They decreased the need to think about the nature of the money. All parties in a trade could assume the coins had an identical value and thereby spend more time negotiating about price. Their minted existence as perfect copies made them universal: their promise of uniform stability empowered market negotiation and sped up exchange.[6]

In fact, in daily use, identical coins wore out differently, and might lose value as they grew lighter. Men and women "clipped" coins, snipping off tiny amounts of metal as the coins passed though their hands. The milled edge still found on the U.S. dime and quarter originated as a measure to thwart "clipping" of gold and silver coins. The unscrupulous counterfeited coins as well: they stamped new copies from base metals. Coinage promised a security it did not deliver.

Even in periods of gold and silver coinage, people fundamentally disagreed on what gave the coins their value—was it the precious metal

FIGURE 4.1. Sears, Roebuck and Company, *Spring Features in Women's Apparel* (1909). Courtesy, The Winterthur Library: Printed Book and Periodical Collection.

content, or was it the stamp of the king's authority? If the latter, what made a well-produced counterfeit any less viable in the market? The actual king, after all, never made his majestic way into most people's affairs, nor touched the money. As mentioned earlier, stamped coins had a different value and a different utility than an equivalent lump of similarly alloyed metal. Did the coin embody the intrinsic value of gold, or symbolize the king's authority?

Printed paper money promised the same uniform security, and similarly failed to deliver: the uniform perfection of paper copies promised to level and standardize one troubling aspect of exchange—the money form—and free both parties to negotiate about price. But paper money, no matter how well printed, was always an imperfect copy of the thing it symbolized. The ten dollar National Gold Bank Note of 1871—yet another of the many varieties of paper money Americans used—made this relationship clear. Its reverse side showed an engraving of a stack of gold coins.[7] Each coin was theoretically a perfect copy, the bill was a copy of the value of the coins, and in the theory of the gold standard each bill ostensibly reflected that value perfectly. As we have seen, in practice counterfeit paper money abounded, and in daily life Americans used forms of paper with little or no discernable connection to gold.

By 1895 Americans had extended the promise and potential of mass-produced uniformity, realized first in coins and paper money, to daily life. But the uniform production of mass commodities, like the uniform production of coins and bills, only heightened anxiety about the security of value and character. To accumulate commodities was also to accumulate symbols—symbols of status, of "culture," of class. Immigrants might come to America and buy themselves a new set of identities. A man on the make might easily counterfeit the style of a man of settled substance. What did a chromolithograph of Rembrandt's *Night Watch* symbolize? Did it symbolize Rembrandt's actual painting in the way a silver coin symbolized actual silver? Or did it symbolize the artistic authority of the Dutch master, in the way a silver coin symbolized the king's authority? Perhaps it represented Rembrandt's actual labor in the way a greenback symbolized the labor of American citizens. Or did the print, simply because it looked pretty, contain a distinct value of its own?[8]

Historians sometimes describe a "crisis in subjectivity" in the Gilded Age, a fancy way of saying that it got harder and harder to know with any certainly who was who, or who was what. Identity, who we appear to be, is always to some extent a performance—a set of mannerisms or

PICTURESQUE AMERICA

FIGURE 4.2. Harry Grant Dart, *Picturesque America*, from *Life* v. LI, June 18, 1908 p. p. 681. Digitized by Google.

verbal styles, a set of visual cues in clothes and hair, a "series of success-ful gestures."[9] A mass-consumer society made the props, the gesturing, more readily available, more easily acquired, and more obvious. In fact, it shouted their presence literally from the rooftops. Ben Singer uses the term "hyperstimulus" to describe the era: a sense of bewilderment and anxiety at the dazzling extent of modern possibility.[10]

The 1909 image by Harry Grant Dart in figure 4.2 captures this sense of anxious possibility. Pedestrians are inundated by advertising for sur-realistically implausible goods—the "Pushard Auto car," "Seaming-less Underwear," "Fatal Wedding Rye." Clocks promise "correct time," but they all disagree. "We will make you look exactly like a magazine cover for $18.95," promises a billboard. In the chaos of urban possibil-ity, a small sign for a detective agency barely registers in the profusion of mixed messages and false possibilities.

Even outside of the cities, the Sears or Montgomery Ward's catalogs allowed anyone with enough money to purchase the trappings of an en-tirely new identity, unique to them but composed out of mass-produced copies, mass-produced "props." It is that exact "crisis of subjectivity" that Walker describes in the quote at the start of the chapter, and which Dart's illustration captures—a world where cheap money and mass pro-duction have made it almost impossible to tell the true from the false.[11]

The "American dream" promised that no one need be confined by the circumstances of birth. A powerful idea, it implied negotiability of all identities; at its boldest and simplest, it suggested that any man at least could be whatever he wanted, whatever his will and drive, tal-ent and imagination allowed. We often remember the Gilded Age as the apex of the "self-made man."

But the gilded coin had a flip side: if American culture emphasized the possibility of self-making, of acquiring new gestures for success, it also emphasized the necessity of pinning identity and character down. It is no coincidence that the age of the self-made man was also the age of the detective and of forensic sciences; the age that celebrated self-transformative "rags to riches" stories was the age that adopted finger-prints as discrete, ineluctable markers of identity. John Kasson advanced Harry Houdini as the prototypical man of the day: stripped nearly na-ked in performance, reduced to his essential body, typically locked in police handcuffs and local prisons, Houdini managed to miraculously escape confinement. His career embodied the simultaneous fascination with pinning character down and with escaping, with freedom in self-transformation and the idea of a fixed self, a self which could not "pass" and which authorities of all sorts, not just the police, could arrest from circulation.[12]

As it celebrated the circulation of commodities and the new possibilities they brought, the Gilded Age, and particularly the decade of the 1890s, saw an intensification, a hardening, of biological essentialism. American political rhetoric spoke constantly about true manly virtue, about the essential qualities of men and women. Americans toyed with these ideas as an alternative to market negotiability.

*   *   *

Charlotte Perkins Gilman offers a good example of how new possibilities arrived encumbered by new kinds of restraints. A woman of strong, original, and erratic opinions, she wanted to write, and to lecture, and to enjoy a career. When she married in 1884 and bore a child, she fell into a deep depression. She loved her daughter and her husband, but not marriage and the dreary work of childrearing. Concerned, her husband in 1887 convinced the twenty-eight-year-old Charlotte to see Silas Wier Mitchell, one of America's leading physicians and a specialist in "neurasthenia," the catch-all phrase then used to describe a wide range of mental agitations and symptoms. Mitchell subjected her to his famous "rest-cure," which involved complete and total isolation and inactivity: bland, baby-ish foods, solitude, soft light, and no work with either hands or brain.

Most readers know Gilman from her fictionalized account of this ordeal, "The Yellow Wallpaper." In the harrowing short story the narrator slips into madness under the strain of isolation and forced inactivity. After she left Mitchell's care, Gilman resumed her career as a writer and activist for women's equality. Her second most famous work, *Herland*, imagines a utopian society of women isolated from male contact.

She also wrote on women and economics, and extensively on eugenics. This latter work is troubling to modern readers: while Gilman stands as a feminist, she also betrays the racial and ethnic prejudices typical of her era and her class. Like others of her generation, she both desired market freedom and imagined new ways to restrain it.

In *Women and Economics*, published in 1898, Gilman attempted a grand theory of gender difference. The book is a bizarre amalgam of feminism, socialism, Lamarckian evolution, and eugenics. Gilman looked at other mammal species—"lower" forms of life—and noticed that the females of these other species were not typically weaker or less capable than the male, or at least not much so; female bears, lions, or wolves required no males to defend themselves or to hunt. She argued that gender dimorphism, the tendency of the sexes to vary in body type, was much less pronounced in other mammals than in humans. From this she concluded that among our "primitive" ancestors men and women must have looked much more alike: alike in size and strength and general capacity. In primitive societies, she argued, men and women competed equally as male and female animals did. This, she argued, was because they did not exchange, they did not have markets and economics.

Markets, Gilman reasoned, perverted human development: they selected for social traits that reflected nothing more than whim and prejudice. "Note the marked race-modification of the Hebrew people under the enforced restrictions of the last two thousand years," she wrote: we see now "the effect of the economic conditions—the artificial development of a race of traders and dealers in money, from the lowest pawnbroker to the house of Rothschild; a special kind of people, bred of the economic environment in which they were compelled to live."[13] She was sorry to conclude that Jews had evolved genetically into moneylenders: been made biologically distinct by market exchange. The market, she argued, creates racialized, essential difference.

Just as market exchange had bred a race of moneylenders, so too exchange had bred women into passivity. "We are the only animal species in which the female depends on the male for food, the only animal species in which the sex-relation is also an economic relation."[14] Over time, she argued, an emphasis on certain "sex-related" characteristics—reproduction, adornment, femininity—produced an exaggerated, inflated market for those qualities, so exaggerated that women became physically weaker, more dimorphic, less capable: they lost their natural, inherent value and instead became commodities of unstable, inflated value in false, dangerous, speculative markets. The market had bred women to emphasize secondary sexual characteristics and to promote economic dependence, much in the way from "wild cows" farmers bred "milch cows" which could not survive in the wild.[15]

Gilman linked this perverted market to the decorative, sexualized commodities with which late-nineteenth-century women were so closely identified. She compared the perversion of the natural market to the wearing of a corset. Warped notions of the sexes in exchange created false values in human relations as a corset distorted the body in caricatured ways.[16]

Gilman's argument directly confronted Adam Smith, who had argued similarly that without markets, without free exchange, all men (and presumably all women) were basically alike. But through market exchange, Smith argues, men came to notice differences of talents, and those differences widen by degree, until diversification of labor begins as generic farmers become coopers, wheelwrights, farriers, clockmakers, and finally perhaps even economists. Smith hailed this "diversification of labor" as the freeing of human creativity and liberation from the inertia of custom. Gilman saw it instead as a kind of tulip mania,[17] a speculative market in false and damaging values. Her solution, imagined in *Herland* and *Women and Economics*, involved eliminating exchange altogether.

Throughout her work Gilman, like the partisans of gold or silver, looked for intrinsic value in nature, in a condition of human relations untainted by cultural, political, or social manipulation. In *Herland*, Gilman's feminist utopian novel, this state of nature depended on parthenogenesis—asexual reproduction. In this socialist utopia women conceived spontaneously at age twenty-five and gave birth only to other women. No choosing of mates went on, no competition for better partners, no market in desirability, and so the society ran with a harmonious logic that freed it from the false, inflated, unreliable whims of industrial capitalism. Counterfeiting, indeed false value of all kinds, was impossible in this society, because money and markets had disappeared.[18]

In his essay on the gold standard and naturalist literature, Walter Benn Michaels points out the odd way in which gold bugs, by calling for gold as money, actually imagined gold as a kind of "not-money," a thing which never circulates, never changes its value, never inflates or contracts. Gold sits in a dark vault while its nimble, thin agent, paper money, does the circulating. The desire for a gold standard in commerce in effect marked a retreat from the implications of commerce and exchange itself; it marked a desire for stasis rather than boundless exchange, a realm of non-negotiability and fixed meaning.[19]

We might view Gilman's attraction to parthenogenesis, and to eugenics, in the same way. The racist desires *less* exchange and less variation in exchange; the racist wants to marry someone as much like himself as possible. The famous question "would you want your sister to marry one?" implies that the asker wants to marry his sister: his worst racial nightmare involves the sister desiring the other, not the self. If eugenicists found a blue-eyed blond who matched a specific phenotype, they sought out a second blue-eyed blond who matched the phenotype as exactly as possible. Racism is in that sense incestuous, a desire to marry one's sibling and finally either to have reproduction and genetic exchange without difference or to reproduce one's self without the necessity of exchange, like the women of *Herland*. Gold bugs tended towards racist ideas because they wanted to stop the promiscuous circulation of goods and people and meanings, the negotiation of identities.

*   *   *

At the turn of the nineteenth century, American politicians talked constantly about manliness and honor, about the necessity for male aggression and the threat posed to it by women, by the genetically inferior, and by the supposedly enfeebling qualities of modern life. In the 1890s Americans embraced radical forms of racial essentialism, ideas frequently termed "social Darwinism" or subsumed broadly under the umbrella of eugenics. White elites worried about "race suicide" and decline, about the debasing effects of inferior blood. North and South embraced a three-pronged attack on African American participation in American life: formal legal segregation, systematic disfranchisement, and a campaign of "spectacle lynching" designed to reinforce white supremacy. The decade saw massive immigration from Eastern and Southern Europe, men and women who faced revitalized racial typologies asserting their essential difference from "Anglo-Saxons" or "Nordic Teutons." These same typologies asserted themselves in the rhetoric of imperialism, and they too are connected to the problematic political economy of money, value, and identity.[20]

When the United States moved away from slavery, it undermined the racial constant that had both given value to loose paper money and ensured the security of elite, white identity. In the Gilded Age the absence of slavery, coupled to the dazzling possibilities of a mass-consumer society, led Americans to reinvigorate both the gold standard and radical racism. But in the 1890s the money debate stressed not so much white/ black relations as the problematic character of ethnic immigrants.

Supporting this claim requires a review of monetary policy. In the National Bank Acts, passed during the Civil War, the Union tried to standardize and centralize the paper money system, and in its tentative moves towards "resumption" it attempted to establish a gold standard.

Neither attempt wholly succeeded.[21] Inflationary pressures never entirely went away, and so acts related to the currency question between 1870 and 1890 lurched from hard money positions to compromises designed to ease the bite of the deflation. The major pieces of legislation passed between 1870 and 1890 reflect the mixed motives and cultural baggage attached to the money question, and they also tend to make little sense at first to most readers, because they reflect an understanding of money very different from our own.

For example, take the arcane business of "mint ratios," which would come to consume American politics by the 1890s. Alexander Hamilton, readers may recall, had established both gold and silver as the foundation of the nation's money supply, and after studying the composition of the various dollars then circulating, established a standard dollar of either 371.25 grains of pure silver or 24.75 grains of pure gold. At rates then prevailing, the ratio of silver to gold was fifteen to one—that is, it would take fifteen ounces of pure silver to buy an ounce of pure gold. If you dug up some silver and gold, you could carry the bullion to a mint and, for a small fee, they would make it into coins, valued according to the fifteen-to-one ratio. But gold and silver have a market value as commodities independent of their use in coins. In real life the amount of gold and silver in the marketplace changes—a new discovery of gold in California, new mining technologies, or simply a change in trade flows between nations could result in a change in the relative scarcity of each metal. In the antebellum U.S. after 1849 gold became more common than it had been in 1792, which meant that in terms of what constituted a dollar, silver was undervalued at the mint, and gold was overvalued. So those paying attention hoarded silver and coined gold, or they used silver to buy gold and coined the gold. By 1860, though we had a *de facto* bimetallic standard, silver coins had vanished from circulation. In 1873, Congress passed the Coinage Act of 1873, later made famous as the "Crime of '73." The Coinage Act declared gold to be the sole basis of the economy. Two decades later, the act would form the core of conspiracy theories about attempts to crush silver, an international conspiracy to press a crown of golden thorns onto the brow of mankind.[22]

Dealing with mint ratios makes little sense to the modern reader, accustomed to legal tender paper money. Neither the mint ratio nor the elaborate conspiracy thinking *can* make sense without understanding that debates about money were also debates about other things: about the nature of value, about character, about the genuine and the false.

The Coinage Act sheltered bondholders from inflation, but it also grew from the sense that gold formed the "natural" money of the Anglo-Saxon races and that only "Pagan Asiatics" and Latin Americans used silver.[23] Later critics of the Coinage Act understood the gold standard as a cause of deflation and saw it as an elite trick to rig the economy in favor of capital, and they talked about silver as "the white metal," the "dollar of our daddies."[24] But in 1873, when the act itself passed, the money debate still focused largely on the greenback question, and whether or not the U.S. could continue on "fiat" paper money.

As part of that debate, in 1874 Congress had passed the Specie Payment Resumption Act, which limited circulating greenbacks to no more than $300,000,000 and specified that on January 1, 1879, the U.S. would start redeeming greenbacks for gold at face value. The Treasury established a "redemption fund" for those who wanted to exchange paper for gold; few did so, because paper is so much more convenient than gold. The result was declining prices, deflation. The currency in circulation suddenly gained value, seemingly a good result but disastrous for some sectors of the economy, especially farmers and small producers. The Greenback Party's arguments against resumption failed, despite the fact that it had elected fourteen congressmen and polled a million votes in 1878. After 1879, greenbacks still circulated, but in amounts limited to the gold reserve in the Treasury. The act put the U.S. on a gold standard—sort of.[25]

As the greenback argument failed, inflationist forces turned to silver. Remonetizing silver—it had only been officially *de*monetized in 1873—would cause more "real" money to magically appear, bringing inflation and lowering interest rates. Inflationists, backed by mining interests from the Western states, began lobbying for silver. Silver-backed money would increase the money supply and also offer the happy fantasy of intrinsic value. "Silver had charisma," says economic historian Richard Timberlake.[26] Silverites passed the Bland-Allison Act in 1878: the act required the Treasury to buy two to four million dollars worth of silver each month, and coin it into money. The Treasury Secretary could choose how much to buy each month, and the act did not require the money to circulate. It only required it to be minted (or printed: "silver certificates," paper money backed by silver, began appearing shortly after). The act gave the secretary some of the role of a central bank, in that he could add silver to the economy and slightly increase the money supply. Sometimes called "limping bimetallism," the policy represented a compromise of sorts between the gold bugs and the inflationists.[27]

Legislative enthusiasm for silver peaked with the Sherman Silver Purchase Act of 1890, which required the Treasury to buy an additional $4.5 million in silver each month, on top of the two to four million required by the earlier Bland-Allison Act. This guaranteed, subsidized market for silver caused production to rise, which lowered the price of silver as more came into markets. But the official definition of a silver dollar remained the same. If you brought silver to the Treasury rather than to a private dealer, they paid you for it in Treasury notes—paper money— which you could redeem for either gold or silver. Most chose to redeem them in gold, and the resulting drain on Treasury gold reserves figures as a major cause of the financial panic of 1893, in which drains of gold from the U.S. treasury required the personal intervention of J. P. Morgan, who lent the United States $64 million in gold to cover the shortfall. The Panic of 1893 reignited the money debate with renewed passion.[28]

That debate peaked in the election of 1896 between Republican William McKinley and Democrat/Populist William Jennings Bryan, which famously centered on the money question. The Populist Party, formed in the 1880s and strongest in the South and the Plains, inherited the Greenback Party's emphasis on pure paper money. It mounted possibly the most effective third party challenge in American history. But Populists fell increasingly under the spell of silver and engaged in overheated rhetoric about the "Crime of '73." In the presidential election the Populists "fused" with the Democrats, who subsequently lost resoundingly to McKinley's "hard money" gold standard platform. The Gold Standard Act, passed in 1900, settled the question by naming gold as the only medium for redeeming paper money. Elites especially assumed they had finally driven a stake through the heart of the rag baby.[29]

One salient fact here is that through 1890s it was *still* very hard to say exactly what money really was. The U.S. enjoyed the gold standard—sort of. It also had a halfway silver standard. Was money gold and silver, but not copper? What about the paper notes still circulating? Did they represent a paper promise to pay, or a legal compulsion? Were they a symbolic representation of labor, or a symbolic representation of precious metal? A socially convenient medium of exchange, a store of value, or a material with intrinsic properties governed by natural law? The United States in 1896 had "probably the most heterogeneous system of money of any of the civilized countries," wrote the Deputy Assistant to the Treasurer. Gold and silver coins circulated along with "greenback" United States notes, National Bank Notes, Treasury notes of 1890, and gold and silver certificates. Subsidiary silver, copper, and nickel coinage also circulated, "and it is due solely to the unbounded faith of the people in the unlimited credit of the nation that all these kinds [of money] have for so many years circulated side by side."[30] The currency's heterogeneity in 1896 mirrored the nation's ethnic, racial, and economic diversity: paper money's controversial relationship to the original it imitated made the money question central to debates about value in imitation and the limits to a self made of "gestures." Looking at the case of a celebrated immigrant counterfeiter helps bring mass-commodification, money, and racial theorizing together.

*   *   *

Emanuel Ninger and his wife arrived in America from Germany in 1882. They set about raising four children in the small farming community of Flagtown, New Jersey. His neighbors believed that Ninger enjoyed a pension from the German government, because while Ninger worked at times as a sign painter, and did some farming, he did not appear to do enough work to earn the good living he and his family apparently enjoyed.

In the 1880s, saloonkeepers and storeowners in New York City began finding unique, extraordinary counterfeit bills. They looked at first like ordinary paper money, but close inspection revealed them as handmade, painstakingly drawn with pencil, pen, and brush. Impressed, one saloonkeeper had a bill framed and hung on his wall, where in 1891 it drew the notice of the *New York Times*. The *Times* reporter marveled at the drawing's extraordinary realism, and marveled even more when he discovered that other bills, similarly hand-drawn, now resided in the Secret Service curio room, in the Treasury Department offices in Washington, and in the hands of private collectors. The bill's astonishing realism extended even down to the lathe lines, the web of tiny, scrolled engraving that still marks American currency. "Nine persons out of ten would take it for the genuine article," the reporter continued. Government officials acknowledged a great deal of fruitless hunting for the counterfeiter. But they also concluded that he posed little danger. Such painstaking, labor-intensive work could hardly make economic sense—they regarded the bills as "a fad, or perhaps a mania, on the part of the person who does them."[31]

A few weeks later the *Times* noted that more of the bills had turned up, all coyly missing some aspects of the genuine note they imitated. For example, genuine ten dollar "silver certificates" bore the words "this cer-

FIGURE 4.3. One of Emanuel Ninger's fakes, courtesy United States Secret Service; and a real bill of the same denomination, courtesy Paper Money Guaranty LLC.

tifies that there have been deposited in the Treasury. . . ." The unknown "maniac" rightly omitted them, for no silver backed this note's value—only the artist's skill allowed it to pass. Nearly a year later the *Times* reported another "marvelously fine piece of work" by the same man, this time missing only the phrase "Engraved and Printed at the Bureau of Engraving and Printing."[32]

This mysterious counterfeiter's bills had reached Subtreasury offices in New York as early as 1880, by some accounts. According to the *New York Herald*, the Treasury Department in Washington had even canceled one of them—that is, retired it from circulation, its serial number duly recorded in a ledger. Only when the real bill arrived for retirement did the Secret Service realize just how good the artist was.[33] For over fifteen years the unknown counterfeiter had made perhaps as few as ten or as many as sixty or seventy astonishingly impressive notes a year, pass-

ing them in saloons and liquor stores in downtown Manhattan. His success and skill made him something of a folk hero.[34] In 1896 they caught
him; he was of course Emanuel Ninger, the ostensible Flagtown farmer.
His capture set off a brief flurry of newspaper celebrity, in part because
it recapitulated a number of the decade's most vexing public issues.

Ninger took advantage of the plethora of American paper money, but
he also took advantage of prevailing criminological and social stereotypes about the relationship between appearance and character. Police,
the Secret Service, and average citizens mistook him, and not just his
bills, for the thing he imitated.

On Friday, March 27, 1896, Ninger came to New York to pass seven
of his hand-drawn counterfeits, all fifty and one hundred dollar notes.
He managed to spend all but one, either by using them to buy something or, even more audaciously, handing over a large bill and asking for
change. He entered a downtown saloon at 10 p.m. on Saturday, bought
a cigar with real money, and then requested change for a fifty dollar bo-
gus note. The bartender gave him the change but spotted the fake when
the ink ran on the wet bar top. Ninger offered him five dollars to keep
his mouth shut, then ran out when the bartender refused. Guessing he
would head for the ferry, the bartender found a policeman and had
Ninger arrested.[35]

At least the Secret Service told it that way; newspapers gave a different account. Ninger told the Secret Service and the police several stories. First he gave his name as "Joseph Gilbert," farmer, a country rube
duped into taking bad bills by a wily urbanite, the classic victim of the
confidence man. Later he admitted, encouraged by the Secret Service, to
being Emanuel Ninger's confederate—the "boodle carrier" who merely
passed the bills. Newspapers published both versions in front page stories on the days following the arrest, partly because the Secret Service
also had doubts about their suspect's identity. Ninger/Gilbert didn't con-
form to common notions of what a skilled forger should look like.

"His appearance was such I did not think he could be the maker,"
reported William P. Hazen, Chief of the New York Bureau of the Secret Service; "specially as I had him write his name and he did it very
clumsily."[36] But after Secret Service agents tracked down the other bills
Ninger had passed, and witnesses identified him, Ninger broke down and
confessed all.[37] Still, Hazen and the other agents remained unconvinced.
"I called attention to his big clumsy hands," agent G. Raymond Bagg
wrote, and his "coarse and poor penmanship." Ninger began talking

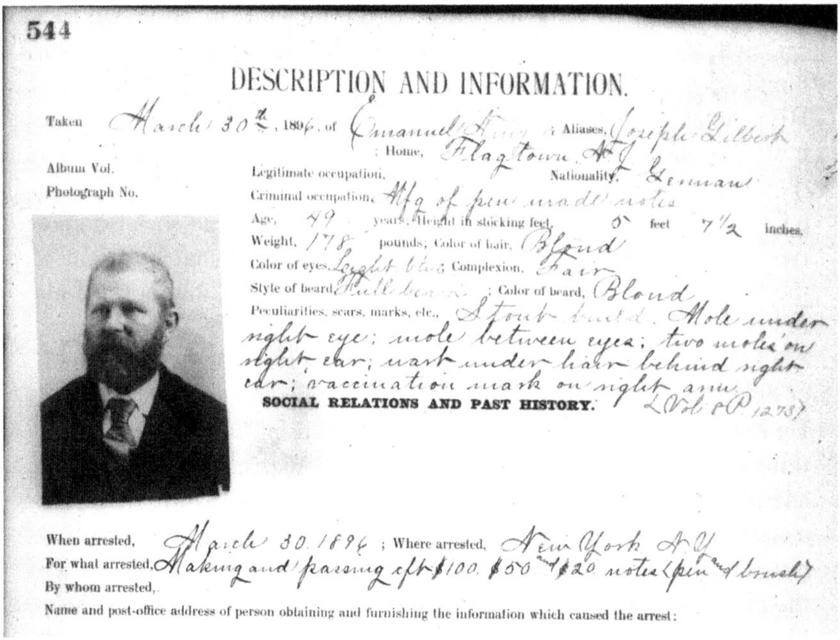
544

DESCRIPTION AND INFORMATION.

Taken March 30th, 1896, of Emanuel Ninger ; Aliases, Joseph Gilbert
; Home, Flagtown N.J.
Album Vol. Legitimate occupation, Nationality, German
Photograph No. Criminal occupation, Mfg of pen made notes
Age, 49 years; Height in stocking feet, 5 feet 7 1/2 inches.
Weight, 178 pounds; Color of hair, Blond
Color of eyes, Light blue Complexion, Fair
Style of beard, Full beard ; Color of beard, Blond
Peculiarities, scars, marks, etc., Stout build. Mole under right eye; mole between eyes; two moles on right ear; wart under hair behind right ear; vaccination mark on right arm.

SOCIAL RELATIONS AND PAST HISTORY. (Vol 8 P 1273)

When arrested, March 30 1896 ; Where arrested, New York N.Y.
For what arrested, Making and passing cft $100. $50 & $20 notes (pen & brush)
By whom arrested,
Name and post-office address of person obtaining and furnishing the information which caused the arrest:

FIGURE 4.4. Emanuel Ninger's Arrest Record. Secret Service Division, United States Treasury Department, *Description and Information of Criminals* v. 25, p. 544. National Archives.

more freely and even showing off—the poor penmanship vanished. He copied signatures and other parts of some currency, even forging Chief Hazen's signature from his business card. "It is excellently done," Bagg reported: Hazen seemed less enthusiastic.[38] Ninger even boasted that "he could make a picture from a photograph just like an engraving."[39] Ninger proved who he really was by imitating other people's markers of identity. His ability to mimic signatures, ironically, helped establish his real identity—just as, in newspaper accounts, his ability to imitate the mass-produced and uniform steel engravings on paper money marked him as unique.

Newspapers treated Ninger as a double counterfeiter, both a maker of fake money and a man of false identities. Several of the New York papers put the Ninger story on the front page and included portraits of the counterfeiter, whom they dubbed "Jim the Penman" after an eighteenth-century forger.[40] All accounts included descriptions of his appearance—his height and weight, but also other supposed marks of character. A reporter for the *New York Herald* also noted Ninger's "big, fat, clumsy looking hands, like a farmer's," and marveled that they could do such work; the *Press* called him a "plain, homely, decent looking old farmer," with "a distinctly German cast to his features" and a "high forehead." With "mild blue eyes that seemed the mirror of innocence," observed the *Sun*, he "looked the farmer from head to foot." All accounts noted that he was a German, and some connected this to an "intelligent look."[41]

In the 1890s, law enforcement fell increasingly under the sway of criminology, a line of inquiry that aimed to find a relationship between appearance and crime. Cesare Lombroso, the Italian author of *Criminal Man* (1887), claimed that tendencies to crime revealed themselves in the face and body, and further that different sorts of criminals looked alike — swindlers like swindlers, burglars like burglars, shoplifters like shoplifters. New York police compiled their "Rogue's Gallery" of criminal photographs not to help victims identify the man who robbed them but to figure out if all pickpockets looked alike. New York's "Rogue's Gallery" presented the faces of murderers, pickpockets, forgers, and burglars, all sorted by their crime.[42] Elaine Abelson, in her study of women shoplifters, has noted that "phrenology had a strong following in the last decades of the nineteenth century among those entrusted with policing the department store."[43] Phrenology promised a relationship between physical appearance — specifically, the shape of the skull — and fundamental character.[44] Stephen Jay Gould has retraced the evolution of intelligence testing and its relation to criminology. Forensic attempts to connect character to appearance proved especially attractive in America, where they seemed to give order to America's racial and ethnic diversity.[45]

Many of his peers found Lombroso's claims exaggerated.[46] But their attraction for Americans seems clear. Arthur MacDonald, specialist in the Bureau of Education, claimed in 1893 that forgers "have an artlessness, and something clerical in their manner . . . some have a haggard look, very small eyes, and the face of an old woman." He argued that when it came to counterfeiters, "imprisonment in advance applies," because their predilection to crime was so automatic.[47] They simply *were* counterfeiters, by nature. Secret Service agents underwent a substantial professionalization in the late nineteenth century, after a series of corruption scandals rocked the fledgling bureau. This training included up-to-the-minute theories of the appearance of criminals. Such descriptions must have influenced the Secret Service's interpretation of Ninger.[48]

Although MacDonald represents an extreme, hereditarian or biological notions of criminality had largely displaced earlier emphases on individual moral failure by the 1890s, at least in academic circles.[49] In interviews with reporters, Treasury agents had referred to Ninger's counterfeiting as a "mania," a word with very specific meanings in the 1880s and 1890s. "Manias," like pyromania, kleptomania, or nymphomania, emerged in the late nineteenth century where criminology and psychology met.[50] Faced with apparently irrational desires to do wrong, behavioral researchers came up with the idea of manias, internal drives too strong to control. "Maniacs" acted mechanically, driven to crime by a biological, essential disposition. Abelson notes, for example, how psychologists connected women's kleptomania to disorders in their reproductive organs. Their propensity to crime, in other words, lay not in the social construction of gender roles but in the biology of sex. The period's most vicious stereotype of compulsive essential criminality, the "bestial black rapist," motivated the radical restructuring of Southern society. Both the rise of "manias" and the theory of genetic or racial criminality had a powerful attraction for Americans in the late nineteenth century.[51]

Records of Ninger's arrest repeatedly refer to his ethnicity. The same attempts to pin down character in criminals appeared in attempts to locate and stabilize the *economic* character of immigrants, and they make Ninger's *economic* behavior especially interesting. John Higham first documented the rising fear of immigrants following the Haymarket riot, a fear that in the 1890s resolved into racial stereotypes of Jews, Slavs, and Italians.[52] The consistent emphasis on Ninger's "German–ness" reflects this concern—agents and reporters were searching for a way to properly *value* him, a way to make sense of him. This concern with his essential value also points to the much larger political debate about labor, value, and the money supply in which immigrants were enmeshed.

*   *   *

In the 1890s, many Americans responded strongly to racially based economic arguments about the low character of imported workers. Alarmed by the census of 1890, and the massive increase in immigration for Eastern and Southern Europe, Francis A. Walker drew on "Teutonic germ" theories of democracy to warn that new immigrants would beat down wages. "They have none of the inherited instincts and tendencies" compatible with self-care and self-government, Walker urged: "they are beaten men from beaten races, representing the worst failures in the struggle for existence." Walker blamed their poor wages on their poor genetic stock, their willingness to settle. Poor nations try to escape poverty by issuing paper money, he argued in *Money, Trade and Industry*, "in defiance of the laws of its distribution," instead of recognizing that such poverty stemmed from "vices of industrial character," that is, bad racial character.[53]

Most turn of the century economic theorists argued that recent immigrants lacked the drive that made the U.S. so dynamic. Henry Pratt Fairchild, in his treatise on immigration, told a story of Theodore Roosevelt visiting Ellis Island. "He wished to observe the effect of a gift of money on an immigrant woman," Fairchild claimed, and so he arranged to have it given "to the first woman with a child in her arms who passed along the line." According to Fairchild, "the woman took the coin, slipped it into her dress, and passed on, without even raising her eyes or giving the slightest indication that the incident had made any different impression on her than any of the regular steps in the inspection." The point? She failed to react properly to a gold coin—immigrants do not understand the value and meaning of money.[54] They do not understand exchange.

Mathew Jacobson describes the sense, by 1890, that the U.S. suffered from overproduction—too many goods, and not enough desire for goods—and that immigrants, because they lacked basic economic instincts necessary to a modern economy, made the problem worse. He quotes Josiah Strong: "A savage, having nothing, is perfectly contented so long as he wants nothing. The first step toward civilizing him is to create a want." But immigrants hoarded: rather than "wants," they displayed "racial parsimony" or compulsive hoarding. Jacobson also quotes American missionary Arthur Smith's observation that Chinese clothing had no pockets, no place to carry "a pocket-comb . . . a boot-buttoner, a pair of tweezers, a folding pair of scissors." Their lack of pockets demonstrated a basic lack of desire, of ambition, their unfitness for industrial society.[55] Sociologist E. A. Ross regarded recent immigrants as "low wage races" with different needs. "Reilly can *outdo* Ah San," Ross wrote, "but Ah San can *underlive* Reilly."[56]

Political economists increasingly saw immigrants as problems of exchange relations: the new immigrants were genetically predisposed to underconsume. Nathan Shaler, writing in 1893, conceded that while immigrants had a desire for gain, "the peasant who attains a fortune rarely alters his scheme of living." Instead, the wealthy peasant simply hoards the money, "a true miser."[57] As Lawrence Glickman and others have argued, native workers feared immigrants as poor consumers, people with few needs who needed only small wages. Undistracted by consumption, unambitious, they simply hoarded with what novelist Frank Norris called the "instinct" of "peasant blood," "saving for the sake of saving, hoarding without knowing why."[58] In Norris's novel *McTeague*, none of the immigrants understand money properly: they all either squander it or hoard it mindlessly. Driven by instinct, they mistake junk for gold and even stories about gold for the gold itself.[59]

So when newspapers described Emanuel Ninger's activity as a "mania," they expressed the sense that some people, immigrants especially, simply lacked the "economic instinct": they understood neither borrowing, nor lending, nor spending, nor saving, and could not function in the modern economy. Rather than seeing Ninger's actions as an example of practical economic self-serving, they saw them as signs of a deficient character, the irrational act of a person lacking the right economic genes.

But if immigrant underconsumption posed a problem, immigrant consumption posed another, equally vexing problem. Consumption equaled assimilation: if civilization originated, as Strong put it, as a set of "wants," did a "savage" who satisfied those wants become civilized? By the early twentieth century advertisers had firmly linked consumption with patriotism, loyalty, and "Americanism."[60] The I.Q. tests devised by Lewis Terman and Robert Yerkes to screen out undesirable immigrants included a great many multiple choice questions about consumption, including the consumption of goods: "Bull Durham is the name of a . . ."; "An air-cooled engine is used in the . . ."; "Soap is made by . . . ." They also included questions about leisure time activities, for example, asking test-takers to identify George Ade and Laura Jean Libby. The tests sent a clear message: knowledge of the consumer marketplace equals intelligence and worthiness.[61] Consumption, and knowledge of the landscape of goods, offered immigrants "assimilation" and erased the difference between immigrant and native. This very capacity posed a grave danger. "These immigrants adopt the language of the native American; they wear his clothes; they steal his name," warned Madison Grant, "and while he is being elbowed out of his own home the American looks calmly abroad and urges on others the suicidal ethics which are exterminating his own race."[62] If immigrants acquired the commodities, the clothes, the gestures of the native, they threatened to erase racial distinctions, or make them negotiable.

Reporters who trooped out to Ninger's farm gave conflicting accounts of his domestic life. Some reporters found a deserted-looking farmhouse kept by an "untidy German woman," with Mrs. Ninger and their four children "ill cared for" in "ragged garments." That is, they conformed to the stereotype of immigrant economic ineptitude. Others saw a "pretty little home" on a "modest but rich estate" kept by a comely wife. The former suggested that Ninger and his family simply did not understand money properly, like the immigrant mother at Ellis island. The second suggested normal middle-class economic habits: an assimilated entrepreneur. Family and home sweet home failed to definitively explain Ninger's criminal motives, or to describe any solid sense of his real character. A *Herald* headline announced that "Ninger Shed Tears" when his twelve-year-old daughter saw him in prison—reassuring evidence of a real emotional core. But when the United States Marshal questioned Ninger's family, reported the *Sun*, "he got nothing of value from them."[63]

Ninger's disguise as a solid family farmer only reinforced his look of honesty when he came to pass his bills. According to Secret Service interviews, all those who took Ninger's hand-drawn counterfeits recognized him immediately as a farmer, and found the identity reassuring. With hard work, a farmer produces something real from the earth itself, where gold—"real" money in 1896—also comes from. By imitating—counterfeiting—a farmer, Ninger called to mind the presumed connection between work, economic value, and "real" products of nature. In real life Ninger only imitated a farmer, his identity as a farmer appeared mostly as gestures, as his bills only imitated paper money, itself only an imitation of the value supposedly inherent in gold or silver.

To resolve the tension between an ideal of racial character and the possibility of self-transformation, late nineteenth-century America revolutionized record keeping and identity tracking, the techniques of forensic science and the bureaucratic, administrative apparatus of Weberian rationality. The Secret Service file on Ninger included a "mug shot,"[64] and along with the photo came a description of his appearance, including "peculiarities, scars, marks etc." Here Treasury agents noted "mole under right eye; mole between eyes, two moles on right ear, wart under hair behind right ear, vaccination mark under right arm." It listed his nationality as "German," with "legitimate occupation" left blank. The record allowed a positive and ostensibly permanent record of ineluctable marks, making it possible on the one hand to pin Ninger's identity down (a *counterfeiter*, not a farmer who made bad bills) and on the other to compare Ninger to other counterfeiters and so perhaps identify them by their looks.[65]

From its inception, writes Alan Sekula, photography raised the problem of the archive—photographs as a record of identity, a means of tracking. Photography very quickly entered the arsenal of state surveillance and forensics. Ninger's photo would have appeared in a wide and developing intellectual apparatus aimed at classifying criminals by type and assessing the specific behavior of a given criminal against emerging criminological norms.[66]

But photographs proved less reliable than police had hoped. Criminals grew or shaved their facial hair. Scars or bruises present at one moment might fade. Suspects would often move their heads back and forth, blurring the image—many early mug shots include the hands of the police, on either side of the suspect's head, holding it in place so the slower cameras of the day could get a usable picture. Subjects for the mug shot would distort their facial features for the camera, puffing out their cheeks or making grotesque faces in an attempt to make the mug shot useless.

A stunning example of these techniques, vivid in its depiction of the mixed feeling the public held towards police and criminality, appears in the 1904 film *A Subject for the Rogue's Gallery*. This very short film begins with an attractive woman being led willingly before a camera. The woman twirls in a flirty manner, removes her hat and jacket, smoothes her hair, and sits down. The police, standing on either side of her, grasp her hands and hold their palms flat against the side of her head, so she cannot move and ruin the picture. The camera moves slowly closer as the woman makes s series of comic, distorted faces, then finally breaks down in sobs. The film's voyeuristic fascination with the woman, its sadistic desire to pin her in place, combined with its identification with her resistance and flash of sympathy for her pain, mark two poles of feeling about crime, punishment, and the self.[67]

The public found Ninger fascinating, but the Secret Service, like police departments across the country, wanted a bureaucratic and scientific answer to the slipperiness of Ninger's character—he would henceforth be the person recorded in the file.

Ninger's arrest happened just before fingerprints came into general use, when police and prosecutors were experimenting with alternative methods of pinning identity down. Use of fingerprints as markers of iden-

tity began in the British Empire, advanced partly by colonial Indian bu-
reaucrats who claimed Indians "all looked alike,"and partly by adminis-
trators who needed better means of identity than the easily forged marks
of illiterate subjects. Francis Galton, Charles Darwin's cousin, hoped
that among other things fingerprints might provide a stable sign of racial
character—that there would be Caucasian fingerprints and Asian fingerprints, and that theoretically fingerprints might resolve cases of uncertain race. Simon Coles, in *Suspect Identities*, argues that Americans
adopted fingerprints with little or no scientific evidence to support the
notion that all fingerprints are unique, and with little or no acknowledg-
ment that identifying fingerprints taken from a crime scene constituted a
highly subjective, highly uncertain interpretive enterprise. That is, their
desire for an ineluctable, fundamental marker of identity outstripped evidence for such a marker's actual existence.[68] Ninger's case points out the
contrast between a public, market life often marked by shifting identity
and compelling fraud and the quest for fixed and stable markers of identity revealed in Ninger's file.

*   *   *

Though newspapers described him as unique, other men besides Ninger
drew facsimiles of American money in the 1890s. Practitioners of illu-
sionistic or *trompe l'œil* painting including William Harnett, John Fre-
drick Peto, and John Haberle painted minutely detailed facsimiles of
mass-produced material objects, including American currency. Each was
either arrested or questioned on suspicion of counterfeiting by Secret
Service agents looking for Ninger.[69] Trompe l'œil painting had a long history; in the U.S. it particularly reflected the influence of the Peale family in Philadelphia. Trompe l'œil painters of the late nineteenth century
loved to depict the detritus of mass culture, and they frequently painted
money alongside other forms of mass print. Characterized by sly humor,
their work called attention to the uncertain meaning and value of money
in daily life.

One of John Haberle's money paintings so astonished a Chicago
critic that he accused Haberle of pasting a real bill to his canvas and
then painting over it. Incensed, the painter hurried to Chicago to prove
the critic wrong. Haberle thereafter occasionally included painted newspaper accounts of the incident in his work, along with other clippings

marveling at his skill and extolling his ability to work, like Ninger, without a magnifying glass or any artificial aids. The money painters, like Ninger, exploited the ambiguity of value and authenticity.[70]

John Haberle was one the wittiest of the trompe l'œil money painters. His most famous painting, *The Bachelor's Drawer*, depicts a physically impossible space loaded and cluttered with things a man might keep in his pockets—the things "Chinese garments" had no space for.

Haberle announces both a self—his self—which transcends commodities, which masters by imitation, and an identity entirely composed of commodities. The paintings finally mock the possibility of clarity—in *Bachelor's Drawer* the objects and printed matter hang improbably on the vertical face of a drawer, an impossible space which highlights the tension between Haberle's imitation and the original.[71]

Most of the trompe l'œil painters made a modest living on the fringes of the "highbrow" art world. Their work appeared in saloons (like Ninger's bills), trade fairs, department stores, and men's clubs, and art critics dismissed it as mechanical and shallow. The prevailing understandings of art disdained mass-produced objects as vulgar, and saw the imitation of them as pointless.

Lawrence Levine has described the new understandings of cultural hierarchy that emerged following the Civil War—what came to be called "highbrow" culture. Like criminologists, theorists of high culture fantasized a relation between appearance and intellectual development, in which "lowbrowed" individuals lacked the essential qualities necessary to make or appreciate art.[72] In this view "high" culture's value came in part from its essential qualities, which in turn resulted from the artist's intrinsic genius. In his extremely influential essay on "The Political Economy of Art," originally published in 1857, John Ruskin directly compared great artists to a nation's limited supply of "artistical gold." "You can't manufacture" the great artist, he wrote, "any more than you can manufacture gold." "A certain quantity of art–intellect is born annually in any nation . . . or race of men; but a perfectly fixed quantity annually, not increasable by one grain." This artistic gold standard demanded careful management: Ruskin worried that "there may be two or three Leonardo da Vincis employed at this moment in your harbors and railroads: but you are not employing their Leonardoesque or golden faculty there, you are only oppressing or destroying it."[73] That is, art consists in an essential, individual genius revealed, an element discovered and then burnished, like gold, through careful labor. A sort of artistic mercantilism prevails in the notion of a "limited national art intellect," and the relation of artistic value to gold.

In 1896, Ninger's "high, protruding forehead," as the *New York World* described it, gave away the special talents behind the humble demeanor. Was he a Leonardo, laboring in the wrong field? Like Ruskin's concern with the essential nature of genius, the emphasis on Ninger's appearance in both popular and official accounts reflects a pervasive desire to link appearance or practice with reality, to have signifier and signified agree. But Ninger's productions also created the value they represented—their value came from their capacity to literally embody Ninger's matchless skill.[74]

In 1896 another, more obscure money painter, Victor Dubreuil, painted *Cross of Gold*. In an obvious reference to William Jennings Bryan's famous speech of the same year, Dubreuil painted five greenbacks and silver certificates arranged in the shape of a crucifix. Gold tacks, one each at the "head," "feet," and two "arms," hold the money in place. Dubreuil, "a poor devil who . . . painted money because he never had any," seemed to take a neo-populist line in depicting inflationary greenbacks and silver certificates pinned to the wall by gold tacks.[75] But he also made reference to American society's fabled love for or "worship" of money, in this case a merely representative paper money which specie economists critiqued as a sort of false idol. Then again, the gold tacks pin the money in place, stabilizing it—as gold supposedly stabilized value in commerce.

* * *

The ambiguity of the money paintings, their lack of a coherent, consistent point of view, hardly makes them different from the orthodox and respectable economic theories and positions of the day. It was extremely difficult to make sense of the relation between money, labor, and value. The late nineteenth-century gold fetish, relatively unstudied by historians, presents an extraordinary wealth of preposterous and incoherent claims about essential value.

Most historians tend to see the partisans of the gold standard as the more rational. Richard Hofstadter famously depicted the silver camp as paranoid and "agrarian," out of step with modernity. James Livingston similarly sees the gold standard camp as bringing modern capitalism into being: he chides the Populists for a simplistic one-to-one-understanding of the relationships between things and people. A recent history of the money debates recognizes that "in the face of the silver challenge, defense of the gold standard became more shrill, binding nature's laws ever more tightly to gold alone." But gold bugs and silverites *both* believed in natural law, natural value. What most historians miss is the congruence between theories of natural law in money and theories of natural law in racial character. The gold bugs grew more shrill, and more obsessed with the "natural" rise of the gold standard, not because of silver but because of racial and ethnic diversity and the "crisis of subjectivity."[76]

Proponents of specie money consistently saw nature as their foundation. "Who or what gave these metals . . . their peculiar qualities for serving as coined money?" asked "A Currency Primer" of 1896. "Men did not," came the answer: "Law did not. Government could not. It was done by *Nature*." "Nature has decreed of what materials our money should be, and has even indicated the proportions of money to be made of each metal"—that is, the ratio of gold to silver—"and nature is more potent than legislation."[77] The resort to natural truth, pushed to its conclusion, made little sense. An 1897 textbook on the money problem, for example, argued that only gold was real money, and that "the ultimate value of real money rests on the market value of itself."[78] In other words, its value is its value, which is itself—its intrinsic properties. "Sound money must mean money that under all conditions, unaided, will be able to establish, *by force of its own virtue*, its own supremacy in the markets of the world" (my italics). Since only gold had this virtue, "therefore, *sound money* consists *only* of gold" (italics original).[79]

In his famous critique of the Populists' tendency to racism, Richard Hofstadter rightly pointed out how they tended to anthropomorphize silver, to depict it as a humble sturdy yeoman suffering under elite tyranny. But "Coin" Harvey's language found clear echo in this vision of gold battling its bare-handed way to supremacy, living "the strenuous life" in a manner Theodore Roosevelt would surely approve. Recall this period as the height of American imperialism, and the rhetorical similarity becomes broadly apparent. Consider, for example, Theodore Marburg's comment on the Spanish–American War: "The Spaniard and his American descendent are very much the same people they were several centuries ago," and "the impartial observer must admit the superiority of our race, the Anglo-Saxon, in the qualities that contribute to human advance. . . . [A]ny nation that blocks the way of human progress must expect to be brushed aside by more powerful and vigorous blood."[80] The rhetorical similarity of gold bug arguments to social Darwinist justifications for imperialism seems unmistakable.

Gold bugs consistently established historical monetary progressions, mineral hierarchies with gold at the top. In these accounts primitive peoples—thanks in part to "indolence and want of initiative," Francis A. Walker argued—used base materials as money. "Iron once served the Lacedæmonians as money," he continued, "but it would be an impossible money today for any but a nation of savages."[81] Over time, humble materials give way to increasingly more valuable metals. "The history of money and the history of the civilization of the human race are intertwined," argued "A Currency Primer." "Gold is the standard of civilization and Christianity," insisted another gold bug: "As Mexico adheres to the implements of which the farmers of the United States discarded fifty years ago, so does it adhere to a standard of value [silver] which this country . . . discarded in 1834."[82] "The brass 'cash' of China," "A Financial Catechism" announced, "indicate[s] that the people are in an extreme state of degradation; the silver dollar of Mexico represents a higher condition of the people; the gold coin . . . of the United States . . . represents the highest condition." Like monotheism, suggested one businessman-turned-politician, "gold mono-metallism is the unavoidable destiny of this country."[83]

Edward Wisner's bimettalist *Cash vs. Coin: An Answer to "Coin's Financial School"* often asserted that value originated in labor. But it began by stating: "All money is a medium of exchange, but intrinsically valuable money, only, is a measure of values."[84] What can such a statement possibly mean? In other words, its value is its value, which is itself, its intrinsic properties, as judged by the market—peculiar reasoning indeed. Hofstadter also characterized the desire for specie money as "folkish" and primitive, but the nation's leading businessmen and economists shared these fantasies of intrinsic value. William Trenholm, a founder and director of the U. S. Rubber Company and comptroller of the currency under Grover Cleveland, admitted in *The People's Money* that value "does not exist in the things said to possess it, but is imputed to them by human intelligence." But he also argued that "there must be a natural law . . . which tends always to establish as a standard of value the material of highest intrinsic value available at the time," and that "it is obvious that, in fixing upon silver and gold to be the standards of value, modern nations have simply followed a natural law."[85] Gold does, of course, possess certain intrinsic physical properties. But did nature (or God) make it money? Rejecting the old greenbacker's contention that value emerges from social and individual labor, arguments for specie insisted that nature had installed timeless, universal, and intrinsic money properties in precious metals.[86]

As noted above, Gilded Age discussions of immigration, and immigrant labor, saw immigrants in racial terms. Facing intense competition and deskilling in the 1890s, many workers found a tool for promoting solidarity in nativism, and in racial typologies that posed essential differences between Anglo-Saxon, "Latin" [Italian], Semitic, Slavic, black, and Asian workers. In this view black Americans were simply not "union material," and as Samuel Gompers later put it, "the Caucasians . . . are not going to let their standard of living be destroyed by negroes, Chinamen, Japs, or any others."[87] In the 1890s, native white workers responded strongly to racially based arguments about the low character of imported workers—arguments made most convincingly by economists.[88] But it is clear that many American saw both the immigrants *and* the money they earned, the wages they took in pay, in racial terms as well.

Arguments for gold aimed at the working class frequently linked gold to both a high standard of living and the superiority of the Anglo-Saxon race. "Take a look at the company before you sit down at the feast," an anti-silver tract warned workingmen. Who had silverites invited? "Half civilized, half clad peoples, who are weak and ignorant, who have little or no commerce; where bullfights abound and schools do not; where human labor is in sharp competition with the meek and lowly jackass; where the breech-clout is preferred to a full suit."[89] A "sound money" cartoon published and distributed free to newspapers in 1896 depicted three workingmen labeled "English," "American," and "German" standing in front of a barker's wagon (fig. 4.5).[90] The barker sells "Minowners [*sic*] silver elixir: Indorsed by India, Japan, China and Mexico." The barker's sign describes the elixir as "especially good in restricting emigration." Gaunt, poorly clad stereotypes of Mexican, Chinese, Japanese, and Indian workers sit beneath the sign looking lean, hungry and sinister. "If those are its cures," says the caption," we don't want that medicine."

The cartoon linked a high standard of living to the gold standard, a common enough ploy for gold bug forces. But it also linked both to the essential racial difference between northern European whites and "darker" peoples. Two other cartoons from *Sound Currency* make a similar point. In "Mexico's Object Lesson" (fig. 4.6) a barefoot man struggles with a huge pack labeled "Mexican peon's wages." Behind him

FIGURE 4.5. Chorus—"If those are it cures, we don't want the medicine." "Sound Currency Illustrated," in *Sound Currency* 2 (October 1, 1895), 429.

stands a well-dressed American, and a factory labeled "American factory gold standard wages."[91]

In "Don't Monkey with the Buzz-Saw" (fig. 4.7), Chinese, Mexican, and Indian caricatures have their fingers cut off by the "free coinage buzzsaw."[92]

Finally, in "Uncle Sam's Wooing" (fig. 4.8) bearded Uncle Sam sits

(33) **MEXICO'S OBJECT LESSON.**

FIGURE 4.6. "Mexico's Object Lesson." "Sound Currency Illustrated," in *Sound Currency* 2 (October 1, 1895), 486.

next to "Prosperity," an unimpeachably white woman with flowing hair and bare shoulders. She ignores his moneybags full of silver and says "I want a gold engagement ring; a silver one won't do."[93]

That such arguments carried the day for gold should come as no surprise. Albert Beveridge's famous defense of the Philippine War called on similar assumptions of Anglo-Saxon superiority and Filipino inferiority. "The Filipinos are children," he wrote in 1900; "they are not capable of self-government. How could they be? They are not a self-governing race. They are Orientals, Malays. . . . What alchemy will change the oriental quality of their blood and set the self-governing currents of the American pouring through their Malay veins?" Beveridge legitimated imperial conquest in essentialist terms—the Filipinos lacked the essential qualities of Americans, and no "alchemy" could change their blood.[94] Arguments for gold and silver buttressed this tendency, eliminating the "alchemy" of difference in exchange by founding exchange in fantasies of natural law and natural, intrinsic value: Anglo-Saxons could not be a "silver" people.

Late nineteenth-century political economists unmistakably associated gold as money with civilization, advancement, and racial superiority. By linking gold to the social Darwinist rhetoric of imperialism, they naturalized social inequality. They made money the sign of what the difference between peoples meant—money made sense of difference. "Turn your eyes to the countries having the silver standard

(43) DON'T MONKEY WITH THE BUZZ-SAW.

"We all have silver standard."

FIGURE 4.7. "Don't Monkey with the Buzz-Saw." "Sound Currency Illustrated," in *Sound Currency* 2 (October 1, 1895), 493.

(41) UNCLE SAM'S WOOING.

PROSPERITY—"I want a gold engagement ring; a silver one won't do."

FIGURE 4.8. "Uncle Sam's Wooing." "Sound Currency Illustrated," in *Sound Currency 2* (October 1, 1895), 491.

alone—Mexico, South America, Asia—and those having the gold standard," an American gold bug wrote, "and there is no room for argument. The latter countries are prosperous, intelligent, and progressive; the former embarrassed, poor, and ignorant." The difference shows up in their lower wages—their price—and their cultural inferiority.[95]

A gold bug tract of 1892 argued similarly that "fair tests of the state of civilization in any country" included "the kind of money it uses," and that only the poorer nations of the world used silver. "Congress cannot cause us to be born again, and into the Hindu, Chinese, Japanese or even into the Mexican or South American silver–handling type," it concluded.[96] "Silver has served a useful purpose as a standard," another tract argued, "but it has yielded to the survival of the fittest."[97] Drawing on Herbert Spencer's social Darwinist political economy, these authors connected gold to an interracial economic struggle, further linking America's racial "value" to gold's intrinsic superiority.

Although it seems clear that anxiety about immigrants informed the gold bug position, I am not trying to argue for a strict causal link, or for a consistent explanation of individual or group positions on either the money question or on race. In 1896 the Republican Party endorsed both the gold standard and a "multicultural" immigration policy, allowing its members to have both cheap labor and an intrinsic value standard governing social hierarchies. More recent immigrants responded to this more tolerant approach and supported McKinley in 1896. If drawn away from exclusionary racism by their desire for cheap labor, the Republicans certainly participated in the social Darwinist political economics of imperialism. The Democrats, and organized labor, endorsed Bryan, silver, and immigration restriction, thus gaining some limited inflation and anti-monopoly rhetoric, along with "the dollar of our [white] daddies"—a metal also linked to intrinsic value arguments about racial tradition.[98] Support for the gold standard does not always correlate to racist positions.

What this discussion points out, however, is the absurdity of talking about money, or even "the economy," as if these things had a distinct, objective existence outside of culture—as if the were "natural facts." Few of those engaged in the money debates of 1896 even agreed on what money, the supposed bottom line, really was. When they talked about money, they imbued their language with racial metaphors. They used the same logic to talk about gold that they used to talk about race, because in an economy devoted to constant renegotiation and reinvention, linking race and money made both seem more substantial. While economic interest may have determined voting on the money question, the parameters of economic interest—the range of choice available between gold, silver, and greenbacks—make little sense without reference to racial or essentialist theories. "What prevents Congress from legislating the value of a dollar?" asked "a financial catechism" of 1895: Is it the Constitution? "Not the Constitution of the United States," came the answer, "but the constitution of man."[99]

Frances A. Walker looked at the 1890 census and saw immigrants overwhelming native stock as they strained resources and drove down wages; they "lacked the enterprising spirit" and so would swamp the economy. It is their fault wages decline, he argued, their lack of self-respect and economic drive. He proposed a "money test" for admission—all immigrants must present a deposit of one hundred dollars to gain entry—presumably in gold. That they earned money would demonstrate their fitness; their possession of money would mark their difference from the "degraded peasantry" who daily begged in the cities' streets.[100] The time had come, Walker argued, when "the nation's birthright shall no longer be recklessly squandered" in open-door immigration.[101] The Anglo-Saxon "birthright" included a high standard of living derived from an enterprising character, from an essential nature. Those gains vanished, squandered like easy money, when lazy immigrants accepted less and drove good character out of the market. For Walker and his peers, immigration was an economic issue, but their economic principles were the principles of racial exchange.

A strong class affinity linked these men—like many descendants of old elites, they felt their social position eroding under the dual pressures of capitalism and immigration. Many of the leaders of the movement for "sound money"—Walker, David Wells, the Adams brothers, Horace White, or Charles Conant—came from or had close ties to this old elite. But their argument's success with ordinary voters takes us beyond class analysis. James Livingston has noted that some of the most effective propaganda for gold came from the "Sound Currency Committee," formed by leading businessmen and economists to lobby for hard money. The committee published a periodical, *Sound Currency*, which it offered free of charge to newspapers, magazines, and interested parties generally. The committee's publications deliberately aimed at a mass appeal, and it is these publications which have supplied many of the gold bug cartoons and quotations for this essay. Why did people who were not members of the elite—in many cases the children of the very immigrants so threatening to the likes of Walker—respond to gold bug irrationality?

Here again the answer must lie in the nature of exchange, in the indeterminacy of value and place in capitalism. How, in exchange between people, could difference become equivalence, yet still remain difference? Gold bug arguments did indeed make a certain kind of economic and cultural sense—if a Chinese, black, or Mexican worker could do the same work as the Caucasian, if their labor could be rendered equivalent, what separated the two? A "silver–handling" character amenable to low wages? An essential lack of self-respect or ambition? Using gold money allowed a fantasy of natural stability and true value in exchange. Relying on a notion of race similarly set standards for meaning in exchange. It made both race and money comprehensible in the same terms, and mutually reinforcing. While economic interest may have determined some voting on the money question, the parameters of economic interest—the range of choice available between gold, silver, and greenbacks—were yoked to questions of racial character.

Racializing the money debate had more than metaphorical effects. By

1903, for example, American workers on the Panama Canal had been segregated by task and by pay into two groups—white workers, known as "gold" workers, took their pay in gold, working on the "gold roll," while black workers, the "silver workers" on the "silver roll," took silver coins home. Gold and silver workers had to use separate restrooms; they ate and slept in segregated quarters. "If white Americans are needed, I think we should employ them on the gold roll," wrote one canal official; "the silver roll was not created for [white] Americans any more than the gold roll was created for negroes."[102] Economics and racism worked together to produce the basic categories for organizing labor.

Americans adopted these ideas, these fantasies of golden racial value, in response to the "crisis of subjectivity" American society experienced starting in the 1890s. The dynamic American economy opened up new possibilities: it created new identities and new accessories to furnish those identities. It rendered "self" negotiable. In the 1890s, Americans responded to the promise of the American dream by drawing a line of non-negotiability around gold, and by insisting on a fixed racial identity even in the face of common-sense facts.

The famous case of *Plessy v. Ferguson*, 1896, makes this point: Homer Plessy was an extremely light-skinned man, the product of generations of "race mixing." He could easily have passed for white, but he identified himself firmly as an African American. His attorney, Albion W. Tourgée, hoped that pointing to Plessy's light skin would demonstrate the absurdity of classifying people as black or white. Why should the law imagine a distinction that nature did not respect or observe? The Court simply refused to consider the idea, relying implicitly on the "one-drop rule": racial identity was not negotiable.[103]

The triumph of the gold standard represents the same impulse as the triumph of segregation: a retreat from the solvent tendencies of the American dream. The economic arguments of the 1890s make no sense considered away from their similarity to arguments about the nature and authenticity of self. If arguments about economic cause are arguments about individual self-interest, they explain nothing without an understanding of the ways "self" was constituted.

CHAPTER FIVE

A Bank in Human Form

Fort Knox and Phantom Gold

MR. UNTERMYER. Is not commercial credit based primarily upon money or property?
MR. MORGAN. No, sir; the first thing is character.
MR. UNTERMYER. Before money or property?
MR. MORGAN. Before money or anything else. Money cannot buy it. . . . Because a man I do not trust could not get money from me on all the bonds in Christendom.[1]

In the twentieth century the debate over money changed significantly. The Federal Reserve System largely moved the subject of money out of the realm of popular politics and into the domain of experts, and with that change the crude racial language surrounding money faded. White supremacy continued to be linked to the gold standard, but the new era of managed money weakened the link. The twentieth century also saw the end of the white supremacist consensus established in the Jim Crow era, and the rise of the modern civil rights movement. If establishing the gold standard and the Federal Reserve took most public questions about money off the table, ending the gold standard opened up some new discursive possibilities about value, character, and where they originated. This chapter surveys the way Americans remade and redefined money in the twentieth century. It looks particularly at Franklin Roosevelt and the way Roosevelt used the newly constructed Gold Bullion Depository at Fort Knox to create a sense of solidity that his own actions had undermined. It argues for a general affinity between FDR's abandonment of the domestic gold standard and his administration's slow embrace of racial equality.

*   *   *

In 1907, shortly after they finally established the gold standard, Americans experienced a serious financial panic, centered on Wall Street. In the panic of 1907, J. P. Morgan worked closely with leading bankers and with the secretary of the treasury to avoid a larger financial collapse, shoring up shaky banks with drafts of private and public capital. Hailed as a hero by the Wall Streeters whose fortunes he saved, he drew the ire of Americans who noticed that a very small number of men appeared to be co-running all the nation's leading financial institutions. These men, it seemed, had a near total control over the nation's supply of money and credit. In the wake of the panic Morgan, nicknamed "Jupiter" on Wall street for his godlike greatness, found himself summoned to Washington in late 1912. Congressman Arsène Pujo of Louisiana, chairman of the House Committee on Banking and Currency, wanted to hear his testimony as part of a Congressional investigation into the "money trust."

At the Pujo hearings Samuel Untermyer, as counsel to the House Committee, subjected Morgan to a very long cross-examination. Untermyer, a self-made millionaire, son of Jewish immigrants, set out to demonstrate how interlocking directorates formed a "money trust," a virtual monopoly on the money supply. Their remarkable exchange suggests either that Morgan lied under oath or that one of the richest men in the world simply had no coherent understanding of the relationship between money, character, and credit.

Untermyer began one session by asking about "the control of money":

MR. UNTERMYER. The control of credit involves a control of money, does it not?

MR. MORGAN. A control of credit? No.

MR. UNTERMYER. You do not think so?

MR. MORGAN. What I call money is the basis of banking.

MR. UNTERMYER. But the basis of banking is credit, is it not?

MR. MORGAN. Not always. That is an evidence of banking, but it is not the money itself. Money is gold, and nothing else.

MR. UNTERMYER. Do you not know that the basis or banking all over the world is credit rather than gold?

MR. MORGAN. It is the basis of credit, but it is not the basis of money.

The exchange makes little or no sense. The subject—the "it"—keeps shifting. Morgan says definitively "money is gold, and nothing else." But if money is gold, what is credit? Well, credit would be, we assume, money lent in expectation of producing more money, a bet on the possibility of more money (gold) appearing. Untermyer continued:

> MR. UNTERMYER. I say, the basis of all banking is credit, is it not, and not money?
> MR. MORGAN. No; I do not think so.
> MR. UNTERMYER. Do you not know that it is?
> MR. MORGAN. A basis of banking is credit, but not a basis of money.
> MR. UNTERMYER. The basis of banking is credit?
> MR. MORGAN. Yes.
> MR. UNTERMYER. And you know, do you not, that in no part of the world is the supply of gold anything like sufficient to meet the outstanding obligations in the form of notes representing credit?
> MR. MORGAN. That is so.

So both men agree there is not enough gold in the world to equal the amount of credit the owners of that gold have extended to borrowers. Untermyer concluded: "Therefore, when money is issued by a Government it is issued largely on the basis of credit, is it not? It has [not] got dollar for dollar of gold to support it, has it?" Morgan agreed: "well no, not always."

This leads Untermyer to conclude that "a man or a group of men who have the control of credit have control of money, have they not?"

> MR. MORGAN. Yes.
> MR. UNTERMYER. Is not that so?
> MR. MORGAN. No, sir; not always.
> MR. UNTERMYER. That is generally so, is it not?
> MR. MORGAN. No.

Here Morgan baldly contradicts himself, first agreeing, then disagreeing. So Untermyer presses him—if you had control of all that represents the assets of the banks of New York, you would effectively "have the control of money—of all that money"? Morgan disagrees. Untermyer says that since money is gold, money is a commodity, subject to the laws of supply and demand. Morgan agrees with this, but when Untermyer extends this argument to suggest that money can be "cornered" like wheat or tin or oil, Morgan again disagrees, and in interesting ways:

MR. UNTERMYER. And it is conceivable that every commodity could be controlled, is it not?

MR. MORGAN. Except money.

MR. UNTERMYER. I say, every commodity except money?

MR. MORGAN. Yes.

MR. UNTERMYER. And money is a commodity?

MR. MORGAN. I do not like to think of it as a commodity.

"I do not like to think of it as a commodity," says Morgan. So for Morgan, money is "gold and nothing else," just a commodity, but at the same time he does not like to think of it as a commodity. What then, *does* he like to think of it as?

MR. UNTERMYER. It is not conceivable that one man would have the credit and the other the money, is it, because the credit is based upon money?

MR. MORGAN. But money can not be controlled.

MR. UNTERMYER. Is not the credit based upon the money?

MR. MORGAN. No, sir.

MR. UNTERMYER. It has no relation?

MR. MORGAN. No, sir.

MR. UNTERMYER. None whatever?

MR. MORGAN. No, sir; none whatever.

So now Morgan astonishingly claims that money and credit bear no relation to each other—"none whatever!" By "credit" here perhaps Morgan means "trustworthiness," and he wants to say, perhaps, that the amount of money one possesses is not in and of itself a sign of one's trustworthiness:

MR. MORGAN. I know lots of men, business men, too, who can borrow any amount, whose credit is unquestioned.

MR. UNTERMYER. Is that not because it is believed that they have the money back of them ?

MR. MORGAN. No, sir; it is because people believe in the man.

MR. UNTERMYER. And it is regardless of whether he has any financial backing at all, is it?

MR. MORGAN. It is very often.

MR. UNTERMYER. And he might not be worth anything?

MR. MORGAN. He might not have anything. I have known a man to come into my office, and I have given him a check for a million dollars when I knew he had not a cent in the world.[2]

Morgan here sounds like someone out of Horatio Alger—"a man" comes off the street with not a penny and Morgan cuts him a check for a million dollars, because he has an honest face or possibly because Morgan, the yatchsman, "likes the cut of his jib." Untermyer, hard headed, will have none of it:

MR. UNTERMYER. Is not commercial credit based primarily upon money or property?

MR. MORGAN. No, sir; the first thing is character.

MR. UNTERMYER. Before money or property?

MR. MORGAN. Before money or anything else. Money can not buy it.

MR. UNTERMYER. So that a man with character, without anything at all behind it, can get all the credit he wants, and a man with the property can not get it?

MR. MORGAN. That is very often the case.

MR. UNTERMYER. But that is the rule of business?

MR. MORGAN. That is the rule of business, sir.

If that is the case, Untermyer continues, quite reasonably, "why do the banks demand, the first thing they ask, a statement of what the man has got, before they extend him credit?"

MR. UNTERMYER. For instance, if he has got Government bonds or railroad bonds, and goes in to get credit, he gets it, and on the security of those bonds, does he not?

MR. MORGAN. Yes.

MR. UNTERMYER. He does not get it on his face or his character, does he?

MR. MORGAN. Yes; he gets it on his character.

MR. UNTERMYER. I see; then he might as well take the bonds home, had he not?

MR. MORGAN. Because a man I do not trust could not get money from me on all the bonds in Christendom.[3]

Here again Morgan sounds like a Horatio Alger character, and describes, apparently seriously, a world of face-to-face contact between men of character, in which money is completely irrelevant—the would-be borrower "might as well leave the bonds," the collateral, "at home." Morgan agrees, because they bear no relation to the issuance of credit, since credit appends to character alone. This ends up making Untermyer's case: if the world of Wall Street is a world of face-to-face contact in which a small number of men of "good character" lend each other money on face-to-face evidence and trust, then it looks a great deal like a private club or a cartel.

Morgan offered comforting mystifications. Yes, money is a commodity, just like all other commodities, but simultaneously it is not a commodity and magically not subject to "cornering." Money comes to (and from, we must assume) those of good character; it is "gold only" but also character. Physical assets, other commodities like land or bonds or money, have no bearing whatsoever on the lending of money—he actually says this in front of Congress, with no eye winking or any ironic muggery whatsoever. In banking "character" generates money, and generates money in excess of the gold upon which it is theoretically based, even though according to Morgan, "gold is money and nothing else." Money is simply gold, yet at the same time Morgan "does not like to think of money as a commodity." He likes instead to think of it as some kind of incidental byproduct of "character."

Morgan's emphasis on character extends, without the racial language, the logic of the gold standard described earlier. Of course no one would lend money to an untrustworthy person, and of course assets, collateral, serve as a hedge and buttress to trust and risk. No one would lend a man with bad character money, unless the man had a lot of collateral. And as the *New York Times* commented: "The man who goes about the city seeking credit solely on the strength of a good character will find this a hard, cold, and doubting world."[4]

"Character" marks an attempt to escape the market, to set up a realm outside market negotiation that nevertheless enables market transactions and gives them meaning. In their accounts of immigration turn-of-the-century economists imagined immigrants as having racial, genetic money-handling characteristics: they imagined "silver-handling peoples" and "low wage races"; peasants who hoarded but never spent; theoretical Chinese consumers with no pockets for holding consumer goods, lacking the gene for consumption. Economists, as we have seen, saw the way immigrants and natives used money as a sign of racial character, a genetic political economy. Their insistence on the gold standard grew from their ideas about the racial character of Anglo-Saxons. Gold went with and to those of good racial character. Morgan does not use racialized language here, but he thinks of money in much the same way, as an incidental byproduct of character, of necessity only gold but not really a commodity.

Morgan simultaneously insists that money must be gold but that money bears no relation to gold; that money is just a commodity and yet uniquely cannot be commodified or controlled; that accumulated wealth is meaningless in credit relations and that young Ragged Dick, the honest bootblack of Horatio Alger fame, is just as likely—in fact *more likely*—to walk away with Mr. Morgan's check for a million dollars, because he has character. Morgan wants to elide the entire question of money as an object of politics and thereby make money, gold, and character analogous: rich men are men of good character; their money is a physical manifestation of their selves.

This is precisely the kind of self-flattering mumbo-jumbo that always infuriated advocates of paper money. Morgan repeats, in effect, the assertions made by the anonymous author in chapter 1, regarding the South Sea Bubble: "had there not been Men of Substance in this Country . . . you might have made Paper Bills till you had been blind, they would never have fed your Bellies, nor have clothed your Backs."[5]

Morgan wants money to express not some purely negotiable, arbitrary, fluctuating set of social values, but essential character. He has money because he has character: he lends money to men of character regardless of how much money they have. Because character cannot be bought, and bears no relation to money, no one can control money, and yet character produces money. "John Pierpont Morgan," declared a headline in the *New York Times*, was "a bank in human form."[6]

Indeed! Morgan seems to imagine himself precisely this way. He has reserves of golden character which secure his wealth; his wealth is practically meaningless except that he uses his good character to judge the character of others and to lend them money, which makes more money even though money is gold only. But the exchange is not an exchange of money, really; it is a fraternity of character. Morgan renders money into both a magical commodity, outside the market, and a product of character, also something also outside the market.

*   *   *

The Gold Standard Act of 1900 largely ended public political debate about the basis of money. In those earlier debates, as repeatedly shown, Americans had linked their notion of money to their notion of racial character—both "race" in the sense of black and white and race in the sense of ethnicity. Gold triumphed as the natural mineral of the Anglo-

FIGURE 5.1. From *Puck*, February 2, 1910. Caption reads "The Central Bank—Why should Uncle Sam establish one, when Uncle Pierpont is already on the job?" Prints and Photographs Division, Library of Congress.

Saxon race. Its character was their character. Formalizing the gold standard in law resolved the debate about gold, silver, and paper that had characterized much of the preceding century.

The triumph of the gold standard came, not coincidentally, at the high tide of racial essentialism and eugenics: Jim Crow in the South, anti-immigrant nativism in the North. Establishing a gold standard coincided with the well-documented emphasis on manliness and gender essentialism described in the work of Gail Bederman, Kristin Hoganson, John Kasson, Mathew Jacobson, and others.[7] Not just racial essentialism but gender essentialism strongly marked the era of the gold standard, with its fears of "race suicide" and the dangerously fertile immigrant "moron" called into being by I.Q. tests. H. H. Goddard coined the term "moron" in 1910, to describe "persons with a mental age of eight to twelve." Such persons, he admitted "are often normal looking with few or no obvious stigmata of degeneration and frequently able to talk fluently. . . . So strong is their resemblance to the normal person that altho they are well understood by those who have studied them and have dealt with them in Institutions, yet there are many people even to-day who refuse to admit that they cannot be trained to function like normal people. Yet they are the persons who make for us our social problems."

The problem, for Goddard, was *passing*: the racially defective person could pass for normal, hold a job, marry, and reproduce. Like a counterfeit bill the moron entered commerce and debased general social values. Not surprisingly, Goddard found high percentages of "morons" among recent immigrants.[8] He wanted this debased currency removed from circulation.

Mutually reinforcing, both the gold standard and the emergence of radical race and gender essentialism expressed anxiety about market negotiation, about exchange, about false value, about the integrity of racial difference. Establishing the gold standard marked the appearance of an essentialist consensus about value and race. And the end of the gold standard in the 1930s was accompanied by a breakdown of the white supremacist consensus.

This early twentieth-century racial consensus legitimated formal legal segregation and disenfranchisement. It looked the other way when spectacle lynchings recurred in the South and when race riots broke out in the North. In the schools and colleges, racial consensus in history emphasized worldwide racial competition and the inevitable superiority of the Anglo-Saxon. Courts of law assumed the subordinate status of nonwhites and undermined the protections established by the 14th and 15th amendments to the Constitution. "You understand," a white Alabaman told Robert Moton, principal of Tuskegee Institute in 1923, "we have the legislature, we make the laws, we have the judges, the sheriff, the jails. We have the hardware stores and the arms."[9] Given that commitment to the gold standard correlated so closely with commitment to white supremacy, it is not at all surprising to find Virginia politician Carter Glass, a "sound money," gold standard Democrat, declaring in 1901: "Discrimination! Why, that is precisely what we propose: that, exactly, is what this convention was elected for—to discriminate to the very extremity of permissible action, under the limitations of the Federal Constitution, with a view to the elimination of every Negro voter who can be gotten rid of, legally, without materially impairing the numerical strength of the white electorate."[10] Glass spoke these words as a Virginia State representative, but he later chaired the House Committee on Banking and Currency, where he worked closely with Woodrow Wilson to revise the design of the Federal Reserve System. He served as Wilson's secretary of the treasury and in the 1930s, co-authored the Glass-Steagall Act, regulating commercial and investment banking. His belief in the gold standard and federal management of the money supply fit perfectly with his belief in the necessity of white supremacy and the legal management of racial inequality.

Carter Glass was not a racist because he believed in the gold standard, nor did belief in the gold standard compel him to racism. But when he defended the gold standard, Glass wrote: "The ghost of Andrew Jackson stalked before my face in the daytime and haunted my couch for nights."[11] He meant not the Jackson who hated central banking—Glass is one of the fathers of the Federal Reserve System. He meant instead Jackson the slaveowner, who insisted on the gold standard and saw paper money, and the changes it fostered, as "artificial." That is, Glass bound up his support for the gold standard within his sense of the traditions of white supremacy in Southern politics. He talked about the new banking system as "scientific," in the sense of "scientific management," a Progressive-era fad, but he meant scientific in the sense of natural law. Carter Glass's philosophy of both race and money required an idea of non-negotiability, things that money, exchange, could not buy or alter. The gold standard served this purpose in exchange. The white supremacist commitment similarly drew social lines which could not be crossed.

The white supremacist consensus was stubborn and long lasting, but after 1934, when Roosevelt took the U.S. off the gold standard in domestic exchange, the racial climate began to change—by the late 1970s, when the U.S. had abandoned the gold standard altogether, the white supremacist consensus had been significantly diluted and reduced. Here again, it would be far too simple to suggest a strict causal link between the two. But just as it is not a mere coincidence that the establishment of the gold standard coincided with the height of the white supremacist consensus, it is most likely not an accident that the rise of civil rights, and the ethic of nondiscrimination, coincided with the end of the gold standard and the rise of a centrally managed, fiat currency. It is similarly not surprising that the election of the first African American president in 2008 should coincide with a wild rise in gold prices and the revival of political arguments for the gold standard among his opponents. Talk about money has almost always been linked to talk about race.

One of the first effects of the gold standard, following 1900, was to change the way Americans talked about money, to take race talk out of money talk by removing money from political debate. In 1900, Milton Freidman concluded, "the gold standard had finally triumphed," and "the money issue retreated from the center of political controversy."[12] The gold standard let the U.S. hold its head high among other Anglo-Saxon nations. But the Panic of 1907 highlighted some of the most serious fiscal problems with a gold standard, and it led directly to the establishment, in 1913, of the Federal Reserve System. The establishment of the Federal Reserve further discouraged debates about money in the early twentieth century, by distancing money from politics—money theorists and cranks still pamphleteered, but the subject would not dominate American politics again until the early 1930s. The Federal Reserve, a true central bank, changed the discourse of money. It took money debates out of common parlance and rendered money largely "unthought," a subject for technocrats and experts. This is part of what central banks are supposed to do—to get money creation out of the realm of politics—and the Federal Reserve System largely succeeded. It took the mysterious process of money creation out of democratic view.

Conspiracy theorists and pamphleteers frequently denounced the Federal Reserve, often with little or no understanding of what it was and how it worked: they liked—and still like—to repeat a statement alleged to have come from Henry Ford: "It is well that the people of the nation do not understand our banking and monetary system, for if they did, I believe there would be a revolution before tomorrow morning." It is not at all clear that Ford ever said this—I have not been able to find the original source—but the quote has resonated down the years and even now that exact quotation results in more than eight thousand hits in a Google search. The money question receded from the political mainstream but nagged continually at the political unconscious.

*   *   *

The Panic of 1907 highlighted a problem critics of the gold standard had always pointed to: "inelasticity." In any economy demand for money fluctuates. In the United States in the first decade of the twentieth century, demand for money, for credit, tended to peak in autumn. Farmers brought their crops to market: it took money to buy them. Farmers in turn sought loans for next year's crop. Grain merchants and farmers borrowed the money from local banks; local banks in turn borrowed from Eastern banks. Money had to flow to those locations where demand went up, *when* demand went up. If it didn't, then prices went down, injuring the farmer and his buyer; interest rates soared, further injuring the farmer and his erstwhile customer, the grain merchant. Money, drawn always by the gravity of New York and the East Coast, grew scarce in the Midwest. Understanding money as "gold and nothing else," as Morgan claimed he did, meant that lending money ultimately required the presence of physical gold in the lending bank, or some credible symbol of the actual gold which would soon arrive, by train or by boat. If no such gold arrived, grain buyers and farmers would simply have to pace in frustration while miners, driven by increased demand, rushed out to pan up more gold and smelt it into bullion. In the absence of a central bank, it was even difficult to get the paper symbols of gold, and the credit they enabled, where they needed to be at the moment of demand. Inelasticity, in the example above, would describe a farmer with grain to sell, and a buyer with a ready market for his grain, but simply no money available to enable the exchange, not unlike the situation with the Puritans and wampum in chapter 1.

This kind of problem had always struck greenbackers, rightly, as an obvious flaw in the idea of a gold standard. For Populist farmers, for example, labor produced value in the form of wheat, wheat had value by virtue of its being edible, but the need for gold seemed both arbitrary and dangerous: at best a superstition, at worst part of a plot to "corner" the supply of money, to artificially limit money and thereby to control interest rates and prices. Talk of the superior character of bankers only added insult to injury. In the panic of 1907 both the problem of inelasticity and the problem of a "money trust" came together.

The Panic had many causes. The San Francisco earthquake, striking in April 1906, caused an intense demand for credit in San Francisco, to fund rebuilding. An attempt by Otto Heinze & Co. in 1907 to control the market in stock of the United Copper Company led to a spectacular rise in the value of Copper stocks and an even more precipitous fall. When Heinze's effort failed, banks that had lent money to buy stock at higher prices found their loans close to worthless, triggering runs on the bank by nervous depositors. At its height the bank panic brought down the Knickerbocker Trust, the third largest bank in New York. When the stock market collapsed in late October 1907, it caused money—or perhaps more accurately value—to vanish from the economy. That made credit—despite Morgan's later claim that credit depended entirely on character—scarce.

A central bank would at this point have "injected liquidity" into the market, a fancy way of saying, "printed more money." In 1907, J. P. Morgan had to press English investors to ship gold to the U.S., and while they waited for the ship, had to organize a consortium of wealthy men to scare up enough money to stave off panic, literally by locking them in a room until they reached agreement.[13]

The Pujo Committee, convened to investigate Wall Street in the wake of the panic, strongly deplored the concentration of ownership in the hands of a few men, and it called for greater regulation of banks and the stock market. Their investigation, and Morgan's sentimental evasions quoted above, opened one path to the establishment of the Federal Reserve.[14]

The Panic of 1907 had centered clearly in New York banks and Wall Street. For that reason, J. K. Galbraith observed, "it was far more serious," not so much because its impact on the country was greater than other panics, but because "its impact was on much more important people."[15] A year after the panic Congress passed the Aldrich–Vreeland Act, which established a National Monetary Commission to investigate reforms to American banking. Senator Nelson Aldrich of Rhode Island dispatched himself to Europe for two years, to see how they did it over there. Aldrich returned brimming with enthusiasm for central banking. He convened an unnecessarily and somewhat comically secret meeting of eminent bankers to discuss the matter at the posh Jekyll Island club in Georgia. *Forbes* magazine, prone to gush, later told the story this way:

PICTURE a party of the nation's greatest bankers stealing out of New York on a private railroad car, hieing hundreds of miles south to an island deserted by all but a few servants, and living there a full week under such rigid secrecy that the name of not one of them was once mentioned lest the servitors learn their identity and disclose to the world this historic episode in American finance. I am here giving to the world the real story of how the famous Aldrich currency report, the foundation of our new currency system, was written.

Aldrich invited Henry P. Davison of J. P. Morgan & Co.; Frank A. Vanderlip, president of the National City Bank; Paul M. Warburg, then of Kuhn, Loeb & Company, and A. Piatt Andrew, assistant secretary of the treasury. After a journey hedged with the utmost secrecy, the party were landed in a small boat at the deserted Jekyll Island:

> "The servants must under no circumstances learn who we are," cautioned Senator Aldrich.
> "What can we do to fool them?" asked another member of the group. The problem was discussed.
> "I have it," cried one. "Let's all call each other by our first names. Don't ever let us mention our last names."
> It was so agreed.

With this clever dodge, and despite the chronic shortage of poorly informed servants, the men managed in a week to draft a first version of what became the Federal Reserve. Then, "as quietly as they had left," *Forbes* tells us, "the authors of the epochal Aldrich report disappeared from Jekyll Island and slipped into New York undetected."[16] Their actions presented a virtual gift to conspiracy theorists: into the twenty-first century interested citizens can buy, for example, copies of *The Creature from Jekyll Island*, an anti-Fed tract that treats the fed as the monstrous child of island conspiracy.[17]

Bankers designed the initial plan of the Federal Reserve to serve bankers. It serves the public only incidentally, to the degree that we all depend on the regular and reliable flow of credit. Although it reflected the interventions of Woodrow Wilson and Carter Glass, who inserted measures giving the president appointment power over the board of governors, the Federal Reserve System established a genuine central bank. Like the Bank of England, it has a unique combination of public and private features.

The act that created the Federal Reserve set up twelve regional Federal Reserve Banks in Boston, New York, Philadelphia, Cleveland, Richmond, Atlanta, Chicago, St. Louis, Minneapolis, Kansas City, Dallas, and San Francisco. These banks own the system. Like their forbears, the Bank of England and the late First and Second Banks of the United States, the Federal Reserve banks are *the* bank of the United States government. They handle the Treasury department's payments, buy and sell government securities, and more or less do for the government what a bank does for you. Other banks can become members of the Federal Reserve System by buying stock in the twelve regional banks. In return they get discount borrowing but also stricter reserve requirements.

The long and rich history of opposition to central banking shows up in the way the banks are governed. Each regional bank has a board of directors who serve three-year terms. Each board is divided into three "classes" of three persons each. Class A directors represent commercial banks that are members of the Federal Reserve System—they are the regional banks' stockholders. Class B directors were intended to represent the public and the full range of what "the public" does for a living. They may not be officers, directors, or employees of any bank. Class A and B directors are elected by member banks in the regional district. The final class, class C, also represents the public and cannot be directly involved in any bank: these persons are appointed by the board of governors of the Federal Reserve to one-year terms.

This complex structure reflects the public/private nature of the system, and the mixed feeling Americans have always had about money and money creation. The Class B and C directors, theoretically "just folks," are there to insure that the Federal Reserve Bank looks beyond the interests of bankers themselves and the country clubs at which they dine. But bankers elect or appoint them; they were and are basically tokens. The Fed responds to the impulses of democracy mostly through its board of governors.

The president of the United States appoints the seven governors, each named to a fourteen-year term. One of them, the chairman, gets a four-year term renewable at the president's pleasure. This is democracy's moment to influence policy.[18]

The Federal Reserve Banks issue "Federal Reserve Notes," which now serve as our only paper currency. The system affects the quantity of money, the amount in circulation, in several ways. One is the Federal

Open Market Committee, composed of the board of governors, the president of the Federal Reserve Bank of New York (always the largest and most powerful of the twelve), and the presidents of four other regional Federal Reserve Banks, who serve on a rotating basis. The Open Market Committee buys or sells government bonds. When it buys bonds, it puts money into the economy. When it sells bonds, it takes money out of the economy. The committee can also adjust the reserve requirements of member banks and thereby rein in or encourage lending. More significantly, the Open Market Committee also adjusts the interest rate at which member banks can borrow money—known as the "discount rate." As of this writing, member banks of the Federal Reserve can borrow money at practically zero interest. They can lend this money to other banks and to private individuals, and eventually what they borrow for nearly nothing you borrow for, say, 6 percent.

At each stage in this lending chain, money is created in a multiplier effect. Imagine the Fed loans ten million dollars to a member bank. Economists call that initial loan "high powered money," because it will increase as member banks loan it in turn. The member bank takes that ten million and loans twenty million to its customers, most likely businesses and local banks, and those banks in turn then lend forty million dollars to their customers: voila: money has been created. [19]

Why, you may ask, do member banks get to borrow against our collateral for nearly free and then lend it back to us for profit? Ideally, they are profiting for the service of "the efficient allocation of credit": the keen eye for likely businesses, the assessment of credit worthiness, the assumption of risk that the borrower may default—the recognition and possession of "character" as imagined by Morgan. When I would explain this to my classes back in 2008, at the height of the subprime mortgage crisis, I typically only had to wait silently for a few moments before someone would raise a hand to point out the magnitude of this pretty supposition's collapse. But money creation has never been free of insider advantage, never been free of mystification, and it has rarely been particularly democratic. And at this point, in 1913, the U.S. still enjoyed a gold standard, and the idea that "real money" was a magic commodity, limited by nature, which nevertheless "backed" American money.

The Federal Reserve System shows the influence and reputation of J.P. Morgan, the "bank in human form." It places its trust in the wisdom of bankers, acting in concert to judiciously encourage enterprise and restrain enthusiasm, and in gold. It also depends on the legacy of the Bank of England.[20] In that sense, it is similar to the First and Second Banks of the United States, and it is open to similar objections.

"The Federal Reserve System is the visible hand of the Invisible Empire picking the pockets of the producers of real wealth," declared *The Federal Reserve Monster* in 1922: "It is the most leviathan parasite. . . . It is an industrial vampire sucking industry's life blood down its bottomless maw." The elite directors of the Fed believe, the authors warned, "that wealth is produced for its exploitation; that production of values exists for its parasitical plunder; that Shylockery is a virtue and that the fruits of industry belong not to its producers but to its despoilers." The ninety-five pages of this volume appeared originally in *Jim Jam Jems*, a North Dakota magazine of political commentary which promised and delivered "Zinc! Vinegar! Vitriol!" to its readers. The authors correctly saw the Fed as the legatee of Biddle's Bank. "Twice the people violently repudiated the Central Bank banditry. Hence in the fertile brainery of predacity was born the idea of the Federal Reserve System—a camouflage, a deception and a mere cloak of Pecksniffian hypocrisy."[21]

The authors invoked Shylock, Shakespeare's Jewish moneylender. The Fed, this "subter-human super-Shylock," far outdoes its literary antecedent: the Federal Reserve "commandeers capital" for profits that "make Shylock look like a philanthropist." They denounced the Federal Reserve's "ruthless methods of plunder, its machinery of despoilment, its monopoly of money and credit, its pawnbrokery and Shylockery and its huge mounds of pillage."[22]

"Shylock" and "Shylockery" of course have a distinctly anti-Semitic cast. It was difficult to make the charge that the Federal Reserve represented a Jewish influence, since its founders and allies—Morgan, Carter Glass, Nelson Aldrich, and Woodrow Wilson, represented the high WASP aristocracy. Proponents of the supposedly Jewish character of the Fed found a target, however, in Paul Warburg, the German-born banker who had been among those hiding his last name at the Jekyll Island meeting. *The Great Conspiracy of the House of Morgan and How to Defeat It* cited the influence of "a German Jew by the name of Paul M. Warburg," "a member of the banking firm of Kuehn, Loeb & Co., of New York," as the major influence on Morgan's conspiracy. The author correctly noted Warburg's influence on the formation of the Federal Reserve: "Soon after associating himself with the American House, be began a study of our American system, and in a series of pamphlets outlined our deficiencies, and advocating the better system, which so attracted the attention of J. P. Morgan and associates that he was induced to become an American citizen, that he might be the better able to assist in making the change." It was a vicious conception, he continued, "the very worst in the world's history." Warburg had accomplished this system "with almost cruel, Jewish-German efficiency."[23]

Theories of the Federal Reserve System as a Jewish conspiracy reached their height in the pages of Henry Ford's *Dearborn Independent*. In his Michigan magazine Ford retooled old claims about the Rothschilds and the Bavarian Illuminati dating back to the Crime of '73. *The Dearborn Independent* became the roosting place of anti-Semitic theories about Jews, banking, and the Federal Reserve. In 1920 the *Independent* admitted that though Jewish influence was strong, "this is not to say, however, that Jewish influence in American financial affairs is paramount. At one time it threatened to be, but American financiers have always been silently aware of the International Jewish Financier, and have endeavored quietly to block his game. Time and again the contest has seemed to turn in favor of the Jew, but when the widespread secret wrestlings of the two powers have been suspended for a moment, it has been found that American finance has maintained its superiority, if only in a slight degree."[24] But by 1926, the *Independent* concluded, the game had ended: "the international Jew invented our financial and interest system, and is today in direct control of all financial centers of government, including the United States Federal Reserve system, which he organized and is now perfecting according to his original plan."[25] Ford was widely criticized for these views even in his day, and pressured into a public apology. Anti-Semitic conspiracy theories have never entirely gone away, though they have certainly faded in public discourse.

But note that Ford was discussing the bank, not the money it issued: again, establishing the gold standard and the Federal Reserve had the effect of ending most public debate about the character of *money*. Warburg appeared to the crackpot Ford as part of an international Jewish banking conspiracy, but of the money Warburg and he banked Ford had no doubts. The Federal Reserve provided for a managed, gold-backed, elastic currency and a hybrid public/private central bank with limited control by politicians. Ford could conjure up a Jewish conspiracy in the system's management but not a defect in the money.

There were other grounds, rational coherent grounds, for criticizing the Fed's management after 1929. The onset of the Depression brought bank failures, unemployment, declining prices, and catastrophic deflation. When the stock market crashed in 1929, it took fourteen billion dollars with it. Where had that money gone? The Federal Reserve, run by bankers for bankers, responded to the crash and the deflation by assuming that prices had gotten "too high" and that a period of belt-tightening was necessary, to restore "real" values and prices. That view dominated orthodox economics. "There is too much of the old inflation to be gotten rid of before business can be put on a sound basis," one economist insisted: "temporary inflation would only result in a postponement of the inevitable deflation and readjustment." "Readjustment"—readjustment to what? Why is deflation "inevitable"?

This kind of thinking recurs constantly today, as when newscasters refer to declines in the market as a "correction." There is no "correct" price: the price is what people are willing to pay, and that changes. The persistent idea that there are real and false prices and values speaks again to a fundamental ambivalence about the kinds of negotiations the market allows. It imagines a real price and a false price, a genuine value and a value born of bad character. Trying to imagine these price differences as somehow "natural," rather than the product of human social negotiation, turned out to be disastrous in the 1930s.

Bankers in the Federal Reserve System understood the crash and Depression as a symptom of "un-natural" acts or bad character, and they aimed to either restore character in backsliders or purge the economy of bad men. "They tended to regard bank failures as either regrettable consequences of bad management or bad banking practices," wrote Milton Friedman, "or as inevitable reactions to prior speculative excess."[26] "Speculative excess": a lovely phrase, meaning close to nothing except in hindsight, the idea again implies some kind of natural limit to speculation. "If a patient dies," wrote Lynn Talley, chairman of the Dallas branch of the Fed when the Depression began, it is "quite impossible to bring the patient back to life through the use of artificial respiration or injections of adrenaline."[27] Herbert Hoover recalled his secretary of the treasury, Andrew Mellon, telling him the Depression "will purge the rottenness out of the system . . . people will work harder, live a more moral life. Values will be adjusted, and enterprising people will pick up the wrecks from the less competent people." Mellon, a banker and the son of a banker, had J. P. Morgan's conviction of the relation between money, prices, and character. "He insisted," Hoover recalled, "that when people get an inflation brainstorm, the only way to get it out of their blood is to let it collapse."[28] The system had suffered moral rot. Hard times and low prices, physical suffering (by people other than Mellon), would restore its character. The Federal Reserve initially responded to the Great Depression in exactly this way—contracting the money supply and aiming to restore "real" prices and values.

*   *   *

By the 1930s, however, other approaches to hard times had begun to take hold. Histories of economics attribute these changes in thinking to John Maynard Keynes. Mellon saw hard times as a manifestation of bad character and excess, and wanted to cut back and restore "real" values. But in hard times, Keynes observed, people instinctively do the worst possible thing. They tighten their belts; they spend less; they hoard what they have. This action by millions of individuals compounds the problem: it reduces consumer spending, which reduces demand, which leads to cuts in the workforce, which leads to less consumer spending. The solution, Keynes suggested, lay in government spending—the government should prime the economic pump by spending money as quickly as possible, flooding the economy with money, raising prices, and causing consumers to peer out from their caves and hoards and start spending again. If Mellon acted like the stern and punishing daddy, Keynes reflected the progressive tradition, aiming to shape behavior by cultural means, to reshape mass psychology. Keynes's approach suggested the Fed should have lowered interest rates and pumped money into the economy as quickly as possible.[29] It did the opposite.

Disgusted with the conservatism of the Fed and of orthodox economists, "for whom gold was a religion,"[30] and increasingly swayed by Keynesian theory, Roosevelt took the United States off the domestic gold standard in the Gold Reserve Act of 1934.[31]

The act made it illegal for private citizens to hold "monetary gold," insisting that they sell any such hoards to the Treasury in exchange for paper dollars. It also required banks to transfer title to what gold reserves they held to the United States government, again in return for dollars. These dollars might take the form of "gold certificates," especially in large transactions, but no longer might paper dollars be redeemed for gold, except at the discretion of the secretary of the treasury (a provision designed for foreign exchange: the U.S. remained on the gold standard in foreign exchange until 1971). Now nothing backed the paper currency but the good faith and credit of the government itself. Under the act individuals could still own gold jewelry or keep their gold dental fillings. But the act forced anyone owning "monetary gold"—coins or bullion—to sell it to the federal government.

The federal government now declared that it owned all monetary gold, but that gold no longer backed the currency, except in the sense that *all* assets of the federal government, *all* property owned by the federal government, secured the issue of paper money. It made gold simply another piece of government property like land or tanks or surplus office furniture.[32]

It is worth looking at the way Roosevelt managed this transition, and in particular at the way he gave the impression of a gold standard while effectively abolishing it. Roosevelt established and publicized a new vault, at Fort Knox in Kentucky, mostly for the purpose of dramatizing the secure warehousing of gold. Fort Knox, late into the twentieth century, would serve to symbolize the security the gold standard allegedly established. But what it actually marked was a new understanding of the federal government and its relationship to money and value.

The crisis of the "first hundred days" helped make this radical departure acceptable, and the Gold Reserve Act passed with remarkably slight opposition. Congressman Louis McFadden of Pennsylvania revived anti-Semitism when he denounced the bill for vesting too much authority in the secretary of the treasury. The secretary, he reminded the House, "is by family, tradition, neighbors, association, and friends tied in with the international Jewish financial group who are associated closely with the ruling financial officials of the British Government and the Bank of England."[33] Robert Luce of Massachusetts pointed to the portraits of Washington and Lafayette on the walls of the House chamber. "Metaphorically they may give you backing," he argued, "but surely no one would say you are 'secured' by their presence. . . . The value of no piece of paper will be enhanced because it says there is gold somewhere." Memory without tangible connection to the past lacked authority, he argued; this bill amounts to

> the death and burial of 8,000 pounds of precious metal. In the future when a guide takes a tourist around the Capital, he will tell of the burial vault under the grim old treasury, itself suggestive of a mausoleum, and will point to a tablet reading: 'Here lies gold. Sterilized and chloroformed. (Long it served mankind. Now it shall slumber until the day of resurrection).'[34]

But an opponent looked at the portraits and claimed, to his colleagues' applause: "I have looked upon that serene figure of Washington many a time since this depression began," he said, and "I would rather have the faith, the hope and the courage that even the picture of Washington inspires than to have all the destructive bickerings of the gentleman from Massachusetts and all who believe as he does." Here then is the anti-essentialist position, the greenback position: money was founded in social values, in shared commitment, in the idea of the United States and the things its citizens accomplished rather than in its material assets. These things alone, knowledge of shared enterprise reflected in history, could stabilize paper money if all believed.[35]

Roosevelt himself defended the Gold Reserve Act in misleading ways. "By making clear that we are establishing permanent metallic reserves in the possession and ownership of the Federal Government," he told Congress, "we can organize a currency system which is both sound and adequate."[36] But this makes no sense—the U.S. already had "metallic reserves" before the act: the act actually eliminated that gold's legal function as reserves—paper money was no longer redeemable in gold. The government would now own all the gold, but what would that gold's function be? Roosevelt's emphasis on the "bullion base for the currency" was more symbolic than actual: "sound and adequate" meant a money supply tied to the neo-Keynesian economic theories of his closest advisors, not to any natural scarcity or abundance of precious metal. He also asserted "the inherent right of Government to issue currency and to be the sole custodian and owner of the base or reserve of precious metals underlying that currency." Such an inherent right had never been imagined before. True, the Constitution implied that the federal government had sole power to issue currency, and for much of the nineteenth century Americans had ignored this claim. But nowhere in the Constitution does it say that the government has a right to be the sole custodian and owner of the gold which now did not in fact underlie the currency. "With this goes the prerogative of Government to determine from time to time the extent and nature of the metallic reserve. I am confident that the Nation will well realize the definite purpose of the Government to maintain the credit of that Government and, at the same time, to provide a sound medium of exchange which will serve the needs of our people."[37]

Like Lincoln during the Civil War, Roosevelt asserted the government's right to control the money supply, and as in the Civil War, national emergency formed a justification. But Roosevelt had managed something unprecedented and entirely new: he took control over the money supply out of the hands of bankers and the market and put it in the hands of politicians and social scientists. That he did so little with this power speaks to the fundamentally conservative outlook he always claimed for himself.

Roosevelt insisted to Congress that the 1934 act would vest in the government of the nation the "title to and possession of all monetary gold within its boundaries."[38] To help establish this, he appointed Marriner Eccles as Federal Reserve Board chairman in 1934. Eccles strongly supported Roosevelt and acquiesced in virtually every New Deal program. By 1934 the Treasury had nearly complete control of the money supply, which it enjoyed for the next twenty years.[39]

Adding to the need for a physical demonstration of security and ownership, in 1936 the Treasury announced a "gold sterilization policy," whereby it would purchase foreign gold with its own income (from taxes and tariffs) and then retire that gold from any possible monetary function—that is, not allow it to serve as a reserve for loans. The Treasury had been buying gold since 1934, in an ill-conceived attempt to raise commodity prices by causing inflation. Although it produced an unprecedented influx of gold into the U.S., as foreign nations rushed to take advantage of a price higher than the open market, it never worked to produce inflation.[40] Nor were Roosevelt's advisors entirely sure they wanted it to—they initiated the "sterilization" program to *stop* inflation. After 1934, when gold bullion began pouring into the United States, it "was feared that the additions to our monetary and credit structure . . . might result in too great an expansion of credit."[41] The government in effect bought the gold to cause inflation, then reburied it to prevent it.[42] This confusing policy stemmed from the experimental character of New Deal finance, and from Roosevelt's conservative temperament.[43]

Compare FDR, for example, to Huey Long, governor of and then senator from Louisiana. Long wanted actively redistributive economic policies; he wanted wealth to move down towards the poor, and he told reporters in 1933 that he wanted inflation, and that "he did not care how inflation was brought about." Whether by devaluing the dollar or printing more money or adding silver-backed currency, he simply did not care. "I was raised in the South," he told reporters in a truly remarkable moment, "and lots of my life has been spent among the Negroes." "They get to recognize certain basic factors," Long continued, and "I remember one time a Negro said: 'a white man gets worried about money and worries and worries and worries and blows his head off. A Negro gets worried about money and goes to sleep.'" Long wanted inflation, by any means, and he dismissed worries about inflation by citing the imaginary observations of an imaginary negro. He conjured up a gold bug's nightmare, an economy in which the whimsical and folksy sayings of fictitious African American peasants govern monetary policy. He would, he added, shorten working hours: "if necessary he would shorten the year." "It's all in the Scriptures," he told reporters. Long would the use "the Bible and Negro Philosophy" to end the slump, the headline said.[44]

Long, who generally did not engage in race baiting and enjoyed acting the buffoon on occasion, played on American racial division to justify inflation. He deliberately tweaked the pomposity of bankers and economists, their self-congratulatory blather about "character," by suggesting the relaxed attitudes and needs of the American underclass should govern policy, not gold or silver or the alleged character of bankers.

But Roosevelt talked about the importance of gold reserves even while abandoning gold's function as a reserve. He asserted that only "a deep seated desire for added certainty" explained the historic need for gold reserves. He noted: "nations, at various times, have placed it now in their public treasuries and again in private or semi private fiscal institutions forming a part of their financial structure" (like the Federal Reserve). But, he argued, only "the national government provides that permanence which is in keeping with a lasting custodianship which is of such importance; and the government furnishes a base of responsibility as broad as the public welfare to be safeguarded, since its interests are always those of the entire nation."[45] Rather than a natural economy, founded in "character," natural law, and biological fact, FDR proposed an economy derived from democratic association, with a money system based on mutuality, an "imagined" thing. The *New York Times* had imagined J. P. Morgan as "a bank in human form." Roosevelt here imagines not the human form of an individual but the human form of the American people as a whole. It is a construction of value that implies generalized equality.

On the subject of race Roosevelt kept much of his personal beliefs hidden. He grew up imbibing Theodore Roosevelt's "strenuous life" racism, and before his election to the presidency he had, like most Democratic politicians, taken great care not to offend the South, where segregation ruled and where any deviation from white supremacy provoked outrage. Though he admired Japanese culture and had Japanese personal friends of long standing, he had no hesitation about locking Japanese Americans up in concentration camps after Pearl Harbor.[46] Most historians credit his wife, Eleanor Roosevelt, for pressing him on civil rights issues. Eleanor Roosevelt genuinely detested racial bigotry, and she worked to give African American leaders like Mary McLeod Bethune a voice in the White House. She and Franklin came to view Mrs. Bethune, a woman of iron resolve and unfailingly gracious manner, as a personal friend; Bethune was a key part of the informal circle of African Americans that came to be known as FDR's "black cabinet."

Many of FDR's advisors shared Eleanor Roosevelt's views and contributed to the general climate of anti-racism that began chipping away at the white supremacist consensus in the 1930s. At the same time, by 1936 African Americans in the North had emerged as a crucial electoral bloc, and both parties worked hard to secure their votes.[47]

The combination outraged "Dixiecrats." Carter Glass, an architect of the Federal Reserve and fierce advocate of the gold standard, complained to a friend that Roosevelt was more committed to civil rights "than any President except Lincoln." This has "incensed me beyond expression, and but for the very peculiar political situation at this time I would bitterly denounce it in a public statement." He later argued that Southern Democrats might need to bolt the party to face down the "new Reconstruction era that northern so-called Democrats are menacing us with." Glass thought loose money and racial equality equally bad: other Dixiecrats complained, James Patterson observed, that New Deal relief spending "raised the negro to the white man's level." Patterson quotes Martin Dies of Texas, in a debate on efforts to standardize wages in relief spending, declaring to a chorus of rebel yells: "there is a racial question involved here. . . . Under this measure what is prescribed for one race must be prescribed for another, and you cannot prescribe the same wages for the black man as for the white man."[48]

Beyond wages, Southern racial conservatives saw the New Deal promoting general social equality. Senator Ellison "Cotton Ed" Smith of South Carolina loved to tell and retell the story of how he walked out of the Democratic National Convention in 1936 rather than listen to an invocation by a black minister: "By God, he's as black as melted midnight! Get outa my way! This mongrel meeting ain't no place for a white man!"[49] Eugene Talmadge, governor of Georgia, distributed photos of "Mrs. Franklin D. Roosevelt being escorted to her car by a Negro member of the faculty of Howard University." Talmadge accused Roosevelt of calling on "Republicans, socialists, Communists and Negroes to tell him how to run these good old United States."[50]

Dixiecrats recognized that the New Deal's reconfiguration of the money system, and federal authority, had changed the rules: they saw that "a liberalized Democracy under an all-powerful executive was a threat to white supremacy."[51] The New Deal called for a sense of even-handedness in the distribution of government largess. FDR's evocation of money as an expression not of gold, not of "natural value," but of the people themselves, implied equality. But Roosevelt, ever a canny politician, put Southern elected officials in a difficult position. Southern states benefited greatly from New Deal spending, and because they were hit hard by falling crop prices, Southern politicians tended to favor inflation and back the New Deal. Carter Glass may have clung to white supremacy and the gold standard, but Talmadge once suggested, apparently seriously, that the government should "print a lot of $10 and $20 bills and scatter them over the country by throwing the money out of airplanes."[52]

How did a racist like Talmadge come to support inflation? Roosevelt famously managed Southern politicians by making sure that control over federal dollars remained as much as possible in local hands, perpetuating local traditions of white supremacy wherever possible. Mississippi governor Theodore Bilbo, who became notorious for his relentless race baiting in the 1940s, rarely missed a chance to flay the race question or to spend New Deal federal dollars: one biographer calls him a "redneck liberal."[53] That FDR presided over a party that included both Bilbo and Mary McCleod Bethune speaks volumes about FDR's political genius.

Roosevelt also reassured Dixiecrats, and the American people generally, by talking about gold in ways that suggested the currency had solid backing. He used the construction of Fort Knox to create an impression of permanence and natural solidity that his other actions undercut. Fort Knox appeared to protect and preserve the nation's gold precisely at a time when that gold had lost its "redemptive" function, and when the federal government had embarked on a wide range of new approaches to government and the economy.

*   *   *

The Fort Knox vault appears to have been almost entirely a public relations project. There were no calls for a new vault from the Treasury or the Federal Reserve. The only record of request for funding the Bullion Depository at Fort Knox that I have found came from the U.S. Mint. According to the assistant director, "the continued receipt of an accumulation of gold bullion in the mints and assay offices made it necessary to provide additional storage facilities." The Treasury's gold—that is, gold other than that kept at Federal Reserve Banks—had resided at the mints in San Francisco, Philadelphia, and Denver, and in the assay office in New York, but these were apparently growing too small and would have cost too much to expand. "Therefore it was decided to construct a special depository and the Fort Knox site was determined upon."[54] Funding came from the Deficiency Appropriations Act of June 22, 1936, after a transfer of land at Fort Knox from the Army to the Treasury, and the PWA oversaw construction. The vault opened in October 1936.

Lack of space might have offered sufficient reason—the country's stock of gold tripled between 1933 and 1936.[55] But consider also that it does not take much space to store gold. William "Coin" Harvey had famously pointed out in his 1895 pamphlet that "all the gold in the world could fit into the wheat trading pit in Chicago." In an enlightening contrast of cultural style, J. M. Keynes himself had later calculated it might all fit easily into the cargo hold of an ocean liner.[56] The *Annual Reports of the Director of the Mint* before 1936 mention "congestion" hindering the speed of processing newly acquired gold, but not a shortage of storage space.[57] The *exterior* dimensions of the Fort Knox vault itself are only forty by sixty feet, so clearly the gold required no vast space. Then as now, the existing Federal Reserve Banks probably offered more than adequate physical space, and safety, for gold deposits. At the height of the Cold War, for example, the Soviet Union stored millions of dollars of its own gold in the Federal Reserve Bank in New York City, with no apparent concern for space.[58] Space may have been short, but it also seems likely that creating and publicizing a new fortress offered a kind of mental security.

In the bank panic of 1792, Bray Hammond wrote, the Bank of North America tried to stave off a run by its customers by having its porters "carry its specie busily to and from the cellar in order to give a magnified notion of what it had." The bank's managers, he added, "ostentatiously brought in deposits of gold and silver that had unostentatiously been carried out a little while before." The show of specie money reassured the jittery customers, saving the bank from failure. Hammond himself recalled, as a young bank clerk in Iowa during the Panic of 1907,

FIGURE 5.2. The Gold Bullion Depository at Fort Knox. Prints and Photographs Division, Library of Congress.

employing the same dodge: heaping impressively large piles and sacks of low value coin in plain view, and ostentatiously counting it, in order to give the impression of overflowing vaults.[59]

With Fort Knox, FDR attempted something similar. The government made a great show of moving its bullion to Kentucky. Press releases described the elaborate precautions necessary to move six billion dollars worth of gold. "Fifty armored trains to carry Federal gold," announced the *New York Times*.[60] Armed soldiers and submachine-gun-toting Treasury agents rode with the gold as it moved by rails along a secret route. False "dummy" trains decoyed would-be thieves. Tanks and soldiers on foot protected armored transports as they drove the yellow bars from railhead to vault. It cost well over a million dollars to move the gold, many times more than it cost to build the vault. Although the Treasury kept both the actual moving day and the amount moved secret, it took pains to call attention to the fact of the move and to the gold's enormous but unspecified value. The *Literary Digest* noted that "the gold itself, which miners once dug from the earth, the government now returns to the earth. And the fortress at Fort Knox, with its feudalistic moat, is simultaneously a memorial to the gold standard and an emblem of managed money."[61] The elaborate and well-publicized precautions demonstrated unmistakably that the U.S. owned the gold, that the gold was immensely valuable, and that it now sat in an impregnable fortress in the nation's heartland.

"It is the greatest treasure of all time," wrote *Popular Mechanics*: "the strongest, best guarded, least expensive, most sensible strongbox owned by any nation."[62] Popular magazines and newspapers quickly seized on the vault as a symbol of security and strength. Several accounts noted that any potential invaders would have to "first fight their way across the Appalachians" just to approach the fort, associating the vault's impregnability with the nation's geography.[63] They also repeated Treasury Department press releases describing the vault's extraordinary security measures, including electric fences, a moat, steel and concrete walls of unknown but doubtless staggering thickness, a bombproof roof, poison gas booby traps, and an emergency flooding system. The Treasury hinted at other forms of protection too secret and awful to mention. "We thought Fort Knox would be a safe place," treasury secretary Henry Morgenthau answered cryptically when a reporter asked why he chose Fort Knox: "you know what I mean—*safe.*"[64]

Despite, or perhaps because of, the combination of elaborate and well-publicized hoopla and secret, unnamed contrivances and stratagems, the vault made some observers uneasy. Roger Ward Babson, described as the "prophet of the 1929 crash," argued that such a concentration of American gold made too tempting a target for fascists and communists—"the key to nearly one half the world's gold supply is hanging on the wall of the President's private office!" "The one greatest step our nation has taken to prepare the ground for revolution," the "sage of Wall Street" continued, "was the taking of this gold from millions of banks, insurance companies and individuals and putting it together under the control of one man."[65] "Who Owns the Money? Who Owns the Gold?" demanded Montana Representative Jacob Thorkelson. "They want us to believe that our hocus pocus money is good enough and gold is not necessary. Yet the New Deal has deprived the people of all gold and has set it aside for the money kings" Why? "It is set aside at the present time for one purpose, and that is to place the invisible government and its disciples in complete control of the United States."[66] Conspiracy theories aside, the Bullion Depository at Fort Knox emerged into popular culture as an embodiment of the nation's financial and spiritual strength.[67]

Indeed, argued *Travel* magazine in 1962, Fort Knox was "More than Gold": it was an important destination for the patriotic tourist. *Travel* described the vault as built "just after the United States decided that pa-

per currency was preferable to heavy gold coins." The comment, suggesting that mere convenience led to the abandonment of gold coins, echoed
the common perception that the gold at Fort Knox still backed the currency. The writer noted the electric fence and the loudspeaker at the
gate, which warned visitors to advance no further. "Only the realization
that over 13,000 tons of gold are stored inside this mammoth strongbox
turns tranquility into an eerie atmosphere of mystery and pounding curiosity." The vaults had served the nation as more than a bullion depository, the writer noted: "during the Second World War the bricks made
way for other precious items of national interest, namely the Declaration
of Independence, the Constitution, one of the Gutenberg bibles and the
original manuscript of Lincoln's Gettysburg address."

Storing national treasures in the gold vault associated the gold itself
with the nation's heritage, an association *Travel* strengthened when it observed that Fort Knox housed both an historically important cavalry unit
and "an unknown number of historic cemeteries . . . some say at least
60, others say at least 90." Important figures reposing near the vault included Lincoln's grandmother and his cousin and "childhood playmate
Lucretia Brumfield Allstum." Lincoln's parents married here, it continued, and he may have been born in these same hallowed hills that also
contained close relatives of Daniel Boone, Stonewall Jackson, and other
unknown pioneers. "Few who have not been there think of Fort Knox
as anything but a well guarded treasure chest. Dedicated historians and
perspicacious travelers, however, will find it a gold mine of United States
lore as well."[68] These essays treated the gold, America's historical arti-
facts, and history itself as part of a national patrimony.

The Daughters of the American Revolution, on the other hand, believed that this connection was vanishing. An organization obsessed
with American matrimony, founded on the idea of a genetic link to the
nation's deep past, the DAR charged in 1952 that the Democrats had se-
cretly squandered, stolen, or lost the nation's gold reserve at Fort Knox.
Truman tried to make light of it and offered the DAR members a free
pass to look at the gold.[69] But the charge had its supporters on Capitol
Hill: in 1951 Charles Tobey, New Hampshire Republican, had also demanded an inspection of the Fort Knox gold.[70] Roughly a year later Congressman Carroll Kearns of Pennsylvania himself demanded a count of
the gold, a measure of special urgency "now that the Democrats are leaving office."[71] A few weeks later George Humphrey, the new secretary
of the treasury, named a special committee of bankers and other dark-

suited financial worthies to inspect the vault and count the bars.[72] Halfway through their counting they reported "apparently it's all there."[73]

*   *   *

The DAR figures prominently in histories of the New Deal and civil
rights. In 1939, famously, the Daughters of the American Revolution refused to allow African American soprano Marian Anderson to sing at
Constitution Hall, the Washington, D.C. venue owned by the DAR. The
intensely conservative organization restricted membership to women descended from "patriots of the American revolution," at the time meaning whites only. Although Anderson, Arturo Toscanini claimed, had the
kind of voice only "heard once in a hundred years," the DAR flatly refused to allow her to sing, stating that the hall was open only to "white
artists." Critics mostly denounced the organization. "It's a strange
world," one man wrote Secretary of the Interior Harold Ickes, "when
you find the DAR in the pew with the Klu-Kluxers." Eleanor Roosevelt
publicly resigned her membership, and the NAACP, with her tacit support, organized a free concert on the steps of the Lincoln Memorial,
only a few blocks from Constitution Hall. The concert drew a live crowd
of 75,000 and a radio audience in the millions.

Her performance dramatized the changing racial climate and the government's role in promoting an idea of racial justice. Critics repeatedly
accused the DAR of "lack of Americanism": the DAR's actions are "in-
consistent with the best American traditions, including those which were
born in the fires of the American revolution." The *Christian Science
Monitor* published a letter from George Washington to Phillis Wheat-
ley, praising her talents and welcoming her to visit him. The *Monitor*
called the letter "the genuine American ideal"—"American, surely, and
Revolutionary."[74] These critics understood "Americanism" as a commitment to equality and meritocracy, not as a birthright or a genetic legacy.
While hardly an unmixed triumph, the Anderson concert demonstrated
the New Deal's complicity in undermining the radical racist consensus
that dominated the first half of the century.[75]

When the DAR raised its claims about the Fort Knox gold, it had already therefore become a figure of scorn in progressive circles, widely
lampooned, thanks in large part to the Marian Anderson fiasco. As early
as 1932 the artist Grant Wood had mocked them as "people who are trying to set up an aristocracy of birth in a Republic"; his satirical painting

Daughters of Revolution shows three starchy, pinched, and joyless matrons in front of a monochromatic portrait of Washington crossing the Delaware.[76] "The Daughters of the American Revolution," wrote *Time* magazine in 1955, "have been on edgy terms with the White House ever since Franklin Roosevelt reminded them, in 1938, that 'all of us, and you and I especially, are descended from immigrants.'"[77] *Time* contrasted FDR's invocation of shared, multiethinic nationalism, and immigrant status "we all share," with the DAR's genetic exclusivity and stubborn gold crankery: both rested on claims of fundamental, essential value.

The controversy faded from the press, if not from right-wing political circles. Every year into the 1960s Congressman Kearns, *Time* noted, "has methodically offered a resolution demanding that a congressional delegation be dispatched to recount the gold buried at Fort Knox."[78] Neither the DAR nor the politicians they inspired knew what the gold in Fort Knox actually did or didn't do, but they chose to accept it as a symbol of conservative nationalism, essentialist nationalism, in a time when other standards of value had come under attack. The New Deal stole not gold but the surety of white supremacy.

A 1954 article in *American Mercury* described, with approval, the DAR recount of federal gold. We need to know what lies in the vaults, since "the gold at Fort Knox isn't lying idle . . . it is security for our paper money and it is nice to know that the gold is there to back up our old greenbacks." This it most certainly was not, but the *Mercury* preferred to believe otherwise. A 1958 article in the same magazine worried about the USSR using gold as a weapon against the United States. It quoted assertions about Soviet engagement in a massive build up of gold supplies. "Gold has little or no meaning domestically to the Russians," the author insisted: "the *ruble* in Soviet Russia is as close to being fiat money as any currency could be. The importance to them is solely in international dealings, whether in trade, aid or bribery." But "a sudden announcement of a gold-backed ruble for use in international trade might have as dramatic a propaganda effect as Sputnik, especially in the Near East and the Orient where the boys who run the show have been gold-minded for centuries." The article ended with a report from several "captive German mining engineers who escaped from the Soviets" a few years before; as "slave technicians" in oil fields, they had witnessed a massive Soviet gold build-up. "If you don't watch out," one of them supposedly advised, "one day unexpectedly the Kremlin is going to send its agents out all over the world and shoot at you—with gold bullets. Who will want your paper money then? All you paper money friends then will leave you."[79] Since "gold minded" Near Eastern and Oriental "boys" would rush to the Soviet banner, the U.S. had no choice but to begin its own build-up.

The specter of a "gold gap" haunted *Life* magazine in 1960. *Life* followed a long photo essay on the "gold drain," and a near crisis caused by an imbalance of payments, with a two-page cartoon demonstrating the futility of attacks on Fort Knox. The cartoon showed a golfer arrested for hitting his ball near the vault; a group of teen gang members (in leather jackets with "Kool Kats" on the back) electrocuted by the fence; tourists halting before loudspeakers; sentries in pillboxes shooting gangsters; poison gas stopping tunneling thieves; and bombs bouncing harmlessly off the vault's roof.[80] The article connected the imbalance of payments to national and individual overspending, hinting at a collapse in moral fiber. It also related this apparent collapse to threats to the nation's security, then symbolized that security in the vault, which could withstand even the corrosive social effects of leisure, organized crime, and delinquent rock-and-rollers.

Perhaps the height of the association of Fort Knox with personal and national security appeared in the extremely popular James Bond movie *Goldfinger*, based on Ian Fleming's novel of the same name. In the book sinister billionaire Auric Goldfinger wants to steal the gold from Fort Knox to add to the stock he hoards obsessively. In the 1964 movie, more preposterously, he wants not to steal the gold but to irradiate it, apparently believing this would effectively reduce the world's *usable* supply and thus make his more valuable.[81]

This bizarre premise echoes a number of Cold War America's popular obsessions—with radiation, with subversion, with bodily integrity and hoarding. The famously juvenile and misogynist account of gender and sexuality central to the Bond films only reinforces this point. *Goldfinger*, *Newsweek* argued in a mixed review, "is about sexuality. In the end, the triumph of good over evil is also the triumph of normality over perversion." Indeed, Bond's success in stopping Goldfinger depends entirely on the good graces of Pussy Galore, a physically spectacular and clearly lesbian character played by Honor Blackman. "The central confrontation in the movie is not between Bond and Goldfinger," *Newsweek* continued, "but between Bond and her—a judo match which she finally loses, along with her perverse resistance to his masculine charms." Freed from Goldfinger's bonds by his "liberated" sexuality, Bond saves the gold from sterilization and preserves its potency in the American heartland.

Newsweek concluded that *Goldfinger* "deals with—or at least ex-
ploits—a real problem, the contemporary blurring of male and female
roles. . . . It is an odd entertainment when the hero's strength is as of ten
because his gender is pure." Resolving both gender ambiguity and the
ambiguity of value, Bond's seduction of Galore essentializes both het-
erosexuality and gold.[82]

An interesting update on Fort Knox and gold as symbols of national
and racial character appears in the 1995 film *Die Hard with a Vengeance*.
In the film, more or less a "buddy picture" with explosions, Bruce Willis
plays a rogue cop thrust into alliance with Samuel L. Jackson's black sep-
aratist character. Despite initial racial antagonisms, the two men "bond"
and grow to love each other as they work to stop terrorists from stealing
the gold in the New York branch of the Federal Reserve. The film plays
on racial antagonisms throughout, but in the end desire to rescue the
gold in effect unites black and white.

*   *   *

Americans wanted to believe in a gold standard long after the gold standard ceased to operate. They chose to believe in gold for most of the
same reasons they always had: the gold standard offered an idea of character, or non-negotiable certainty. With Fort Knox, Roosevelt managed
to move off the gold standard while simultaneously giving the impression that it still existed. He was able to gain a remarkable degree of central government power over the money supply: his explanations for abandoning the gold standard stress ideas of value that greenbackers would
have understood—that wealth is socially created, and that money comes
from mutual enterprise: a bank in a much larger human form than Morgan could have imagined.

In the second half of the twentieth century, the radical racist consensus collapsed. Few would seriously argue that racism has vanished, but
public utterances of openly racist sentiment rarely appear without drawing strong criticism: the easy racist consensus no longer holds. Formal
legal segregation vanished, and African Americans regained the right
to vote. It would be too simple to attribute these changes to changes in
thinking about money, but at the same time this book should have made
clear by now that specie money has always been fetishized in association
with stability, tradition, and fantasies of fundamental value.[83] The Federal Reserve System took money out of politics. When Roosevelt aban-

doned the gold standard, he took care, like a worried banker parading his small stock of specie, to give the impression of solidity. Fort Knox gave an impression of national impregnability and stability: like many memorials, this monument to the gold standard protects the stability of our unexamined assumptions.

Words and Bonds

Meum dictum pactum [my word is my bond] was another Latin phrase I used to hear, but that was just a joke.[1]

"The country's going to hell faster than when Roosevelt was in charge," declares the fatherly, avuncular trader Lou Mannheim at the start of Oliver Stone's *Wall Street*: "Too much cheap money sloshing around the world. Worst mistake we ever made was letting Nixon get off the gold standard."[2] Nixon took the United States of the international gold standard in 1971. Roosevelt had suspended the *domestic* gold standard in 1934, but in international exchange, paper dollars were still redeemable in gold. Nixon's decision ended that practice. In Stone's 1987 film, as for J. P. Morgan in chapter 5, Francis Walker in chapter 4, or "Philopatria" in chapter 1, the lack of a gold standard generates bad character in every sense—rapacious greed, wanton bad taste, and the triumph of the wrong sort of people.

Stone called *Wall Street's* villain Gordon Gekko. Michael Douglas, with slicked-back hair and flashy suits, won an Oscar playing Gekko as a cynical, immoral, lizard-like manipulator loosely resembling convicted felon Ivan Boesky. Clearly an arriviste on the Street—he mentions his father's humble origins and mocks "WASPS"—Gekko lures the ambitious Bud Fox, a young broker from a working-class background, into making illegal stock trades based on inside information. In the process Fox, played by Charlie Sheen, rejects and betrays his father, played by Sheen's real-life father Martin Sheen. Martin Sheen's character is a mechanic and union shop steward for a small, struggling airline. Although he makes more money than his father, Bud has to borrow money from him, and Martin Sheen lectures his son repeatedly about his spendthrift ways. But Bud insists that he has to put up a showy front to succeed, and that "there's no nobility in poverty."[3]

Enriched by Gekko's money, Fox embarks on a consumer fling, buys a fancy apartment, and takes up with Gekko's ex-mistress, a trendy interior decorator played by Daryl Hannah. She furnishes him with what the movie wants us to understand as empty and inflated modern art, in an apartment full of fake brick, plastic moldings, and trompe l'oeil furniture. Against his father's opposition Bud Fox tries to put together a deal in which Gekko would assume control of the airline, ostensibly saving it from bankruptcy. Gekko then in turn betrays Fox and his father with a plan to liquidate the company, prompting Bud Fox to seek the aid of Sir Lawrence Wildman (Terence Stamp), a wealthy British financier who we see earlier give a speech about saving companies and making them more productive, rather than destroying them. In the end Bud Fox defeats Gekko with Wildman's help, then testifies to the government about Gekko's illegal machinations, sending him to jail.

By renouncing Gekko and Wall Street, Fox reunites with his working-class father and gives up his aspirations to social mobility. He learns, in other words, to keep his place. "I realized I'm just Bud Fox," he says at the end: "as much as I wanted to be Gordon Gekko, I'll always be Bud Fox." The movie ends up insisting on knowing your place. Throughout the film, the actor Hal Holbrook, as Lou Mannhiem, observes the scene wryly. Holbrook's character represents one of the few figures remaining from Wall Street's old, pre-Gekko days. Holbrook delivers the benediction near the end of the film, after Bud Fox has been arrested for insider trading. He tells Fox that when he "stares into the abyss" he will find "his character," and that this character "is what keeps him out of the abyss." Bud Fox's character will place him back in the working class. The closing credits dedicate the film to Oliver Stone's father Louis, who worked on Wall Street as a stockbroker and who we presume also represents the days when value and character were supposedly stable.[4]

Stone's film marked one of the first popular comments on Wall Street in the 1980s, and it not unreasonably condemned corporate raiders for breaking up companies and laying off workers solely for personal gain. But like J. P. Morgan before the Pujo committee, the film imagines that the older generation on Wall Street, personified by Lou Mannheim and by Stone's father, somehow knew how to make money without losing themselves in it—that they had a stable character that money could never corrupt or alter, while the immigrant newcomers could make money but were no different from the "cheap" money they made. "This movie is about young people and their attitudes towards money," Stone explained in 1987. "There has been a loss of values."[5] Louis Stone, the director's father, was a very prominent stockbroker. A vice president at Shearson Lehman Brothers, he wrote a popular investment newsletter and "was known as a staunch supporter of gold as the basic unit of the currency ... to assure a sound monetary policy."[6] Oliver Stone's problem with Wall Street isn't really that greed is bad, it's that men of character are no longer in charge, and so anyone who can make money might be able to become whatever they want, without limits, and there might be no difference between "us" and "them."[7]

In the Wall Street of the 1980s, Michael Lewis claimed in *Liars' Poker*, skilled bond traders at the right firms could more or less set the value of the goods they traded in. Lewis's firm, Salomon Brothers, pioneered the trade in mortgage bonds—certificates representing pools of real estate mortgages, usually bought from one savings and loan and sold to another. By the mid 1980s, they enjoyed a near monopoly in these mortgage bonds. Combining this monopoly with a cultivated ruthlessness, Salomon traders "whipped and drove" the market; they "jammed bonds" to customers who might not need or even want them, with spectacular results. Lewis Ranieri, the head of Salomon mortgage trading, "would say he thought the market was going up, and buy a hundred million [dollars in] bonds. Then the market would start to go down. So Lewie would buy *two billion* more bonds, and of course, the market would go up."[8] *Meum Dictum Pactum* indeed: the relationship between words and things seems skewed.

The traders like Ranieri, as Lewis depicts them, are gross, coarse; they gorge themselves on greasy food; they bully and swear. Lacking the accouterments of education and "character," willing to adopt any pose to make a sale, they in some ways lack a self beyond their greed. But they also suffer from status anxiety, and in the '80s, "they decided for reasons best known to themselves to invest some of their winnings in buying people like me."[9]

Lewis's autobiographical account stresses his class background. A Princeton art history major adrift among business majors, a "southern boy in a white linen suit" surrounded by rapacious Yankees, a blond WASP among second generation Jews and Italians, Lewis describes Wall Street from an outsider's perspective, as foreign and dangerous but also enticing. During the late '70s and early '80s, Lewis relates, undergraduates at Princeton and other Ivy League schools—Lewis usually refers to this group as "we"—flocked towards economics and business majors, hoping to land a job on Wall Street. Against the generational tide, he writes, Lewis had studied art history to find himself through a traditional liberal arts education. Now he watches his peers from "Harvard, Yale, Stanford and Penn,"[10] "inheritors," as Tom Wolfe put it, "of the *lux* and the *veritas*,"[11] adopt the blunt obscenities of market frenzy. Lewis wants to preserve the worldview of liberal humanism, where what you learn in school confirms your identity, your social position, and your basic difference from the less educated, and where goods in trade can be imagined to have a fundamental, "intrinsic" value apart from market distortions. He imagines, for example, the "goods" of an art history education having an intrinsic value because of their being "self-improving," despite the fact that his classmates regard him as "the class Franciscan." But on Wall Street, Lewis can't figure out if this self really exists any more.[12]

Lewis claims that the M.B.A. he earned after Princeton has nothing to do with success in bond trading, and though he describes Salomon Brothers' "training program" in considerable detail, he mostly scorns it as useless. Success in investment banking, he says, "was less a matter of skill and more a matter of intangibles—flair, persistence and luck." Were these qualities rare, or could anyone acquire or possess them? Are bond traders born or made?

That, says Lewis, "was the question of questions."[13] Most often, he talks about someone being "a born trader" or having "raw trading instinct." In Lewis's description these people are almost invariably Jewish or Italian, sometimes Irish. "I was fascinated," he writes about bond traders, "that such awful looking people could do so well for themselves."[14] Although the lines between the two often blurred, at Salomon Brothers bond *salesmen* usually convinced clients to buy or sell bonds based on the bond *trader's* decisions. Lewis himself decides to become a salesman, rather than a trader, after he looked at bond traders and decided that not one "bore the slightest resemblance to me." "I thought as seriously of being a trader," says Lewis, "as I thought of being Chinese."[15]

The racial metaphor is especially significant to Lewis's account, because in fact he does quite well as a bond salesman—as well as the ethnic types he mostly disdains. The more he learns about bond trading, the more he sees his self disappearing—because if he can do it, then where lies the difference between himself and the fat, loud, and boorish ethnic types he describes as "such awful looking people"? The bonds he sells seem to have no relation to any traditional index of value, and they fluctuate more in response to the whims of Salomon Brothers' Hunnish traders than any market law. The firm cares nothing for its customers, who it sees as dupes, and can barely bring itself to mouth the clichés about raising capital for growth that usually justify investment banking. Even the logic of the free market itself seems useless here, where Salomon Brothers so dominates the market and its clients that it almost seems to print its own money. Without the concept of an inborn, genetic, "racial" difference between himself and other traders, without some extra-market "intrinsic" quality or value, Lewis cannot find any core self at all.

As he gets better at "jamming bonds" Lewis experiences unsettling dreams where he acts like the sort of greedy, vulgar, nouveau-riche person he disdains. In these dreams he is in a hotel, screaming at the top of his lungs at the bellboy because his suite has no bathrobe, or the corners of the first sheet of toilet paper have not been turned back; or flying into a rage because his favorite restaurant has failed to hold his table. The nightmare stems from his fear that there may be no real self, no core of value. "His word" too becomes "his bond"; he loses his "self" in a world where prices rise or fall irrationally, where there is no set value apart from what salesmen and traders create. The bonds fail to bind—instead of affirming a difference between himself and the goods he sells, the market seems to erase it. Limitless self-making becomes Lewis's nightmare.

On the other hand—and here he finds his escape—Lewis stresses repeatedly that a business school education has nothing to do with success in trading bonds. The demand for Ivy League M.B.A.s on Wall Street, he insists, reflects nothing more than status anxiety in the nouveau-riche who do the hiring—no amount of academic training can make a great trader. The best are born rapacious, cunning, and cold. They simply have an instinct, a nose for markets. Lewis consistently depicts successful traders and salesmen as either Jewish or Italian. We are told that Ranieri, for example, recreated his department in his own image—"Italian, self-educated, loud and fat." Their fatness, their loudness, and their ability to trade in a specific way are all linked in the book. If traders are born, not made, and Italians are good traders, then Italians must be as different from Lewis as the Chinese. This ethnic emphasis gets him out of the problem of shifting identity. If the really good traders or salesmen operate on animal instinct—an instinct which may be more common in certain races or ethnicities—then there *is* a final, ineluctable difference between himself and the people he works with. If not, then his Princeton education and blond hair signify nothing.

We might certainly applaud Lewis's rejection of ostentatious vulgarity, and recognize the danger in the mortgage bond market Ranieri helped invent—the very same mortgage bonds that would cause a worldwide financial collapse in 2008. Lewis is no simple bigot—he admires many things about the people he mocks, including their brash honesty and willingness to innovate. The goal here is not to defend either vulgarity or greed, but rather to point out how the critique of both takes on the quality of an ethnic slur. Exactly as in the 1890s, "ethnics" are presumed to have a different economic nature. Lewis, and Oliver Stone, both resolve the ambiguities of market negotiation with appeals to character, and both imagine that character in quasi genetic terms. Their resort to quasi racial notions of essential difference returns us to the themes this book has explored repeatedly, themes that resurfaced with greater force after the 1970s.

* * *

Abandoning the international gold standard in 1971 drew surprisingly little negative comment. Near the end of World War II, the allies had met to establish a new world monetary order in which the United States dollar would serve as the international unit of exchange. The Bretton Woods agreement also established the International Monetary Fund and what became the World Bank. Richard Nixon unilaterally ended the practice of redeeming dollars for gold in international exchange in August 1971. By that point, the gold standard had come to seem crankish and old fashioned. "There is no magic in gold" the *Wall Street Journal* declared. It does not stop inflation, and governments can come and go from it as they please. Gold advocates "hark back to the days of World War I," but "a nation's money needs some flexibility to adjust to the economy's legitimate needs."[16] The *Journal* reflected what had become the Keynesian orthodoxy: that the money supply should rise or fall in response to changing social needs, in response to the psychology of demand. Technocratic experts could monitor the money supply and prevent disaster; they could also adjust the growth of money to compensate for changes in public attitudes. Even the conservative economist Milton Freidman, who advised Barry Goldwater on economic policy, could admit in 1965, to his later embarrassment, that "We are all Keynesians now," and Richard Nixon, just before ending the gold standard, could declare that "I am now a Keynesian in economics."[17]

But Friedman led the new movement, dubbed "monetarism," which overturned Keynesian orthodoxy in the 1980s. From studying American monetary history, and in particular the Federal Reserve in the Great Depression, Friedman concluded that bankers, economists, and politicians could never effectively manage money. Market conditions moved too fast: they would always be "behind the curve" and their interventions would always already be too late. Moreover, their intrusions would always distort the market: their interventions would nearly always make things worse. Instead of technocrats managing the economy, monetarism demanded a fixed, unvarying rate of growth in the money supply. Following Friedman, monetarists pressed for automated money growth, for "rules instead of authorities," as Friedman put it. Freidman saw the Federal Reserve as a major cause of the Great Depression. He wanted it abolished altogether or reduced to a mere administrative formality. The money supply should increase annually at a small, unvarying, and predictable rate, regardless of what the larger economy might be doing. This would allow for growth and keep inflation in check. It would keep prices and values "real."[18]

Friedman's intellectual roots lay in "classical liberalism" or libertarianism. He wanted less government and laissez faire wherever possible. In *Capitalism and Freedom* Friedman had lamented the impracticality of a gold standard, which if it could be made to work would provide a "natural money" beyond reach of governments. In place of the gold standard, a "commodity money," Friedman argued that a fixed rate of money growth could provide the next best thing: an objective, "real" basis for value and social identity which would eliminate "irresponsible governmental tinkering" with economy and society.[19]

For those uncomfortable with the volatility of identity in the market, monetarism made a world of genuine character, a true meritocracy, imaginable—a world where, as Friedman put it, "a man should be judged by what he is and what he does." Presumably these would be the same thing, as Adam Smith had imagined more than two hundred years before; and again as Morgan suggested when he linked money to "character." Friedman nicely expressed the ideal of the free market, race blind and efficient. The fundamental unit of society, he wrote, is "the individual," and if these individuals are left alone they will be free to find their true nature, unconstrained by government. The fundamental threat to freedom, Friedman writes, "is the power to coerce, be it in the hands of a monarch, a dictator, an oligarchy, or a momentary majority."[20]

Non-classical liberals, less enthused by libertarianism, might then ask, "how is the market, relentlessly pressuring individuals to compete in ways they don't necessarily like, not coercive?"

The market avoids being coercive only if you understand "the individual" as a man or woman with an intrinsic, fixed, and fundamental nature which the market will liberate. Freed from political or cultural restraint, the free individual will rise to fulfill his intrinsic potential: libertarians, like social Darwinists, want to imagine a world where all hierarchies are "natural" hierarchies, because what people "are" and what they do is the same.[21]

Friedman often analogized economics to the natural sciences. "In 1953," he recalled, "I introduced a version of the natural-science laboratory" to economic study at the University of Chicago.[22] He argued that "monetary structures" might look bizarre initially, but when seen correctly they appeared as "simply unfamiliar versions of the structures we take for granted, almost as if they were part of the natural world."[23] Though he grew defensive of its deterministic implications, Friedman introduced the economic concept he called "the natural rate of unemployment," effectively social Darwinism in modern guise.[24] In 1973, Friedman wrote, in his column in *Newsweek*, "the biological laws that specify the characteristics of cats are no more rigid than the political laws that specify the behavior of government agencies." The way the FDA behaves, he asserted, is "a consequence of its constitution." A natural scientist, he continued, recognizes "that you cannot assign characteristics at will to chemical and biological entities." "Why do you suppose the situation is different in the social sciences?"[25]

We have seen this kind of language before. From 1895: "What prevents Congress from legislating the value of a dollar? . . . Not the Constitution of the United States, but the constitution of man."[26] Or from 1894: "The natural laws that control the currents of the air, and the formation and condensation of clouds, are not more constant than are the natural laws that control the currents of commerce, and the distribution of capital."[27] These quotes convey the sense in which modern libertarianism is 1890s social Darwinism in trendy dress. But the longing for natural hierarchy goes back farther than that. "Distinctions in society will always exist under every just government," Andrew Jackson had declared in 1832, when he vetoed the recharter of the Second Bank of the United States: "Equality of talents, of education, or of wealth can not be produced by human institutions." The danger, for Jackson, came when government granted "artificial distinctions": when it meddled with the economy and granted "titles, gratuities, and exclusive privileges."[28] Friedman repeats Jackson's arguments about natural character and market freedom: a free market produces a natural, intrinsic self.

It should come as no surprise, then, to find that right-wing libertarians and proponents of the free market often tend to favor genetic accounts of identity. The heroic individualism many libertarians imagine requires a self freed from all social constraints, but at the same time founded in nature—in natural rights and natural talents. The libertarian account of individualism rests on imagining a person free of social and political power. Ayn Rand's *The Fountainhead* ends with her visionary, ego-driven architect standing above the city: "there was only the ocean and the sky and the figure of Howard Roark."[29] That is, nothing but nature and the heroic individual, standing above society: an intrinsic self entirely in possession of itself. In this sense libertarianism embraces not freedom but a kind of genetic determinism, in which "merit" derives not from social whims but from instrinsic qualities and, again, in which all hierarchies are "natural." Rand's clunky *Atlas Shrugged* imagines a world in which all the creative and productive people have fled to a secret location, leaving the rest of us, "looters" and "parasites," flailing helplessly like ants bereft of the queen. Right-wing libertarianism in this way again bears a close relationship to its nineteenth-century antecedent, social Darwinism. It stresses freedom, but also imagines nature as a set of stable confines and success as the proper reward for genetic superiority.[30]

Consider, for example, economist and historian of banking Murray N. Rothbard. A tireless proponent of Austrian economics, Rothbard studied with Ludwig von Mises himself after receiving his Ph.D. from Columbia University. His books consistently and relentlessly stress the benefits of a gold standard. Calling himself both an "anarcho-capitalist" and an exponent of the "old right," Rothbard founded the Ludwig von Mises Institute and the *Quarterly Journal of Austrian Economics*: he co-founded the highly influential Cato Institute but later split with it.

For Rothbard, freedom was best when it wore pants: he blamed the "origins of the Welfare State" on "the legion of Yankee women, in particular those of middle- or upper-class background, and especially spinsters whose busybody inclinations were not fettered by the responsibilities of home and hearth." He regretted the Constitutional amendment that had "imposed" women's suffrage on the nation.[31] Rothbard eventually, with his associate Lew Rockwell, came to call himself a "paleolibertarian," fusing the libertarian emphasis on individualism with conservative notions about social hierarchy.

In 1963, at the height of the Civil Rights movement, Rothbard warned about "the Negro crisis as a revolution." "Demonstrating Negroes," he said, "have taken to a favorite chant: 'What do we want? Freedom! When do we want it? Now!'" One might expect a libertarian to like such a chant, but Rothbard found the idea of freedom for Negroes alarming: they did not understand it properly. Freedom was a "hopelessly ambiguous word as used by the Negro movement," and "the very fuzziness of the goal permits the Negroes to accelerate and increase their own demands without limit. . . . [I]t is the very sweep and vagueness of the demands that make the movement insatiable." An insatiable desire for freedom usually stands in libertarian accounts as the most praiseworthy of human attributes, but Rothbard found the African American freedom struggle alarming. Rothbard worried not just about "insatiable" Negroes, but also about King and his nonviolent protests against "private citizens as store-keepers or owners of golf courses; *their* rights are already invaded, in a 'non-violent' manner, by the established Negro 'Center.'" Rothbard explored ways to stop "the Negro revolution," and his words are worth quoting in full:

> There are two ways by which it might be crippled and defeated. First, the retaliatory creation of a white counter-revolutionary mass movement, equally determined and militant. In short, by the re-creation of the kind of Ku Klux Klan that smashed Reconstruction and the Negro movement in the late 19th century. Since whites are in the majority, they have the capacity to do this if they have the will. But the will, in my opinion, is gone; this is not the 19th century, nor even the 1920's. White opinion, as we have seen, has drastically shifted from racism to egalitarianism; even the Southern whites, particularly the educated leadership, concede the broad merit of the Negro cause; and, finally, mob action no longer has respectability in our society. There have been attempts, to be sure, at mass counter-revolutionary white action: the Ku Klux leader in Georgia told a rally that "we must fight poison with poison," armed conflict between white and Negro mobs has broken out in Cambridge, Maryland, and white hoodlums have repeatedly assaulted Negro pickets in the

Bronx. But all this is a feeble replica of the kind of white action that would be necessary to defeat the revolution; and it seems almost impossible for action to be generated on the required scale.

This exponent of freedom took some comfort in the idea of a "second, and far more subtle, method by which the Negro Revolution might be tamed and eventually crippled: through a 'sellout' by the Negro leadership itself."[32] Rothbard's overall tone regarding the civil rights movement, like his tone regarding women's suffrage, was contemptuous and hostile.

Not surprisingly, the von Mises Institute he founded and ran is allied with the "League of the South," which views the Civil War as a crisis over state's rights and calls for an independent Southern republic and wants, yes, "to return to a sound currency" based in gold. The League of the South laments the fact that "aliens" now govern the former Confederacy, and wants to return rule to the heirs of the "Anglo-Celtic tradition." Rothbard and the von Mises Institute similarly describe the Civil War as an unjust intervention and claim slavery would have vanished on its own. The North, they argue, created racism in what had been a benign natural hierarchy.[33]

Rothbard's version of libertarianism favored genetic accounts of racial difference and social rank. Votes for women, and equality for African Americans, appeared to upset the natural order. Regarding Charles Murray and Richard Herrnstein's *The Bell Curve* (1994), which explored the connection between I.Q., fundamental intelligence, and race, Rothbard praised the book for telling "the home truths which everyone, and I mean *everyone*, knew in their hearts and in private. . . . [T]he almost self-evident fact that individuals, ethnic groups and races differ among themselves in intelligence and many other traits, and that intelligence, as well as less controversial traits of temperament, are in large part hereditary." The book, he wrote, "would put a bullet through the heart of the egalitarian-socialist project" by restoring a natural foundation for inequality.[34] In this line of libertarian thinking, the very existence of racial inequality is itself the sign of freedom. "Egalitarianism," he declared, "is a revolt against nature."[35]

There are of course many flavors of libertarianism, and it would be grossly unfair to simply say that libertarianism equals racism. "Classical liberals" frequently imagine a race-blind society in which individual merit trumps all other factors. Libertarian think tanks like the Cato Institute now sometimes admit the necessity of government intervention in civil rights in the 1960s, and agree that unregulated markets will not magically solve all problems of systemic inequality. Libertarians often genuinely detest what they see as ham-handed attempts by government—Affirmative Action comes up frequently in this context—that they argue only exacerbate the racism they seek to address. They see "race" as a socially constructed tool of domination, a form of collectivism, and pose intrinsic individualism as the alternative.[36]

But the most prominent self-described political libertarian of recent years has close connections to the von Mises Institute. Texas congressman and presidential candidate Ron Paul, a disciple of Ayn Rand and the Austrian school of economics, consistently denounces the Federal Reserve and calls for a return to the gold standard. Paul critiques both the left and the right for increasing the size of government and, through deficit spending, inflating the money supply. Paul's website includes a forty minute movie from the von Mises Institute giving a capsule history of the gold standard and calling for a return to "sound money." The film blames "fractional reserve lending" for nearly all economic woes: that is, the practice of banks lending out more money than they have in their vaults.[37] In this sense, Paul's demand for the gold standard is radical enough to amount to a critique of capitalism itself, and it hearkens back to Jefferson's objections to banking. Paul wants a return to specie money. "If our money were backed by gold and silver, people couldn't just sit in some fancy building and push a button to create new money," Paul writes: "They would have to engage in honest trade with another party that already has some gold in their possession," or "get dirty and sweaty and actually dig up the gold. Not something I can imagine our 'money elves' at the Fed getting down to whenever they feel like playing God with the economy."[38]

In the 1990s, Paul wrote, or allowed to appear under his name, with his endorsement, a series of newsletters which most Americans would find alarmingly racist. Journalist James Kirchik detailed what he found in an article in the *New Republic*. For example, in 1992 the *Ron Paul Political Report* commented on the Rodney King riots in Los Angeles by saying that "order was only restored in L.A. when it came time for the blacks to pick up their welfare checks three days after rioting began." According to the newsletter, the looting came from government promotion of "'civil rights,' quotas, mandated hiring preferences, set-asides for government contracts, gerrymandered voting districts, black bureaucracies, black mayors, black curricula in schools, black tv shows, black tv anchors, hate crime laws, and public humiliation for anyone who dares question the black agenda." "Our rotten liberal culture," the newsletter concluded, "admonishes whites faced by raging blacks to lie back and think of England." In 1992 Paul advised his supporters to take refuge from "the coming race war" in rural strongholds, because "the animals are coming." Of the Martin Luther King Holiday, one Paul newsletter declared: "What an infamy Ronald Reagan approved it!" and concluded "We can thank him for our annual Hate Whitey Day." The newsletter also demonstrated open sympathy for "patriot" militia groups and, Kirchik concluded, classical examples of anti-government political paranoia, frequently involving the Federal Reserve.[39]

Paul has distanced himself from both the newsletters and "paleolibertarianism," but he keeps the hard money focus and the ties to the League of the South. He now chairs the House Financial Services Committee's Subcommittee on Monetary Policy, which allows him to hold hearings on the Federal Reserve and the money supply. When Ron Paul called his first hearing on Fed Monetary Policy, on February 9, 2011, he invited Thomas DiLorenzo, a proud member of the League of the South, to testify on behalf of the gold standard.[40]

Inspired in part by Paul, enthusiasm for gold is on the rise. For example, the National Organization for the Repeal of the Federal Reserve Act and Internal Revenue Code (Norfed) began, in 2007, minting and selling "Ron Paul Dollars" made of copper, gold, silver, and platinum. Since the late 1990s, Norfed had been selling what it called "American Liberty Currency," $1, $5, and $10 dollar notes it claimed were backed by deposits of silver and gold in an Idaho vault. Profits from the sale, Norfed claimed, would go to bringing down the Federal Reserve System. Customers could buy coins but also buy the right to start "redemptions centers," stockpile precious metal, and issue more dollars, with the idea of supplanting Federal Reserve Notes with "real money." Norfed claimed to have issued twenty million in Liberty dollars as part of its attempt to undermine U.S. paper currency with something better. The Southern Poverty Law Center reports that "Many of NORFED's redemption centers are run by men and women connected to the radical right. In Florida, the Tampa Freedom Center is headed up by Charles Eidson, an anti-Semite who last fall denounced the 'damnable eternal Jews.'"[41]

In November 2007, the FBI and the Secret Service raided the offices of Norfed, on the grounds that Norfed was seeking to produce a counterfeit currency and pass it off as the legal money of the United States of America.[42] It resulted in a case with the charming name *United States vs. 3039.375 Pounds of Copper Coins*.[43] Paul and his campaign had no official connection to Norfed, but "'people are pretty upset about this,' said Jim Forsythe, head of the Paul Meetup group in New Hampshire, who said he recently ordered one hundred fifty of the copper coins. 'The dollar is going down the tubes, and this is something that can protect the value of their money, and the Federal Reserve is threatened by that. It'll definitely fire people up.'"[44] In March 2011 the founder of Norfed, Bernard von NotHaus, was convicted of conspiracy and of counterfeiting: federal prosecutors seized seven million in "liberty dollars" and two tons of "Ron Paul dollars," which they hold to be counterfeit because they resemble U.S. coins.[45]

The Ron Paul electoral boom includes the election of his son, Rand Paul, as U.S. senator for Kentucky. Rand Paul has criticized the Civil Rights Act of 1964 as an invasion of private property. He believes not just in the gold standard and the need to abolish the Federal Reserve, but in a secret elite conspiracy to join with Mexico and Canada and impose a new currency, the "Amero." "It's not a conspiracy," Rand Paul claimed: "they're out in the open about it."[46] The "Amero" emerged from discussions among economists about whether or not a North American union, similar to the European union, might be a good idea: there is no plan to adopt such a union or introduce such currency. Nevertheless, the "Amero" attracts conspiracy theorist of all sorts: white supremacist radio host Hal Turner can be found on YouTube claiming that the U.S. government has covertly minted 800 million Ameros in preparation for the collapse of the dollar. A rogue Treasury official, he claims, clued him in.[47] The Amero lives not just in the fever swamps of the political fringe: the *Wall Street Journal's* online *Marketwatch* warned Americans in early 2009 that "The New World Order is upon us, full of hope, promise and a fair amount of fear." We cannot, wrote Todd Harrison, continue with our current money system: we cannot "continue to inject drugs that mask symptoms rather than address the disease."[48] The Amero, he warned, is growing more likely. Congressman Steve King of Iowa said, of the Amero, "My own view is that if you look at all of the signals that are there, look at the evidence that exists and all the dots, and you connect the dots, you can draw that picture."[49] In March 2009 Congresswoman Michelle Bachmann of Minnesota "introduced a resolution that would bar the dollar from being replaced by any foreign currency," partly to stave off the Amero.[50] The gold standard would prevent this kind of monetary mongrelization.

Rumors about the "Amero" coincided with the election of Barack Obama, the nation's first president of African American descent. While inspiring an inane national obsession with his birth certificate, Obama's election also caused a surge of interest in gold among right-wing activists. "Tune into Glenn Beck's Fox News show or his syndicated radio program," wrote Stephanie Mencimer in *Mother Jones*, "and you'll soon learn about the precarious state of the U.S. dollar, a currency on the verge of collapse due to runaway government spending, a ballooning national debt, and imminent Zimbabwe-style hyperinflation."[51] Beck advises his audience—numbered at the time at nearly three million—to rely on "the three G's: Gold, Guns, and God." The federal government is printing money as fast as it can, Beck warns, as part of its campaign to destroy liberty and introduce socialism. The best refuge against the coming apocalypse, he says, is gold. Beck likes to describe FDR's "confiscation act" as a warning: "Back in 1933, FDR said, 'Okay, we're going to take all your gold,' and he confiscated bullion and coins. But he did not take antique coins, 'collector coins,'" says Beck: such coins are even safer than gold bullion.

Beck's biggest advertiser, a gold trading firm named "Goldline International," sells exactly this sort of commemorative coin. The company buys advertising on Beck's program and pays him as a spokesperson. It then sells the gullible not gold bullion but coins alloyed with a lower percentage of gold, on which it takes a hefty markup. That is, it gets people to buy coins that cost more than the value of their gold content. No one would make such a purchase, Mencimer argues, unless ideology trumped reason.

Although some left-leaning radio talkers also promote gold, the affinity between right-wing politics, gold sales, and hostility to the Obama administration is overwhelming. Gold brokers form an advertising bloc behind virtually every right-wing media personality.[52]

Wes Vernon, blogging at RenewAmerica.com, suggests that in a second Obama administration, "the Dark Years will spread around the planet and could collapse the human future for decades, even centuries." He describes looters in the streets and "most people" huddled behind steel bars as roving gangs terrorize the countryside.[53] For more examples, interested readers can simply do a Google search for "Obama, gold inflation, collapse."

RenewAmerica references Craig R. Smith, who draws out the lurid scenario of apocalyptic collapse in his new book *Crashing the Dollar*. Smith, co-author, with Swift-boater Jerome Corsi, of *Black Gold Stranglehold*, is chairman of SwissAmerica Trading, another gold investment firm. He sells gold as "morally-correct money" and notes "Today the U.S. dollar is on the same trajectory as Obama's approval ratings, which have fallen one-third—from 65% to 45%—the lowest level since the election."[54] Gold is the opposite of an African American president: "morally-correct," naturally valuable and uninflated, and it barricades civilization itself. Smith says:

> Let's be brave enough to tell the truth here. . . . America's economy has been skyjacked. And it appears that the big-government crazies at the controls aim to crash the economy and the dollar. They aim to bring about a 'fundamental transformation' of the world in ways that will destroy everything America's founders made, every individual freedom our . . . Constitution enshrines, every opportunity our children were supposed to have in a free society.[55]

Like a character out of chapter 3, comparing greenbacks to "negro soldiers," Smith identifies paper money directly with Obama: it loses value as his popularity declines. And not just prices are at stake: world civilization itself hangs in the balance. Clearly talk about the gold standard involves more than just the value of money.

Fox News host Brian Kilmeade endorses gold trader Rosland Capital, along with G. Gordon Liddy, the Watergate burglar. Kilmeade tells their customers, "Gold is pure. Much like the motives, principles, and traditions of the men who founded our fine country."[56] Gold dealer Lear Capital, which sponsors Rush Limbaugh, Oliver North, Laura Ingram, and others, includes this poem on its website, denouncing the Federal Reserve for "dropping money from the sky":

> Can you hear the helicopters coming
> Sounds of choppers fill the sky
> Whirling birds of destruction
> This is how currencies die . . .
>
> Bernanke's dream is our nightmare
> His solution is our demise

Helicopters filled with money
Dropping from the skies[57]

There is, at this writing, little significant inflation related to the Fed's actions: quite the opposite. To counter the financial collapse of 2008, the Bush and Obama administrations revived Keynesian ideas and embarked on large-scale deficit spending. Despite large amounts of this government "stimulus" spending, the U.S. now appears much closer to a state of deflation.[58] But certain kinds of conservatives see inflation more broadly, as a general social collapse: they mean not fiscal inflation but the inflation of the wrong sort of people to office. For these conservatives, gold money equates closely to white dominance and inflation to the Obama administration.

Gold serves as the alternative. Ron Paul, once a crank, now holds a crucial position of leadership on banking. Fox News has guests arguing that a return to gold is already happening.[59] A German company is apparently making gold vending machines, so that you can insert your credit card and get back a small amount of gold; one of their machines has been installed in a Florida shopping mall. What you will do with one gram gold bars is unclear.[60] In late December 2010, a Georgia state representative introduced a bill to require that all transactions in Georgia take place in gold or silver only. Similar bills appeared in the South Carolina, Utah, and Montana state houses.[61]

Most historians are uncomfortable generalizing about the present. Good history requires the perspective of distance, and history has little predictive value. But it is hard to ignore the affinities between these arguments and previous debates about money and gold. I do not want to argue that all opposition to Obama stems from racial resentment: that would be reductive and unfair. But it seems important to point out how present-day political discourse echoes its grandparent. Inflation appears not just as higher prices but as a generalized destabilization of moral and social values of all sorts. The gold standard offers not just stable prices but the moral purity of the founding fathers and a fantasy of "natural" hierarchies.

*   *   *

This book celebrates the market's *potential*, its capacity for creativity and negotiation and innovation; its cosmopolitanism and multicultural-ism. The dynamic exchange of goods and ideas, the back and forth over meaning and value, lies at the heart of human creativity. The possibility of self-transformation forms the core of any reasonable notion of freedom. But this book also laments the failure of that promise. Again and again, Americans have responded to the possibility of market freedom by reinforcing and reasserting fantasies of intrinsic natural value. Why is "market freedom" so often coupled to genetic determinism? Why does "freedom" so often present itself as an inexorable set of rigid natural laws?

Markets are human institutions set up to serve human needs: they grow from and reflect the social values of the societies that produce them. They offer us ways to rethink and renegotiate our assumptions about value and character. But markets serve us, we do not serve them. We make market law, out of the constantly shifting, continually renegotiated dialogue we all engage in, everyday, about fairness, justice, profit, and individual initiative. Adam Smith argued over two hundred years ago that the major difference between human beings and animals came from our propensity to "truck, barter, and exchange," to trade and negotiate rather than simply take by force.

There are surely natural differences between us. The interesting, and unending negotiation is over what those differences mean. Making a free market genuinely free requires abandoning the gold fetish, and the golden fetters of natural law.

Notes

Introduction

1. Secret Service agent Andrew Drummond quoted in David R. Johnson, *Illegal Tender: Counterfeiting and the Secret Service in Nineteenth Century America* (Washington, D.C., 1995), 177.

2. On the toy money and the chocolate bar, see Johnson, *Illegal Tender*, 177. On the rug, see *Washington Post*, August 14, 1924. Lynn Glaser, *Counterfeiting in America: the History of an American Way to Wealth* (New York, 1968), 112, describes the Philadelphia baker.

3. Richard Powers, "American Dreaming: The Limitless Absurdity of our Belief in an Infinitely Transformable Future," in *The New York Times*, May 7, 2000, reported that on average, at all income levels, 85 percent of Americans "believe it is possible in America to be pretty much who you want to be."

4. See "Selling a Dream of Elegance and the Good Life," *Time*, September 1, 1968, pp. 56–57.

5. Johnson quoted in Jack P. Greene, *Imperatives, Behaviors, and Identities: Essays in Early American Cultural History* (Charlottsville, Va., 1992), 269.

6. This is a cultural history in the sense of the literary or "linguistic turn": it stems from cultural anthropology, particularly Geertz and Mary Douglas, and from Foucault's determination to "denaturalize" ideas of both progress and "the self." I assume that it is impossible to imagine a "financial interest" which is not also a set of ideas about race, and gender, and the possible natures of the self. I also assume that this makes "cause" a very suspect idea. The book also tends towards the "discursive" side of the empathic/discursive divide: it is less about people than about the "webs of signification," as Geertz put it, that they spin around themselves. See James W. Cook, Lawrence B. Glickman, and Michael O'Malley, eds., *The Cultural Turn in U.S. History: Past, Present, and Future* (Chicago, 2009).

Chapter One

1. Venture Smith, *Narrative of the Life and Adventures of Venture, a Native of Africa* (New London, Conn., 1798), 13. This text has been reproduced online at the North American Slave Narratives Collection at the Documenting the American South website (http://docsouth.unc.edu/neh/), a project of the university library at the University of North Carolina, Chapel Hill. The digital text preserves the original pagination. Subsequent references will be to this text, located at http://docsouth.unc.edu/neh/venture2/menu.html.

2. Olaudah Equiano, *The Interesting Narrative of the Life of Olaudah Equiano*, in Henry Louis Gates, ed., *The Classic Slave Narratives* (New York, 1987), 141–42. For another example see Moses Grandy, *Narrative of the Life of Moses Grandy, Late a Slave in the United States of America* (London, 1843), 17: "I asked my master what he would take for me. He wanted 800 dollars, and when I said that was too much, he replied, he could get 1000 for me any minute. Mr. Grice afterwards went with me to him: he said to him, that I had already been more profitable to him than any five others of his negroes, and reminded him that we had been playfellows; in this way he got him to consent to take 600 dollars for me."

3. Gavin Wright, *Slavery and American Economic Development* (Baton Rouge, La., 2006), 2.

4. David Eltis, *The Rise of African Slavery in the Americas* (Cambridge, Mass., 2000), 2.

5. Edmund Morgan, *American Slavery, American Freedom* (1975; reprint ed., New York, 2003); David Waldstreicher, *Runaway America: Benjamin Franklin, Slavery, and the American Revolution* (New York, 2005). For several years the author has asked freshman classes to search the online version of the *Pennsylvania Gazette* for the term "runaway" and compile a database of the results, which are nearly all ads for runaway slaves or indentured servants. The greatest revelation for the students, inevitably, is how little attention the ads pay to race until roughly a decade before the Revolution.

6. Equiano wrote his narrative in the late 1780s from memory. Its accuracy has come under fire, particularly the claim he makes of having been born in Africa and surviving the "middle passage." See Vincent Carretta, *Equiano the African: Biography of a Self-made Man* (Athens, Ga., 2005).

7. See Alden T. Vaughan, *Roots of American Racism: Essays on the Colonial Experience* (New York, 1995); Thomas Gossett, *Race: The History of an Idea in America* (1970; reprint ed., New York, 1997); Winthrop Jordan, *White Over Black* (Chapel Hill, N.C., 1968); Bruce Dain, *A Hideous Monster of the Mind: Race Theory in the Early Republic* (Cambridge, Mass., 2003).

8. See Jordan, *White Over Black*; Vaughan, *Roots of American Racism*, chap. 7; Betty Wood, *The Origins of American Slavery: Freedom and Bondage in the*

American Colonies (New York, 1998), chap. 1; and David Brion Davis, *Inhuman Bondage: The Rise and Fall of Slavery in the New World* (New York, 2008), chaps. 3–6.

9. Equiano, *Interesting Narrative*, 135.

10. Edwin Perkins, *The Economy of Colonial America* (New York, 1988), 200.

11. John Kenneth Galbraith, *Money: Whence it Came, Where it Went* (Boston, 1975); Niall Ferguson, *The Ascent of Money* (New York, 2008), 49–55; Eric Roll, *A History of Economic Thought* (London, 1973).

12. Joyce Oldham Appleby, *Economic Thought and Ideology in Seventeenth-Century England* (Princeton, 1978); Galbraith, *Money*, offers an elegant account of this transition; see also Roll, *History of Economic Thought*. For a massive account see Immanuel Wallerstein, *The Modern World-System*, vol. 2: *Mercantilism and the Consolidation of the European World-Economy, 1600–1750* (New York, 1980).

13. Carretta, *Equiano the African*, makes a strong case that this is not true—that Equiano was born in North America. For the purposes of this chapter it does not matter. Equiano was totally immersed in the world of capitalist exchange and knew how to deploy his race strategically within that world.

14. Daniel Defoe, *Review*, vol. 3 (January 1, 1706), 8.

15. Ibid., vol. 3 (January 5, 1706), 9–10.

16. Ibid., 9–10.

17. Ibid., vol. 6 (June 21, 1709), 134.

18. Ibid., vol. 3 (January 8, 1706), 13.

19. John Locke, "Some Considerations of the Consequences of the Lowering of Interest and the Raising the Value of Money" (1691), in *Locke on Money*, ed. P. H. Kelly (New York, 1991), 1:306–7.

20. *The Pennsylvania Gazette* refers to "a new species of paper, called Treasurer Notes" (December 24, 1783); "stagnation (almost) of every species of business" (August 23, 1786); different forms of paper money as "every species of public security" (July 20, 1791); and slaves as a "species of property" (June 27, 1792).

21. Dain, *Hideous Monster of the Mind*, chap. 1.

22. Defoe, *Review*, vol. 3 (January 5, 1706), 10.

23. Ibid., 16.

24. Equiano, *Interesting Narrative*, 108.

25. Ibid., 119, 122.

26. Ibid., 135–36.

27. On the rampant counterfeiting of the period, see Kenneth Scott, *Counterfeiting in Colonial America* (1957; reprint ed. Philadelphia, 2000) and Stephen Mihm, *A Nation of Counterfeiters: Capitalists, Con Men, and the Making of the United States* (Cambridge, Mass., 2007).

28. E. James Ferguson, "Currency Finance: An Interpretation of Colonial

Monetary Practices," *The William and Mary Quarterly*, 3d ser., 10, no. 2 (Apr. 1953): 153–80; Joseph Ernst, *Money and Politics in America, 1755–1775: A Study in the Currency Act of 1764 and the Political Economy of Revolution* (Chapel Hill, N.C., 1973); and Ernst, *Currency in the Era of the American Revolution: A History of Colonial Paper Money Practices and British Monetary Policies, 1764–1781*, vol. 1 (Madison, Wis., 1962).

29. Perkins, *Colonial American Economy*, 165–70.

30. Some economic historians doubt that there was ever a real "specie" drain. Though England consistently attempted to make gold flow into England, its attempts often failed. Some argue that the colonists merely experienced normal ebbs and flows in trade, and, with the propensity to whining so notable in colonial discourse, blamed it on England. See Ernst and Perkins, above. For our purposes here, the effect is the same—the colonists believed they lacked sufficient specie to do business, and they constantly sought new tools for easing exchange.

31. Herman E. Krooss, ed., *Documentary History of Banking and Currency in the United States* (New York, 1969), 1:4–13.

32. Equiano, *Interesting Narrative*, 148–49.

33. Philopatria, "A Discourse Showing the First Cause of the Straits and Difficulties of this Province of the Massachusetts Bay" (1721), in *Colonial Currency Reprints*, ed. Andrew McFarland Davis (New York, 1964), 2:284–85. According to Davis, the author was probably the Rev. Thomas Paine of Weymouth. I should note here that the pamphlet is not against paper money per se, only paper money not backed by specie. This is typical of colonial politics. As several historians have noted, colonial elites, debtors themselves to England, generally favored some forms of paper money.

34. Present-day libertarian economists similarly detest paper money's volatility: they also see the colonist's use of paper money as a sign of bad character. Murray Rothbard, in his admirably clear because woefully oversimplified *History of Money and Banking in the United States*, writes:

> Constant complaints, both by contemporaries and by some later historians, arose about an alleged "scarcity of money," especially of specie, in the colonies, allegedly justifying numerous paper money schemes to remedy that "shortage." In reality, there was no such shortage. It is true that England, in a mercantilist attempt to hoard specie, kept minting for its own prerogative and outlawed minting in the colonies; it also prohibited the export of English coin to America. But this did not keep specie from America. . . . Americans were able to import Spanish and other foreign coin. (50)

One wonders what "enough" money would mean—enough for who? Paper money does tend to cause "instability," rapid increases or decreases in price, that libertarians like to imagine a pure specie money would avoid.

35. Perkins, *Economy of Colonial America*, 169; Ferguson, "Currency Finance," 180 and passim.

36. Ferguson, "Currency Finance"; Claire Priest, "Currency Policies and Legal Development in Colonial New England," *Yale Law Journal* 110, no. 8 (June 2001): 1303–1405; Curtis Nettels, "British Policy and the Colonial Money Supply," *Economic History Review* 3, no. 2 (October 1931): 219–45; Ron Michener, "Backing Theories and the Currencies of Eighteenth-Century America: A Comment," *The Journal of Economic History* 48, no. 3 (September 1988): 682–92; G.L.M. Clauson, "The British Colonial Currency System," *The Economic Journal* 54, no. 213 (April 1944): 1–25.

37. See chapter 2. For examples of colonial paper money, see Eric P. Newman, *The Early Paper Money of America* (New York, 2008); and on paper currency see John McKusker, *Money and Exchange in Europe and America, 1600–1775* (Chapel Hill, N.C., 1992); Robert Chalmers, *A History of Currency in the British Colonies* (London, 1893).

38. Anonymous, "The Second Part of South Sea Stock, being an Inquiry into the Original of Province Bills, or Bills of Credit" (1721), in *Colonial Currency Reprints*, ed. Andrew McFarland Davis (New York, 1964), 2:313.

39. "The Representation and Remonstrance of HARD MONEY. Addressed to the People of America," *The United States Magazine; a Repository of History, Politics and Literature* 1 (January 1779): 28, 29.

40. Jennifer Baker, in *Securing the Commonwealth: Debt, Speculation and Writing in the Making of Early America* (Baltimore, 2007), argues that paper money "completely detached symbol and referent" (10); in that sense it was, she notes, like language itself—never, ever, the thing it describes. In barter value is tangible; two equivalences are exchanged. With gold or silver coins value is always imagined as physically present. But with paper money the tangible has fled the transaction and taken refuge somewhere else, somewhere, perhaps, close to pure imagination. Paper money, Baker continues, dramatizes how language can never seal the gap between representation and reality.

41. Equiano, *Interesting Narrative*, 144.

42. Benjamin Franklin, "A Modest Inquiry into the Nature and Necessity of a Paper Currency," in *Documentary History of Banking and Currency in the United States*, ed. Krooss, 1:24.

43. Franklin, "Modest Inquiry," 1:29.

44. Ibid., 30.

45. Ibid., 27.

46. Gordon Wood, *The Radicalism of the American Revolution* (New York, 1993), 251. Wood stresses how colonial America was relatively less developed, commercially, than England, in order to argue for the radical meaning of the American Revolution. My research sees financial innovation—wampum money, paper notes—as an early and consistent feature of the colonial experience.

47. Equiano, *Interesting Narrative*, 130.

48. Ibid., 124.

49. Venture Smith, *Narrative of the Life and Adventures of Venture, a Native of Africa* (New London, Conn., 1798).

50. Ibid., 17.

51. Ibid., 19.

52. Ibid., 20.

53. Ibid., 22.

54. The piece originally appeared in *American Museum*, July 1788. It is reprinted in Richard E. Amacher, "A New Franklin Satire?" in *Early American Literature* 7, no. 2 (Fall 1972): 104. Amacher believes Benjamin Franklin wrote the piece.

55. Smith, *Interesting Narrative*, 24. See David Waldstreicher, "The Vexed Story of Human Commodification Told by Benjamin Franklin and Venture Smith," *Journal of the Early Republic* 24, no. 2 (Summer 2004): 268–78; also Robert E. Desrochers Jr., "'Not Fade Away': The Narrative of Venture Smith, an African American in the Early Republic," *The Journal of American History* 84, no. 1 (June 1997): 40–66, and Philip Gould, "Free Carpenter, Venture Capitalist: Reading the Lives of the Early Black Atlantic," *American Literary History* 12, no. 4 (Winter 2000): 659–84.

56. Equiano, *Interesting Narrative*, 115.

57. Smith, *Narrative*, 28.

58. Equiano, *Interesting Narrative*, 240–41.

59. Ibid., 228.

60. Olaudah Equiano, *The Interesting Narrative and Other Writings*, ed. Vincent Carretta (New York, 1995), 332.

61. David R. Roediger, *The Wages of Whiteness: Race and the Making of the American Working Class* (New York, 1991), chap. 4.

62. Frederick Douglass, *Narrative of the Life of Frederick Douglass*, in *Classic Slave Narratives*, ed. Gates, 312–13, 325.

63. Linda Brent (Harriet Jacobs), *Incidents in the Life of a Slave Girl*, in *Classic Slave Narratives*, ed. Gates, 491.

64. Equiano, *Interesting Narrative and Other Writings*, ed. Carretta, 329–30.

65. Smith, *The Wealth of Nations* (New York, 1970), 1:31. It is hard to imagine how an innate desire to truck, barter, and exchange would serve any purpose in Smith's vision of the free market—once true natural law equilibrium was reached the rules of barter and exchange would become completely automatic, with no negotiation possible. The most direct way out of this problem would be to claim that no one ever really reaches their final nature, their true individual identity. But in that case there is no natural law authority for what people become, and so it is equally hard to imagine a lawful market. Another "way out" of

this paradox would be to claim that each generation is free to remake itself, or be remade, in the market—each man is born anew to make himself. Such a claim ignores the power of culture, especially of family, to make character. Smith wrote women out of the wealth of nations, because including women would have forced him to consider the role of nurture in generating difference. Smith seems finally unable, in *The Wealth of Nations*, to fully make up his mind. At times he describes the market itself producing difference, as when he admits that the difference between the street porter and the philosopher "seems to arise not so much from nature as from habit, custom and education." But at other times, he clearly imagines an intrinsic difference rooted in nature, a fundamental identity that the market liberates from the bondage of custom. In a society of shepherds, he speculates, "a particular person makes bows and arrows, for example, with more readiness and dexterity than any other," and so "naturally" "becomes a sort of armourer." Smith never really describes "habit, custom and education" making identity, and the fact that virtually no women contribute to *The Wealth of Nations* strongly suggests that nature, not nurture, makes difference.

66. Robert A. Gross, "The Confidence Man and the Preacher: The Cultural Politics of Shays's Rebellion," in *In Debt to Shays: The Bicentennial of an Agrarian Rebellion*, ed. Robert A. Gross (Charlottesville: University of Virginia Press, 1993), 303, 309.

67. Milton Friedman and Rose Friedman, *Free to Choose: A Personal Statement* (New York, 1980), 137.

Chapter Two

1. William Ogden Niles, *Niles' Weekly Register*, February 24, 1821, p. 429.

2. The exchange is described in Betty L. Fladeland, "Compensated Emancipation: A Rejected Alternative," *The Journal of Southern History* 42, no. 2 (May 1976): 169–86.

3. See Fladeland, "Compensated Emancipation." Lincoln's plan to compensate border state slaveowners proved an exception. See Andrew Weintraub, "The Economics of Lincoln's Proposal for Compensated Emancipation," *American Journal of Economics and Sociology* 32, no. 2 (April 1973): 171–77.

4. David R. Roediger, *The Wages of Whiteness: Race and the Making of the American Working Class* (New York, 1999), 12.

5. The money was initially loaned to England, in installments, by the House of Rothschild. See Kathleen Mary Butler, *The Economics of Emancipation: Jamaica and Barbados, 1823–1843* (Chapel Hill, N.C., 1995), 36–37.

6. The debate is admirably summarized in David Brion Davis, *Inhuman Bondage: The Rise and Fall of Slavery in the New World* (New York, 2006), 237–46. The central texts remain Eric Williams, *Capitalism and Slavery* (Char-

lottesville, Va., 1944) and Seymour Drescher, *Econocide: British Slavery in the Era of Revolution* (Pittsburgh, 1977). See also David Beck Ryden, "Does Decline Make Sense? The West Indian Economy and the Abolition of the Slave Trade," *Journal of Interdisciplinary History* 31, no. 3 (Winter 2001): 347–74.

7. See David Brion Davis, *The Slave Power Conspiracy and the Paranoid Style* (Baton Rouge, La., 1970).

8. Christopher Leslie Brown, *Moral Capital: Foundations of British Abolitionism* (Chapel Hill, N.C., 2006).

9. Davis, *Inhuman Bondage*, 246.

10. Charles Royster, *A Revolutionary People at War* (Chapel Hill, N.C., 1996), 271.

11. William B. Norton, "Paper Currency in Massachusetts during the Revolution," *The New England Quarterly* 7, no. 1 (March 1934): 688; doi:10.2307/359266.

12. Accounts of British counterfeiting often refer to A. Barton Hepburn's 1915 *History of Currency in the United States*, which was an extended version of a pro-gold standard history published in 1903. See Ben Baack, "Forging a Nation State: The Continental Congress and the Financing of the War of American Independence," *The Economic History Review* 54, no. 4, New Series (November 2001): 639–56, doi:10.2307/3091625.

13. *Pennsylvania Gazette*, July 19, 1786.

14. *Pennsylvania Gazette*, August 22, 1787.

15. Gordon Wood, *The Radicalism of the American Revolution* (New York, 1993), 249–50.

16. *Pennsylvania Gazette*, February 16, 1785.

17. See David P. Szatmary, *Shays' Rebellion: The Making of an Agrarian Insurrection* (Amherst, Mass., 1984); Leonard L. Richards, *Shays's Rebellion: The American Revolution's Final Battle* (Philadelphia, 2003); Robert Gross, ed., *In Debt to Shays: The Bicentennial of an Agrarian Rebellion* (Charlottesville, Va., 1993).

18. *The Pennsylvania Gazette*, October 4, 1786.

19. Joseph A. Ernst, "Shays's Rebellion in the Long Perspective: The Merchants and the 'Money Question,'" in Gross, ed., *In Debt to Shays*, 62.

20. See Drew R. McCoy, *The Elusive Republic: Political Economy in Jeffersonian America* (Chapel Hill, N.C., 1980).

21. Alexander Hamilton, "Treasury Report on the Establishment of a Mint, January 28, 1791," in Herman E. Krooss, ed., *Documentary History of Banking and Currency in the United States*, (New York, 1963), 1:95, 99, 100, 108.

22. Krooss, *Documentary History*, 1:106, 116.

23. Ibid., 118.

24. Alexander Hamilton to John Jay, March 14, 1779, quoted in Ron Chernow, *Alexander Hamilton* (New York, 2004), 64–65. See also Michael D. Chan,

"Alexander Hamilton on Slavery," *The Review of Politics* 66, no. 2 (Spring 2004): 207–31, and James Oliver Horton, "Alexander Hamilton: Slavery and Race in a Revolutionary Generation," *The New-York Journal of American History*, issue 3 (Spring 2004): 16–24.

25. John Kenneth Galbraith, *Money: Whence it Came, Where it Went* (Boston 1975), 30.

26. Galbraith, *Money*, 77.

27. Accounts of the Bank of England drawn from John H. Wood, *A History of Central Banking in Great Britain and the United States* (Cambridge, 2005), 8–59; Niall Ferguson, *The Ascent of Money* (New York, 2008); R. D. Richards, "The Evolution of Paper Money in England," *The Quarterly Journal of Economics* 41, no. 3 (May 1927): 361–404.

28. Lord Liverpool, quoted in Robert Chalmers, *History of Currency in the British Colonies* (London, 1893), 38.

29. Chernow, *Alexander Hamilton*, 201; Bray Hammond, *Banks and Politics in America from the Revolution to the Civil War* (1958; reprint ed., Princeton, N.J., 1991); Richard H. Timberlake, *Monetary Policy in the United States: An Intellectual and Institutional History* (Chicago, 1993), chap. 1.

30. Hamilton, quoted in Hammond, *Banks and Politics*, 36.

31. Hammond, *Banks and Politics*, 72, 144; Murray N. Rothbard, *A History of Money and Banking in the United States* (Auburn, Ala., 2002), 70.

32. William M. Gouge, *A Short History of Paper-money and Banking in the United States* (Philadelphia, 1833); William Graham Sumner, *A History of Banking in all the Leading Nations* (New York, 1896); A. Barton Hepburn, *A History of Currency in the United States* (New York, 1915).

33. Hammond, *Banks and Politics*; Galbraith, *Money*.

34. Milton Freidman and Anna Schwartz, *A Monetary History of the United States, 1867–1960* (Princeton, N.J., 1963); Rothbard, *History of Money and Banking*; Timberlake, *Monetary Policy in the United States*.

35. Anti-paper money broadsides, bearing extracts from various persons, dated 1786, 1787, 1811, 1816, 1819, 1832, 1837, 1840, all dealing with the burning question of the day, Philadelphia (1840). Library of Congress, American Memory, http://hdl.loc.gov/loc.rbc/rbpe.1540030c.

36. Jefferson to John Adams, January 24, 1814, in *The Writings of Thomas Jefferson* (Washington, D.C., 1907) 13:76–77.

37. William M. Gouge, *The Fiscal History of Texas, Embracing and Account of its Revenues, Debts and Currency* (Philadelphia, 1852), vii.

38. The anecdote about shinplasters appears in William Wells Brown, *Three Years in Europe; or, Places I have Seen and People I have Met* (London, 1852), 99–104.

39. Brown's life story appears in Brown, *Narrative of William W. Brown, a Fugitive Slave. Written by Himself* (Boston, 1847).

40. Richard G. Doty, *America's Money, America's Story* (Washington, D.C., 1998), 86–88, at 88.

41. Alice E. Smith, *George Smith's Money: A Wisconsin Investor in America* (Madison, Wis., 1966); Richard Sylla, "Forgotten Men of Money: Private Bankers in Early U.S. History," *Journal of Economic History* 36 (March 1976): 176–77.

42. Dean A. Dudley, "Bank Born of Revelation: The Kirtland Safety Society Anti-Banking Company," *The Journal of Economic History* 30, no. 4 (December 1970): 848–53.

43. Hammond, *Banks and Politics*, 626.

44. Sylla, "Forgotten Men of Money," 184.

45. Doty, *America's Money*, 107.

46. "Fiscal History of Texas," *DeBow's Review* 14, no. 4 (April 1853): 381.

47. Larry Schweikart, *Banking in the American South from the Age of Jackson to Reconstruction* (Baton Rouge, La., 1987), 80.

48. Antonio Blitz (Antonio Van Zandt), *Life and Adventures of Signor Blitz* (New York, 1872), 209.

49. Harold Glenn Moulton, *Principles of Money and Banking: A Series of Selected Materials* (Chicago, 1916), 175.

50. Roland P. Falkner, "The Private Issue of Token Coins," *Political Science Quarterly* 15, no. 2 (June 1901): 317. For a fuller account of the astonishing range and number of these, see Russell Rulau, *Hard Times Tokens* (Iola, Wis., 1992).

51. Galbraith, *Money*, 109.

52. Peter Temin, *The Jacksonian Economy* (New York, 1969), 33–37.

53. Printers could assemble a note-printing plate out of standard decorative motifs and features, and the customer would choose a design, as "Emperor" Brown did. Notes tended to have a limited, shared visual vocabulary.

54. See Lyn Glaser, *Counterfeiting in America* (New York, 1968), 104–5; Murray T. Bloom, *Money of their Own* (1957; reprint ed., Port Clinton, Ohio, 1982) 101–3.

55. Stephen Mihm, *A Nation of Counterfeiters: Capitalists, Con Men, and the Making of the United States* (Cambridge, Mass., 2007), 67.

56. Ibid., 65.

57. This figure appears in writings on counterfeiting by members of the American Numismatic Society, but without primary source attribution. See Lyn Glaser, *Counterfeiting in America* (New York, 1968), 104–5; Murray T. Bloom, *Money of their Own*, 101–3. Its accuracy, again, would be colored by the dubious nature of much of the paper money in circulation. Business journals like *Niles' Weekly Register* or *Banker's Magazine* make counterfeiting seem ubiquitous, as does the extraordinary number of "counterfeit detectors" described in William H. Dillistin, *Bank Note Reporters and Counterfeit Detectors, 1826–1866* (New York, 1949), 3–4. This remarkable monograph gives an extremely de-

tailed picture of the day-to-day mechanics of American business in the period. I strongly suspect the figure is more or less accurate, again depending on how speculative paper issues by local banks are regarded. See the table of banks and counterfeits given in Hepburn, *History of Coinage and Currency*, 160.

58. Allan Pinkerton, *Thirty Years a Detective* (New York, 1884), 518.

59. Herman Melville, *The Confidence-Man: His Masquerade* (1857), in *Pierre, Israel Potter, The Piazza Tales, The Confidence-Man, Billy Budd, Uncollected Prose*, ed. G. Thomas Tanselle, Library of America (New York, 1984), 1108–10. A really remarkable account of these curious texts appears in Dillistin, *Bank Note Reporters and Counterfeit Detectors*, cited above. Few historians have looked at counterfeit detectors: for an exception see David Henkin, *City Reading: Written Words and Public Spaces in Antebellum New York* (New York, 1998), chap. 6.

60. Robert Montgomery Bird, *Adventures of Robin Day* (Philadelphia, 1839), 123–25.

61. Larry Schweikert, *Banking in the American South from the Age of Jackson to Reconstruction* (Baton Rouge, La., 1987), 59.

62. Frank A. Montgomery, *Reminiscences of a Mississippian in Peace and War* (Cincinnati, 1901), 32.

63. Richard Doty, *Pictures From a Distant Country: Images on 19th Century U.S. Currency* (Raleigh, N.C., 2004), 58.

64. Richard Holcombe Kilbourne, *Debt, Investment, Slaves: Credit Relations in East Feliciana Parish, Louisiana, 1825–1885* (Baton Rouge, La., 1995), 8, 39, 56.

65. Michael Tadman, *Speculators and Slaves: Masters, Traders, and Slaves in the Old South* (Madison, Wis., 1996), 52.

66. Kilbourne, *Debt, Investment, Slaves*, 7.

67. Ibid., 60.

68. Tadman, *Speculators and Slaves*, 50.

69. Walter Johnson, *Soul by Soul: Life Inside the Antebellum Slave Market* (Cambridge, Mass., 1999), 25–26.

70. Schweikert, *Banking in the American South*, 59.

71. Daina Ramey Berry. "We'm Fus' Rate Bargain: Value, Labor, and Price in a Georgia Slave Community," in *The Chattel Principle: Internal Slave Trades in the Americas*, ed. Walter Johnson (New Haven, Conn., 2004), 64.

72. This is a complicated point. Slaves were clearly priced and rated, in individual sales and at auctions, according to their individual attributes, which might include temperament, strength, health, and other qualities not reducible to a single variable. But they also, in mortgage transactions, and in probate and bankruptcy proceedings, had an abstract monetary value. This is part of the peculiarity of the peculiar institution: slaves had a dual nature as individual laborers and as fixed "immovables" with an intrinsic value.

73. Johnson, *Soul by Soul*, 83.

74. Roger Ranson and Richard Sutch, "Capitalists Without Capital: The Burden of Slavery and the Impact of Emancipation," *Agricultural History* 62, no. 3 (Summer 1988): 134.

75. Alfred Holt Stone, "The Cotton Factorage System of the Southern States," *American Historical Review* 20, no. 3 (April 1915): 557, 559, 562.

76. Harold D. Woodman, *King Cotton and His Retainers* (Columbia, S.C., 1990) 135, quotes a Yankee traveler in 1835: "They sell cotton to buy negroes—to make more money to buy more negroes." The planter's "whole soul is wrapped up in the pursuit. It is, apparently the principle by which he lives, moves and has his being." Woodman stresses cotton, not slaves, as the source of credit, although he acknowledges that slaves formed a central part of the security the planter offered to the factor.

77. Stephen Deyle, *Carry Me Back: The Domestic Slave Trade in American Life* (New York, 2005), 40–41. See also Ralph V. Anderson and Robert E. Gallman, "Slaves as Fixed Capital: Slave Labor and Southern Economic Development," *The Journal of American History* 64, no. 1 (June 1977): 24–46.

78. Deyle, *Carry Me Back*, 60.

79. Ibid., 40.

80. Johnson, *Soul by Soul*, 25; see also footnote on 231.

81. Ferguson, *The Ascent of Money*, 49–55.

82. Galbraith, *Money*; Wood, *History of Central Banking*; Eric Helleiner, *The Making of National Money: Territorial Currencies in Historical Perspective* (Ithaca, N.Y., 2003), part 1.

83. Butler, *The Economics of Emancipation*, 30.

84. *DeBow's Review* 29, no. 6, (December 1860): 799.

85. Edward Rugemer, "The Southern Response to British Abolition," *Journal of Southern History* 70, no. 2 (May 2004): 221–48; Joe Wilkins, "Window on Freedom: South Carolina's Response to British West Indian Slave Emancipation, 1833–1834," *South Carolina Historical Magazine* 85, no. 2 (April 1984): 135–44.

86. George William Bagby, *Selections from the Miscellaneous Writings of Dr. George W. Bagby* (Richmond, Va., 1885), 174. This volume reprints essays published previously by Bagby. I have been unable to find the exact date of this essay. It was written before 1885, but it is not clear when. The general tone is of pre-Civil War nostalgia, which was Bagby's stock in trade, and it speaks of slaves and slavery in the U.S. as an existing institution, which suggests that it was written before the thirteenth amendment. It aims to recapture, at the very least, the antebellum mindset.

87. William Tappan Thompson, *Major Jones's Courtship and Travels* (Philadelphia, 1857), 28.

88. "Basis of Commercial Credit," *DeBow's Review* 16, no. 1 (January 1854): 79.

89. "Canaan Identified with the Ethiopian," *Southern Quarterly Review* 2, no. 4 (October 1842): 375.

90. Calhoun quoted in Lacy K. Ford, *Origins of Southern Radicalism: The South Carolina Upcountry, 1800–1860* (New York, 1988), 93.

91. "Money As An Institution," *DeBow's Review* 29, no. 1 (July 1860): 21–25.

92. John William Draper, *Thoughts on the Future Civil Policy of America* (New York, 1866).

93. L.S.M., "Negro-Mania," *DeBow's Review* 12, no. 5 (May 1852): 519–20.

94. Henry Hughes, *Treatise on Sociology* (Philadelphia, 1854), 240.

95. *American Journal of the Medical Sciences* 6 (1843): 255.

96. "Amalgamation," *DeBow's Review* 29 (July 1860): 3.

97. Josiah Nott and George Gidden, *Types of Mankind* (Philadelphia, 1855), 68.

98. "Abolition vs. Christianity and the Union," *The United States Magazine and Democratic Review* 27 (July 1850): 2.

99. The market for light-skinned slaves, and especially light-skinned female slaves, was mostly confined to coastal cities like New Orleans or Charleston. Light-skinned slaves might be sought as concubines but also to provide a sense of refinement at the table. But their lightness posed the problem of escape.

100. Joshua Rothman's *Notorious in the Neighborhood* demonstrates that in Virginia, before the 1830s, the color line was in fact much more fluid: it was possible for respectable light-skinned families to petition their way to legal whiteness. But by the 1850s Virginia had clamped down on this kind of move, and increasingly sought to harden the racial line between black and white. Rothman makes a strong case for the Nat Turner rebellion, and fear of rebellion generally, as the reason. It is tempting to suggest, and logically consistent to suggest, however, that the rise of "free banking" might have also been a cause. Attempts to legally define a "negro" as someone having "any negro blood at all" clearly reflect a desire to stabilize the nature of slaves and slavery.

101. Johnson, *Soul by Soul*, 25; see also footnote on 231.

102. Temin, *The Jacksonian Economy*, cited above; see Howard Bodenhorn, *A History of Banking in Antebellum America: Financial Markets and Economic Development in an Era of Nation-Building* (Cambridge, 2000); and *State Banking in Early America: A New Economic History* (New York, 2002).

103. Gavin Wright, *Slavery and American Economic Development* (Baton Rouge, La., 2006); Chandra Manning, *What This Cruel War Was Over: Soldiers, Slavery, and the Civil War* (New York, 2008).

104. Seba Smith, *Letters of Major Jack Downing of the Downingville Militia* (New York, 1864), 241.

Chapter Three

1. Frederick Douglass, "Address at a Meeting for the Promotion of Colored Enlistments," Philadelphia, July 6, 1863. Frederick Douglass Papers. Library of Congress, Manuscript Division, http://memory.loc.gov/ammem/doughtml/doughome.html.

2. William Augustus Berkey, *The Money Question: The Legal Tender Paper Monetary System of the United States* (Grand Rapids, 1878), 151. See also John Jay Knox, *A History of Banking in the United States* (New York, 1903), 747; William H. Dillistin, *Bank Note Reporters and Counterfeit Detectors, 1826–1866* (New York, 1949), 63–65, and *Congressional Record*, 43d Congress, 1st sess. (April 8, 1874): 2931.

3. Albion W. Tourgée, *A Fool's Errand* (New York, 1879), 158.

4. James Morris Morgan, *Recollections of a Rebel Reefer* (Boston, 1917), 327–28.

5. Bray Hammond, *Sovereignty and an Empty Purse: Banks and Politics in the Civil War* (Princeton, N.J., 1970); Richard G. Doty, *America's Money, America's Story* (Washington, D.C., 1998).

6. Hammond, *Sovereignty and an Empty Purse*; Richard Franklin Bensel, *Yankee Leviathan: The Origins of Central State Authority in America, 1859–1877* (Cambridge, 1990), chaps. 3–4.

7. John Pendleton Kennedy, *Annals of Quodlibet* (Philadelphia, 1840; reprint ed., Saddle River, N.J., 1970), 58–59.

8. Elbridge Gerry Spaulding, *A Resource of War—The Credit of the Government Made Immediately Available* (Buffalo, N.Y., 1869), 63.

9. Stephen D. Carpenter, *Logic of History: Five Hundred Political Texts: Being Concentrated extracts . . .* (New York, 1864), 325.

10. *New York Herald*, December 23, 1862.

11. Clement Vallandigham, *Speeches, Arguments, Addresses and Letters of Clement L. Vallandigham* (New York, 1864), 482–83.

12. Claudia Dale Goldin, *The Journal of Economic History* 33, no. 1 (March 1973): 66–85.

13. Vallandigham, *Speeches, Arguments*, 483.

14. An excellent account of Carey's economic thinking appears in Anthony F. C. Wallace, *Rockdale* (New York, 1978), 184–200. A contemptuous dismissal appears in Joseph Dorfman, *The Economic Mind in American Civilization* (New York, 1966), vol. 2, chap. 29. On Carey's influence, see Irwin Unger, *The Greenback Era* (Princeton, N.J., 1964), 50–58; and Robert Sharkey, *Money, Class and Party* (Johns Hopkins University Studies in Historical and Political Science, series 78, no. 2 [1959]), 153–56; Walter T. K. Nugent, *Money and American Society, 1865–1880* (New York, 1968) and *The Money Question During Reconstruction* (New York, 1967); Charles H. Levermore, "Henry C. Carey and his Social

System," *Political Science Quarterly* 5, no. 4 (December 1890): 553–82; and Rodney J. Morrison, "Henry C. Carey and American Economic Development," *Transactions of the American Philosophical Society* 76 (Philadelphia, 1986).

15. Edward Kellogg, *Labor and Other Capital: The Rights of Each Secured and the Wrongs of Both Eradicated* (New York, 1849), xv.

16. Ibid., 183–84.

17. Ibid., 65.

18. E. Bowers and Charles Glover, "How Are You Green-backs!" (Philadelphia, 1863). In Historic American Sheet Music, 1850–1920, American Memory, Library of Congress; http://scriptorium.lib.duke.edu/sheetmusic/b/b10/b1071/.

19. The extensive literature on the minstrel show and its ambiguities includes W. T. Lhamon, *Raising Cain: Blackface Performance from Jim Crow to HipHop* (Cambridge, Mass., 2000); Dale Cockrell, *Demons of Disorder: Early Blackface Minstrels and their World* (Cambridge, 1997); Eric Lott, *Love and Theft* (New York, 1995); Michael Paul Rogin, *Blackface, White Noise: Jewish Immigrants in the Hollywood Melting Pot* (Berkeley and Los Angeles, 1998); James Cook, *The Arts of Deception: Playing with Fraud in the Age of Barnum* (New York, 2001) and "Dancing Across the Color Line," *Common-Place* 4, no. 1 (October 2003) (http://www.common-place.org/vol-04/no-01/cook/); and David R. Roediger, *The Wages of Whiteness: Race and the Making of the American Working Class* (New York, 1991), chap. 4.

20. See Cook, "Dancing Across the Color Line"; Mathew Frye Jacobson, *Barbarian Virtues: The United States Encounters Foreign Peoples at Home and Abroad, 1876–1917* (New York, 2001), 15, 37.

21. *Pennsylvania Gazette*, September 20, 1786.

22. Stephen D. Carpenter, *Logic of History: Five Hundred Political Texts; Being Concentrated Extracts of Abolitionism; Also, Results, of Slavery Agitation and Emancipation; Together with Sundry Chapters On Despotism, Usurpations and Their Frauds* (Madison, Wis., 1864), 325.

23. On gold and circulation, see Walter Benn Michaels, *The Gold Standard and the Logic of Naturalism* (Berkeley and Los Angeles, 1988) and David Henkin, *City Reading: Written Words and Public Spaces in Antebellum New York* (New York, 1999), chap. 4.

24. Joseph G. Baldwin, *The Flush Times of Alabama and Mississippi: A Series of Sketches* (New York, 1858), 82.

25. William Gouge, "A Short History of Paper-Money and Banking in the United States" (1833), in *Documentary History of Banking and Currency in the United States*, ed. Herman E. Krooss (New York, 1983), 2:40. See also Benjamin G. Rader, "William M. Gouge: Jacksonian Economic Theorist," *Pennsylvania History* 30 (October 1963): 443–53.

26. "Monopoly and Paper Money," *The United States Democratic Review* 35, no. 6 (June 1855): 440.

27. George Pendleton, quoted in Alexander Harris, *A Review of the Political Conflict in America, from the Commencement of the Anti-slavery Agitation to the Close of Southern Reconstruction* (New York, 1876), 250.

28. *New York Herald*, October 18, 1862.

29. "Monopoly and Paper Money," *The United States Democratic Review* 35, no. 6 (June 1855): 440.

30. Edward Kellogg, *Labor and Other Capital* (1849), quoted in W. A. Berkey, *The Money Question* (Grand Rapids, Mich., 1876), 30.

31. Horace Greeley, *Essays Designed to Elucidate the Science of Political Economy* (New York, 1869), 68. Greeley had some reservations about a purely "irredeemable" paper currency, but was vague about what backed paper money if not gold. He wrote: "Between the bigotry which regards all Paper Money as virtually counterfeit, and the folly which would enrich a people by burying them in shinplasters, there is a happy medium" (80).

32. W. A. Croffut, "Resumption—Greenbacks At Par," *Bourbon Ballads (Songs for the Stump), Written for the New York Tribune by Mr. W. A. Croffut*, Extra no. 52 (1879); American Memory, Library of Congress.

33. Benjamin Franklin Butler, *Autobiography and Personal Reminiscences of Major-General Benj. F. Butler* (New York, 1892), 954.

34. "The Broker's 'Stamp Act' Lament" (July 1862); American Memory, Library of Congress.

35. *The New York Herald*, May 22, 1863.

36. "The Colored Brigade" (Philadelphia, n.d.); American Memory, Library of Congress.

37. *New York Herald*, May 22, 1863.

38. Albany, New York *Atlas and Argus*, January 19, 1863, quoted in Forrest G. Wood, *The Black Scare: The Racist Response to Emancipation and Reconstruction* (Berkeley and Los Angeles, 1970), 44.

39. J.M., "Who Will Care for Old Abe Now? A Parody" (New York, 1864); American Memory, Library of Congress.

40. William Kiernan, "I Am Fighting for the Nigger" (New York, n.d.); American Memory, Library of Congress.

41. "Political caricature. No. 3, "The Abolition Catastrophe. Or the November Smash-up" (New York, 1864); online at the Library of Congress, Prints and Photographs online catalogue; http://hdl.loc.gov/loc.pnp/cph.3a12905.

42. J. F. Feeks, "Shouting our Battle-cry, 'McClellan,'" *The Democratic Presidential Campaign Songster* (New York, 1864); American Memory, Library of Congress.

43. John A. McSorley, "McClellan Campaign Song" (New York, 1864); American Memory, Library of Congress.

44. *New York Herald*, March 6, 1863.

45. *New York Herald*, January 27, 1863.

46. Alexander Delmar, *The Great Paper Bubble, or, The Coming Financial Explosion* (New York, 1864), 54, 30.

47. Manning, *What This Cruel War Was Over: Soldiers, Slavery and the Civil War* (New York, 2008), 199.

48. Manning, *What This Cruel War Was Over*, 221, 123.

49. A much more negative account appears in Reid Mitchell, *Civil War Soldiers* (New York, 1988). Mitchell argues that white soldiers who saw black men in uniform felt their own status lowered. It is also true that minstrel shows were extremely common as entertainment in the Union camps.

50. For the general history of the greenbacks, see Unger, *The Greenback Era*; Sharkey, *Money, Class and Party*; and Nugent, *The Money Question During Reconstruction*.

51. Hugh McCulloch, *Men and Measures of Half a Century* (New York, 1888), 201.

52. Amasa Walker, "Governmental Interference with Standards of Value," *Bankers Magazine* (April 1867): 725.

53. Henry Adams and Francis A. Walker, "The Legal-Tender Act," *North American Review* 110 (April 1870): 321.

54. McCulloch, *Men and Measures*, 514.

55. *Congressional Globe*, 40th Congress, 3d sess. (February 5, 1869), 911.

56. Edward A. Pollard, *The Lost Cause Regained* (New York, 1868), 112–13.

57. James S. Pike, *The Prostrate State: South Carolina under Negro Government* (New York, 1874), 82–83, 35–36.

58. Grant quoted in Darcy Richardson, *Others: Third-Party Politics from the Nation's Founding to the Rise and Fall of the Greenback-Labor Party* (Lincoln, Neb., 2004), 577.

59. Butler deserves a good biography, something less dated than Hans Trefousse, *Ben Butler: The South Called him Beast!* (New York, 1957). He was at the forefront of a number of interesting issues: respectable people detested him, often a good sign.

60. Benjamin Franklin Butler and Jessie Ames Marshall, *Private and Official Correspondence of Gen. Benjamin F. Butler* (Norwood, Mass., 1917), 1:516.

61. Butler, *Autobiography and Personal Reminiscences of Major General Benjamin F. Butler: Butler's Book* (Boston, 1892), 494, 495.

62. On the ambiguity of "prostitute" as a term, see Judith Walkowitz, *Prostitution and Victorian Society* (Cambridge, 1980); Christine Stansell, *City of Women* (Bloomington, Ill. 1987); Kathy Peiss, *Cheap Amusements* (Philadelphia, 1986).

63. Butler, *Butler's Book*, 1036–37.

64. Armstrong, reprinted in *A Documentary History of Reconstruction*, ed. Walter L. Fleming (Cleveland, 1907), 2:434–35.

65. *Congressional Record*, 43d Congress, 1st sess. (January 31 1874), 1089.

66. William C. Harris, *The Day of the Carpetbagger* (Baton Rouge, La., 1979), 291–94; *Congressional Record*, 43d Congress, 1st sess., Appendix (May 22, 1874), 3.

67. Ruth Watkins, "Reconstruction in Marshall County," *Publications of the Mississippi Historical Society* 12 (1912): 198.

68. Linton Stephens, reprinted in Alexander H. Stephens, *The Reviewers Reviewed* (New York, 1872), 245–46.

69. *The Nation* 5 (August 1, 1867): 90. For *The Nation*'s bullionist views, see below.

70. *Congressional Record*, 43d Congress, 1st sess. (April 7, 1874), 2880.

71. Quoted in Eric Foner, *Reconstruction: America's Unfinished Revolution* (1988; New York, 2002), 499.

72. Joseph Story, *Commentaries on the Constitution of the United States* (1833; Boston, 1873), 2:254.

73. *Knox v. Lee* and *Parker v. Davis*, 79 U.S. 457 (1870).

74. *Congressional Record*, 43d Congress, 1st sess. (April 9, 1874), 2973.

75. Mark Emory Elliott, *Color Blind Justice: Albion Tourgée and the Quest for Racial Equality from the Civil War to Plessy v. Ferguson* (New York, 2006), 191.

76. *Congressional Record*, 43d Congress, 1st sess. (January 21, 1874), 801.

77. *Congressional Record*, 43d Congress, 1st sess. (May 22, 1874), Appendix 316.

78. David R. Locke (Petroleum V. Nasby), *The Struggles of Petroleum V. Nasby* (Boston, 1888), 398. The same theme appears in Edward Eggleston's 1873 novel *The Mystery of Metropolisville*, in which a French character, married to a Native American, seeks to "whiten" his daughters. He realizes that his wealth will do the trick, for "Money should wash them also, or at least money should bleach their descendants. For money is the Great Stain-eraser, the Mighty Detergent, the Magic Cleanser." Edward Eggleston, *The Mystery of Metropolisville* (New York, 1873), 128.

79. Charles Francis Adams, "The Currency Debate of 1873–1874," *North American Review* 119 (July 1874): 132.

80. 79 U.S. 457.

81. *Congressional Record*, 43d Congress, 1st sess. (January 31, 1874), 1099. Two months after this speech Mellish died in an insane asylum. "He devoted himself almost exclusively to the study of the currency," noted Garfield, "became fully entangled with the theories of the subject and became insane." That other colleagues drew the same conclusion reveals a great deal about the nature of the money debate. Mellish also supported civil rights. Garfield quoted in Allen Weinstein, *Prelude to Populism: Origins of the Silver Issue, 1867–1878* (New Haven, Conn., 1970), 244.

82. *Congressional Record*, 43d Congress, 1st sess. (April 9, 1874), 2967.

See also March 10, 1874, 2099. Boutwell cited in Sharkey, *Money, Class and Party*, 71.

83. *Congressional Record*, 43d Congress, 1st sess. (March 27, 1874), 2546.

84. Fitzhugh quoted in Ann Fabian, *Card Sharps and Bucket Shops: Gambling in Nineteenth-Century America* (New York, 1999), 127. "What's to be done with the Negroes?" *DeBow's Review* 1 (June 1866): 580.

85. The cartoon appears in David A. Wells, *Robinson Crusoe's Money* (New York, 1876), 97. Foner, *Reconstruction*, gives a good example of Nast's changed vision. See illustrations facing page 386.

86. Wells, *Robinson Crusoe's Money*, 97.

87. David A. Wells, *Practical Economics* (New York, 1894), 52–53.

88. Wells, *Robinson Crusoe's Money*, 52. See also Walter Benn Michaels's description of Wells's book in *The Gold Standard and the Logic of Naturalism*, 145–50.

89. For good examples, see Francis A. Walker, *Money* (New York, 1883), 24–43, 31–34, and *Political Economy* (New York, 1887), 122–27; Walter T. K. Nugent, *Money and American Society, 1865–1880* (New York, 1968), 89–90. Greenbackers also used the same progression, arguing that legal tender represented its next logical step; see William A. Berkey, *The Money Question*, 27–28.

90. *Congressional Record*, 43d Congress, 1st sess. (January 6, 1874), 410.

91. Michael Perman, *The Road to Redemption: Southern Politics, 1869–1879* (Chapel Hill, N.C., 1984), 271–72.

92. See Alexander Campbell, *The True Greenback, or The Way to Pay the National Debt without Taxes, and Emancipate Labor* (Chicago, 1868).

93. Mark A. Lause, *The Civil War's Last Campaign: James B. Weaver, the Greenback-Labor Party, and the Politics of Race and Section* (Lanham, Md., 2001), 39.

94. Stephen Hahn, *A Nation Under Our Feet: Black Political Struggles in the Rural South from Slavery to the Great Migration* (Cambridge, Mass., 2003), 395–97.

95. Historians generally overlook the Greenback Party in favor of its more rustic and easily classified child, the Populist Party. See Gretchen Ritter, *Goldbugs and Greenbacks: The Antimonopoly Tradition and the Politics of Finance in America, 1865–1898* (Cambridge, 1997). The extensive historiographical debate over the Populists' commitment to racial equality is summarized in Lawrence Goodwyn, *Democratic Promise: The Populist Moment in America* (New York, 1976), and Bruce Palmer, *"Man over Money": The Southern Populist Critique of American Capitalism* (Chapel Hill, N.C., 1980), and most recently Charles Postel, *The Populist Vision* (New York, 2007).

96. Charles Francis Adams, "The Currency Debate of 1873–1874," *North American Review* 119 (July 1874): 117.

97. *The Nation* 18 (April 16, 1874): 246, 247. On the Liberal Republicans and

their rejection of racial equality, see Foner, *Reconstruction*, 488–511, 526–29, and John G. Sproat, *The Best Men: Liberal Reformers in the Gilded Age* (New York, 1968), 11–44.

98. "The Negro Problem," *DeBow's Review* 5 (March 1868): 252.

99. Albert Gallatin Riddle, *The Life of Benjamin Wade* (Cleveland, 1886), 288.

100. *Washington Post*, January 27, 1880.

101. Mark Twain and Charles Dudley Warner, *The Gilded Age: A Tale of Today* (New York, 1969), 333, 59; Jean Baker, *Affairs of Party: The Political Culture of Northern Democrats in the Mid Nineteenth Century* (Ithaca, N.Y., 1983), 256.

Chapter Four

1. Frederick Perry Powers, "A Financial Catechism," *Sound Currency* 2 (May 1895): 3. The author likes this quote, having written a book previously on the invention of standard time and daylight saving. In fact the government *can* regulate the length of day and night: not in a cosmological sense, but in every other sense that matters. Twice a year, people convince themselves that while they slept the clocks moved forward or back an hour, and that the sun is now staying up later or rising earlier. It is an example, very much like paper money, of the representation—the clock—becoming the thing it represents.

2. Francis A. Walker, *Money in its Relations to Trade and Industry* (New York, 1889), 242–43.

3. Henry Adams, *The Education of Henry Adams* (1907), in *Novels, Mont Saint Michel, The Education: Democracy, Esther, Mont Saint Michel and Chartres, The Education of Henry Adams, Poems*, ed. Ernest Samuels, Library of America (New York, 1993), 947.

4. Francis A. Walker, *Money and Banking* (1895; reprint ed., Boston, 1902), 13.

5. On the multiplication of commodities, see Miles Orvell, *The Real Thing: Imitation and Authenticity in American Culture, 1880–1940* (Chapel Hill, N.C., 1989).

6. Marc Shell, *Art and Money* (Chicago, 1995), and *Money, Language and Thought* (Baltimore, 1993).

7. Chester Krause and Robert E. Lemke, *Standard Catalogue of U.S. Paper Money*, 9th ed. (Iola, Wis., 1990), 17.

8. Lawrence W. Levine, *Highbrow/Lowbrow: The Emergence of Cultural Hierarchy in America* (Cambridge, Mass., 1988), 160.

9. F. Scott Fitzgerald, *The Great Gatsby* (1924; reprint ed. New York, 2004), 2.

10. Ben Singer, *Melodrama and Modernity: Early Sensational Cinema and its Contexts* (New York, 2001), p. 8, and ch. 3.

11. The idea of a "crisis in subjectivity" at the turn of the nineteenth century is well established in the historical literature. See for example Orvell, *The Real Thing*; Gail Bederman, *Manliness and Civilization* (Chicago, 1996); Kristen Hoganson, *Fighting for American Manhood* (New Haven, Conn., 2000); Matthew Frye Jacobson, *Barbarian Virtues: The United States Encounters Foreign Peoples at Home and Abroad* (New York, 2000).

12. John Kasson, *Houdini, Tarzan and the Perfect Man: The White Male Body and the Challenge of Modernity* (New York, 2002).

13. Charlotte Perkins Gilman, *Women and Economics: A Study of the Economic Relation Between Men and Women as a Factor in Social Evolution* (Boston, 1900), 4.

14. Ibid., 5.

15. Ibid., 43.

16. Ibid., 77–78. The metaphor of the corset is hardly accidental—throughout *Women and Economics* Gilman stresses the relation between gender inequality and consumer goods designed to associate women with consumption instead of production.

17. This is a pun on Luce Iragary's argument on *The Sex Which is Not One*, but not simply a pun. We might conclude the Gilman's *Herland*, and her vision of reproduction without exchange, recalls Iragary's construction of female sexuality as "self-referential."

18. Charlotte Perkins Gilman, *Herland* (1915) in *The Yellow Wall-Paper, Herland, and Selected Writings*, ed. Denise D. Knight (New York, 1987). The only true value in marriage, she was forced to claim, lay in women's "great position as selector of the best among competing males," through which women could "improve the race through right marriage." In this "true love" would appear (*Women and Economics*, 92). Gilman meant the human race, not the Anglo-Saxon race. But she located the final value in genetics, and a supposed "natural," quasi-Darwinian tendency towards selection of the best.

19. Walter Benn Michaels, *The Gold Standard and the Logic of Naturalism: American Literature at the Turn of the Century* (Berkeley and Los Angeles, 1987), chap. 5.

20. On the intensification of racism in the 1890s, see Joel Williamson, *A Rage for Order* (New York, 1986), esp. chap. 4; Amy Louise Wood, *Lynching and Spectacle: Witnessing Racial Violence in America, 1890–1940* (Chapel Hill, N.C., 2009); Robert Rydell, *All the World's a Fair* (Chicago, 1984); and Alexander Saxton, *The Rise and fall of the White Republic* (New York, 1990). The emphasis on race appears everywhere in this period, from Richard Hofstadter's "Social Darwinism" to Theodore Roosevelt's confusion of natural and human

history in *The Winning of the West* (New York, 1889–96), to Thomas Dixon's bestsellers enshrining the Klan.

21. Irwin Unger, *The Greenback Era* (Princeton, N.J., 1964), and Robert Sharkey, *Money, Class and Party*, Johns Hopkins University Studies in Historical and Political Science, ser. 78, no. 2 (1959).

22. Walter T. K. Nugent, *Money and American Society, 1865–1880* (New York, 1968), chaps. 12 and 13.

23. Ibid., 89.

24. "'The Dollar of our Daddies' is the name that has been popularly and affectionately bestowed upon the silver coin which is now occupying so large a share of public attention." "The Silver Dollar," *The Illustrated American* 6 (March 7, 1891): 145.

25. Nugent, *Money in American Society*, still offers the best survey of monetary policy in the period. For an admirably concise account, see Susan Hoffman, *Politics and Banking: Ideas, Public Policy, and the Creation of Financial Institutions* (Baltimore, 2001); and Gretchen Ritter, *Goldbugs and Greenbacks: The Antimonopoly Tradition and the Politics of Finance in America, 1865–1898* (Cambridge, 1997).

26. Richard Timberlake, *Monetary Policy in the United States: An Intellectual and Institutional History* (Chicago, 1993), 147.

27. Irving Fisher, *Why is the Dollar Shrinking? A Study in the High Cost of Living* (New York, 1915), 130–35.

28. Milton Friedman and Anna Schwartz, *A Monetary History of the United States, 1867–1960* (Princeton, N.J., 1963), 89–134.

29. Friedman and Schwartz, *Monetary History of the United States*, 119: "The gold standard had finally triumphed."

30. Maurice L. Muhleman, *Monetary Systems of the World* (New York, 1895), 19. The United States Notes were the greenbacks issued during the Civil War. About $345 million worth of them remained by law in circulation. Gold and silver certificates were redeemable in those respective metals, but Treasury notes were a peculiar hybrid. Issued by the government to pay for silver bullion following the Sherman Silver Purchase Act of 1890, they were redeemable in gold. It is also clear that by 1896 demand deposits, or checking accounts, accounted for roughly 90 percent of business transactions.

31. *New York Times*, April 5, 1891.

32. *New York Times*, May 19, 1891; Murray Teigh Bloom, *Money of their Own* (Port Clinton, Oh., 1982), 38; *New York Times*, May 17, 1892.

33. *New York Herald*, April 2, 1896. The *Herald* claimed the hand-drawn, pen-and-ink notes had reached the Subtreasury in 1880, which is two years before Ninger arrived. It is possible more than one person was drawing counterfeits by hand. It seems highly unlikely that one of the bills was canceled at the Treasury Department, but the story highlights the general anxiety about authenticity.

34. Ninger told the Secret Service that it took him two to three weeks to make a note, working three hours a day. Murray Teigh Bloom, a journalist and numismatist who has made the most detailed study of Ninger's life, suggests that he made as many as five or six a month. See Bloom, *Money of their Own*, 40. On Ninger's hero status, see the *New York Sun*, April 4, 1896.

35. Secret Service Division, United States Treasury Department, "Daily Reports of United States Secrets Service Agents," Report of William P. Hazen, April 1, 1896, p. 3 (marked p. 1253 on microfilm reel). In National Archives, Washington National Records Center, Suitland, Md. Hereafter abbreviated as "SSD," with original page number first and microfilm frame number in parentheses following.

36. SSD, report of Hazen, 5 (1261).

37. Ninger told the agents that he first took high-quality bond paper, soaked it in a solution of weak coffee so it looked worn, then placed the wet blank sheet over a real note. He traced the general outlines with a sharp lead pencil, then went over the tracings with pen, ink, and brush after the new bill had dried.

38. SSD, Report of G. Raymond Bagg, 4–6 (1276–78); report of Hazen, 13 (1285).

39. SSD, Report of Hazen, 13–14 (1285–86).

40. "Jim the Penman" was James Townsend Saward, a working barrister who also led a check-forging ring in London in the 1850s. But "Jim the Penman" was also the title of "one of the greatest triumphs in the history of the New York stage," a society drama by Charles L. Young. Young's version of Saward's career imagined "Jim" as part of an international forgery ring, a man of outward respectability who forged letters to marry under false pretenses. The play ran in New York in 1886–87 and was running in Boston at the time of Ninger's arrest. Quote above from George C. D. O'Dell, *Annals of the New York Stage*, vol. 13 (New York, 1942), 217. Thanks to Jay Cook for this reference. On Saward, see George Dilnot ed., *The Trial of Jim the Penman* (London, 1930), and Charles L. Young, *Jim the Penman: A Romance of Modern Society* (New York, 1912).

41. *New York Herald*, April 2, 1896; *New York Press*, April 2, 1896; *New York Sun*, April 5, 1896.

42. Thomas Byrnes, *Professional Criminals of America* (New York, 1886).

43. Elaine Abelson, *When Ladies Go A–Thieving: Middle Class Shoplifters in the Victorian Department Store* (New York, 1989), 135.

44. Cesare Lombroso, *L'Homme criminel* (Paris, 1895); Abelson, *When Ladies go A–Thieving*, 136–38.

45. Stephen Jay Gould, *The Mismeasure of Man* (New York, 1981), 30–72.

46. Ysabel Rennie, *The Search for Criminal Man* (Lexington, Mass., 1978), 74; Cynthia Eagle Russett, *Sexual Science: The Victorian Construction of Womanhood* (Cambridge, Mass., 1989), 74.

47. Arthur MacDonald, *Criminology* (New York, 1893), 41, and *Abnormal*

Man (Washington, D.C., 1893), 94. Lombroso's introduction to MacDonald's *Criminology* (iv) notes that his work has taken deeper root in the U.S. than in Europe. See also Russett, *Sexual Science*, 73-74.

48. On the history of the Secret Service, see David R. Johnson, *Illegal Tender: Counterfeiting and the Secret Service in Nineteenth Century America* (Washington, D.C., 1995). Charles E. Rosenberg, *The Trial of the Assassin Guiteau: Psychiatry and Law in the Gilded Age* (Chicago, 1968), 224, points out that Charles J. Guiteau's 1881 trial for the assassination of President James A. Garfield became a national test-case for, among other things, the virtues of criminal anthropology.

49. Though these were never without room for environmental factors. Rosenberg, *Trial of the Assassin Guiteau*, 244-48.

50. Ninger was unique in many ways. Most counterfeiters worked in gangs, and used mechanical means. Even in cases where an obsessive "artist" took charge of the actual production of plates and notes—fairly common in instances of counterfeiting—he usually received financial backing from a ring, who were needed to pass the bills effectively. See Bloom, *Money of their Own*, passim. For a modern example, see Charles Black and Michael Horsnell, *Counterfeiter* (New York, 1989).

51. Rosenberg, *Trial of the Assassin Guiteau*, 244; Abelson, *Ladies Go A-Thieving*, 184-96. Manias might also be treatable, which would suggest not a biological but a social cause. But in the popular culture of the late nineteenth century as well as in much formal psychiatric literature they tended to be linked with biological essentialism—Abelson notes especially how often manias were connected to women's anatomy by men like S. Weir Mitchell and George Beard.

52. John Higham, *Strangers in the Land* (New Brunswick, N.J., 1955), chap. 6; Gwendolyn Mink, *Old Labor and New Immigrants in American Political Development* (Ithaca, N.Y., 1986), chap. 4.

53. Francis A. Walker, "Restriction of Immigration," *The Atlantic Monthly* 77 (January 1896): 828; Walker, *Money in its Relations to Trade and Industry* (New York, 1889), 47.

54. On Fairchild and the alleged "racial parsimony" of immigrants, see Katrina Irving, *Immigrant Mothers: Narratives of Race and Maternity, 1890-1925* (Chicago, 2000), chap. 3.

55. Matthew Frye Jacobson, *Barbarian Virtues*, 37.

56. Ross coined the term "underlive" late in the nineteenth century and used it multiple times. The quote above comes from Edward Alsworth Ross, *The Changing Chinese: The Conflict of Oriental and Western Culture in China* (New York, 1911), 47.

57. Irving, *Immigrant Mothers*, 58.

58. Frank Norris, *McTeague* (1899; reprint ed. New York, 1986), 358.

59. Walter Benn Michaels, *The Gold Standard and the Logic of Naturalism*, 153.

60. See Charles McGovern, *Sold American: Consumption and Citizenship, 1890–1945* (Chapel Hill, N.C., 2006), part 1.

61. The test questions given to the Army in World War I appear in Robert Mearns Yerkes, ed., *Psychological Examining in the United States Army* (Washington, D.C., 1921); examples taken from 213 and 234.

62. Madison Grant, *The Passing of the Great Race* (New York, 1916), 81.

63. *New York Sun*, April 4, 1896; *New York Herald*, April 6, 1898.

64. Thomas Byrnes, chief of New York City Police Detective Bureau, first introduced forensic photography to America in the early 1880s, in his famous "rogues gallery." Byrnes had mixed feelings about the connection between appearance and criminality. A reporter asked, "Is physiognomy any guide?" and Byrnes replied, "a very poor one." But he also argued that popular opinions of criminals' appearance were not all wrong, and that experienced men could see a propensity to crime, especially in "low" criminals. Thomas Byrnes, *Professional Criminals of America* (1886; reprint ed. New York, 1969), 55. On the introduction of forensic detection in Europe and America, see Jürgen Thorwald, *The Century of the Detective* (New York, 1964), esp. 90–103. Thorwald claims that as late as 1900 American law enforcement agencies relied on versions of Bertillon's system of identification, a painstaking filing method that demanded a number of measurements and classifications of facial and body size and shape.

65. Secret Service Division, United States Treasury Department, *Description and Information of Criminals*, v. 25, p. 544. Ninger's file did not include fingerprints. Francis Galton's pioneering work on fingerprinting did not appear in the United States until 1892, and apparently the Secret Service was slow to adopt the new techniques, which were not generally accepted in American courts until after 1910—although Mark Twain had anticipated their use in *Life on the Mississippi* and *Puddin'head Wilson*. See Thorwald, *Century of the Detective*, 90–103. The Secret Service began keeping its descriptions of criminals between 1869 and 1874. See above and Walter S. Bowen and Harry Edward Neal, *The United States Secret Service* (Philadelphia, 1960), 147.

66. Alan Sekula, "The Body and the Archive," *October* 39 (Winter 1986): 3–64.

67. American Mutascope and Biograph Company, A. E. Weed, cameraman, *A Subject for the Rogues's Gallery* (1904), in the Paperprint collection, Motion Picture and Recorded Sound Division, Library of Congress, Washington, D.C. Tom Gunning, "Tracing the Individual Body: Photography, Detectives and the Early Cinema," in *Cinema and the Invention of Modern Life*, ed. Leo Charney and Vanessa Schwartz (Berkeley and Los Angeles, 1995), 15–45.

68. Simon Cole, *Suspect Identities: A History of Fingerprinting and Criminal Identification* (Cambridge, Mass., 2002), 63–70, 106, and passim. For a more de-

tailed account of the Indian case, see Chandak Sengoopta, *Imprint of the Raj: How Fingerprinting was Born in Colonial India* (London, 2003).

69. Alfred Frankenstein, *After the Hunt: William Harnett and other American Still Life Painters, 1870-1900* (Berkeley and Los Angeles, 1975), 117.

70. Frankenstein, *After the Hunt*; Doreen Bolger, Marc Simpson, and John Wilmerding, *William M. Harnett* (New York, 1992); and Wilmerding, *Important Information Inside: The Art of John F. Peto and the Idea of Still-Life Painting in Nineteenth-Century America* (Washington, D.C., 1983). The Secret Service may have been right in this suspicion, since according to Bloom, *Money of Their Own*, 47-48, the Treasury's files held pen-and-ink notes which predated Ninger's 1882 arrival in America.

71. For a similar interpretation, see Bruce Chambers, *Old Money: American Trompe L'Oeil Images of Currency* (New York, 1988), 67-77. Chambers offers the most comprehensive account of the money painters; see also Edward Nygren, "The Almighty Dollar: Money as a Theme in American Painting," *Winterthur Portfolio* 23 (Summer/Autumn 1988): 129-50. Nygren notes the similarity between the painted "frame" with its portraits of the presidents and similar iconography in lithographs by Currier and Ives, among others.

72. Levine, *Highbrow/Lowbrow*, 219-31.

73. John Ruskin, "The Political Economy of Art" (1857), in *Unto this Last and Other Essays* (London, 1907), 14. Ruskin argued gracefully for a "higher" standard of evaluation than money or market forces, but in this he echoed the gold bug claims about the intrinsic or essential value of certain standards of reference.

74. *New York World*, April 2, 1896.

75. Chambers, *Old Money*, 67.

76. Quote from Hoffman, *Politics and Banking*, 109. Richard Hofstadter, in *The Age of Reform*, emphasized the silverites' tendency towards anti-Semitism and racism: he treated silver as part of a "paranoid style " in American life. I would agree with Hofstadter about silverites, but point out that gold bugs were just as bad or likely worse. James Livingston, in *Origins of the Federal Reserve System: Money, Class and Corporate Capitalism* (Ithaca, N.Y., 1986) and in *Pragmatism and the Political Economy of Cultural Revolution* (New York, 1994), argues that late nineteenth-century capitalists fought a losing battle against unions and conservative forces who understood subjectivity in a more limited way. Most historians, he argues, tend to a sentimental sympathy with Careyite, Populist "republicanism," which Livingston sees as retrograde. In his account the gold bugs understood the industrial economy correctly. But Livingston has absolutely no interest in, or explanation for, the overwhelming presence of racially charged language in gold bug arguments. Hoffman notes the pervasive emphasis on "natural law" in gold bug arguments but does not connect it to the ways "natural law" worked in other realms.

77. George H. Yeaman, "A Currency Primer," *Sound Currency* 3 (February 15, 1896): 4 and 5. A group of wealthy businessmen and economists, "The Sound Currency Committee of the Reform Club," published *Sound Currency* as an answer to popular arguments for silver and greenbacks. On its extraordinary reach and effectiveness, see James Livingston, *Origins of the Federal Reserve*, 98–100.

78. Charles H. Swan Jr., *Monetary Problems and Reforms* (New York, 1897), 12.

79. Austin W. Wright, "Unwarranted Government Interference," *Sound Currency* 3 (September 15, 1896): 4.

80. Quoted in William A. Williams, ed., *The Shaping of American Diplomacy* (New York, 1956), 429–30

81. Walker, *Money in its Relation to Trade and Industry*, 69, 141; see also 20–25.

82. Josiah Patterson quoted in *Sound Currency* 2 (October 1, 1895): 446.

83. William L. Trenholm, "The People's Money," *Sound Currency* 2 (Mar 1, 1895): 288.

84. Edward Wisner, *Cash vs. Coin* (Chicago, 1895), 6.

85. Trenholm, "The People's Money," 386.

86. On the peculiarity of gold bug arguments, see also Walter Benn Michaels, *The Gold Standard and the Logic of Naturalism*, especially the title essay, which suggests that most gold bugs fantasized gold's final removal from circulation—its value as money stabilized by its never actually being used as money.

87. Mink, *Old Labor and New Immigrants*, 97.

88. Ibid., 125–26; see also Alexander Saxton, *The Indispensable Enemy: Labor and the Anti-Chinese Movement in California* (Berkeley and Los Angeles, 1971); Higham, *Strangers in the Land*, chap. 6.

89. A. J. Philpott, ed., *The White Elephant* (Boston, 1896), 11. Many thanks to Gretchen Ritter for bringing this source to my attention and for sharing some of her findings in this area. For further accounts of the relation between race and discourse on money, see Ritter's *Goldbugs and Greenbacks*, esp. chaps. 3 and 6.

90. "Sound Currency Illustrated," *Sound Currency* 2 (October 1, 1895): 429. These cartoons were distributed in a special volume of *Sound Currency* and were then made available, print ready, for reproduction in newspapers and other periodicals, for shipping costs only. See Livingston, *Origins of the Federal Reserve*, 94.

91. Ibid., 486.

92. Ibid., 493.

93. Ibid., 491.

94. *Congressional Record*, 56th Cong., 1st sess. (Washington, D.C., 1900), 704–5. I have modernized Beveridge's spelling of "Filipino."

95. Julius Burrow quoted in Trumbull White, ed., *Silver and Gold* (New York, 1896), 296.

96. J. Howard Cowperthwait, *Money, Silver and Finance* (New York, 1892), 18, 22.

97. Edward Atkinson, "The Money of the Nation: Shall it be Good or Bad," *Sound Currency* 3 (July 1, 1895): 2.

98. William "Coin" Harvey, as Hofstadter pointed out, shared the tendency of certain Populist extremists to link gold with the "Jewish race" and silver with real Americans. But where Hofstadter saw this as an anomaly, a product of an extreme "paranoid style," I see this tendency pervading American politics and culture. On the centrality of paranoid thinking to American politics, see Michael Paul Rogin, *Ronald Reagan, the Movie* (Berkeley and Los Angeles, 1987), chaps. 1, 2, and 9.

99. Frederick Perry Powers, "A Financial Catechism," *Sound Currency* 2 (May 1895): 3.

100. Walker, "Immigration," *Yale Review* 1 (1892–93): 135–40.

101. Walker, "Immigration and Degradation," *Forum* 11 (1891): 644. On Walker's contribution to nativist racism, see Higham, *Strangers in the Land*, 142–43.

102. Memorandum, H. H. Rousseau to the executive secretary, Dec. 8, 1915, file 2-C-55, pt. 1a, General Records, 1914–34, RG 185, NA. Online at http://www.archives.gov/publications/prologue/1997/summer/panama-canal.html. See the detailed account in Julie Greene, *The Canal Builders: Making America's Empire at the Panama Canal* (New York, 2009), 60–69.

103. Elliott, *Color Blind Justice*, chap. 9.

Chapter Five

1. United States Congress, House, Committee on Banking and Currency, *Money Trust Investigation: Investigation of Financial and Monetary Conditions in the United States*, part 15 (Washington, D.C., 1913), 1084.

2. Ibid., 1081–82.

3. Ibid., 1084.

4. *New York Times*, December 22, 1912.

5. Anonymous, "The Second Part of South Sea Stock, Being an Inquiry into the Original of Province Bills, or Bills of Credit" (1721), in *Colonial Currency Reprints*, ed. Andrew McFarland Davis (New York, 1964), 2:313.

6. *New York Times*, November 10, 1907.

7. Gail Bederman, *Manliness and Civilization* (Chicago, 1996); Kristen Hoganson, *Fighting for American Manhood* (New Haven, Conn., 2000); Matthew

Frye Jacobson, *Barbarian Virtues* (New York, 2000); John Kasson, *Houdini, Tarzan and the Perfect Man* (New York, 2002).

8. Henry Herbert Goddard, *Feeble Mindedness: Its Causes and Consequences* (New York, 1916), 4–5 See also Stephen Jay Gould, *The Mismeasure of Man* (New York, 1981), 30–72.

9. Harvard Sitkoff, *A New Deal for Blacks: The Emergence of Civil Rights as a National Issue* (New York, 1978), 7.

10. Ibid., 7–8.

11. Carter Glass, *An Adventure in Constructive Finance* (New York, 1927), 111. Susan Hoffman, *Politics and Banking: Ideas, Public Policy, and the Creation of Financial Institutions* (Baltimore, 2001), 121, argues for the stress Glass placed on the "scientific" nature of the Federal Reserve.

12. Milton Friedman and Anna Schwartz, *A Monetary History of the United States, 1867–1960* (Princeton, 1963), 119.

13. See Robert F. Bruner and Sean D. Carr, *The Panic of 1907: Lessons Learned from the Market's Perfect Storm* (Hoboken, N.J., 2007).

14. Hoffman, *Politics and Banking*, 116.

15. John Kenneth Galbraith, *Money: Whence it Came, Where it Went* (Boston, 1975), 113.

16. Bertie Charles Forbes, *Men Who are Making America* (New York, 1922), 398.

17. G. Edward Griffin, *The Creature from Jekyll Island: A Second Look at the Federal Reserve* (1994; reprint ed. Westlake Village, Calif., 2002).

18. Concise explanations of the Federal Reserve are hard to come by. Information on the classes of directors taken from Federal Reserve Bank of San Francisco, "How the Fed is Organized," http://www.frbsf.org/publications/federal reserve/fedinbrief/organize.html. Allan Meltzer, *History of the Federal Reserve* (Chicago, 2009), 1–39. See also William Grieder, *Secrets of the Temple: How the Federal Reserve Runs the Country* (New York, 1987), passim.

19. Friedman and Schwartz, *Monetary History of the United States*, 189–96; Geider, *Secrets of the Temple*, chap. 9; Galbraith, *Money*, chap. 10.

20. Allan Meltzer's magisterial three volume *History of the Federal Reserve* devotes an entire chapter to the Bank of England and only a few lines to the failed American antecedents.

21. Jim Jam Jems, *The Federal Reserve Monster* (Bismarck, N.D., 1922), 1, 2, 6.

22. Ibid., 43, 15, 4.

23. Henry Langford Loucks, *The Great Conspiracy of the House of Morgan and How to Defeat It* (1916), 111, 239

24. *The International Jew: Jewish Activities in the United States* (Dearborn, Mich., 1921), 33.

25. *Dearborn Independent*, December 26, 1926, quoted in Neil Baldwin, *Henry Ford and the Jews* (New York, 2001), 215–16.

26. Friedman and Schwartz, *Monetary History*, 358.

27. Ibid., 372.

28. Herbert Hoover, *The Memoirs of Herbert Hoover: The Great Depression, 1929–1941* (New York, 1934), 30.

29. Robert Dimand, *The Origins of the Keynesian Revolution: The Development of Keynes' Theory of Employment and Output* (Stanford, Calif., 1988); Robert Leeson, *The Eclipse of Keynesianism: The Political Economy of the Chicago Counter-Revolution* (New York, 2001); Robert Dimand, Robert Mundell, and Allesandro Vercelli, eds., *Keynes's General Theory After Seventy Years* (New York, 2010); Robert Skildesky, *Keynes: The Return of the Master* (New York, 2009).

30. Galbraith, *Money*, 245.

31. The legal foundation for this act lay in the Trading with the Enemy Act of 1917, which had given the president broad power to oversee trade during war. It was amended and extended in the Emergency Banking Act of 1933, which gave the president authority to combat "hoarding." See Jordan Schwartz, ed., *1933: Roosevelt's Decision: The United States Leaves the Gold Standard* (New York, 1969), vii–xxiii and passim; and Frank Freidel, *FDR: Launching the New Deal* (Boston, 1973), 320–39. But the act did not take the U.S. off the international gold standard: in exchange between nations, U.S. dollars remained redeemable in gold until 1971.

32. On the legality of the act, see James Willard Hurst, *A Legal History of Money in the United States, 1774–1970,* (Lincoln, Neb., 1973), 235. On the ambiguity of this "standard," which still maintained something like gold redemption in international exchange, see Friedman and Schwartz, *Monetary History of the United States*, 90, 462–83; also Richard Timberlake, *Monetary Policy in the United States* (Chicago, 1993), 320–25; G. Griffith Johnson, *The Treasury and Monetary Policy, 1933–1938* (New York, 1939), 10–18.

33. *Congressional Record*, 73d Congress, 2d sess. (January 20, 1934), 971.

34. Ibid., 960.

35. Ibid., 961.

36. Roosevelt, "President Roosevelt Requests Legislation to Organize a Sound and Adequate Currency System," in *Documentary History of Banking and Currency*, ed. Herman E. Krooss (New York, 1983), 4:236.

37. Ibid., 2792.

38. Roosevelt, "President Roosevelt Requests Legislation," in *Documentary History of Banking*, 4:236.

39. Galbraith, *Money*, 214.

40. According to the theories of the influential "farm economist" George Warren, deliberate and sustained purchases of gold would increase its price in

dollars and devalue the dollar, producing an increase in the price of ordinary goods. It would also stimulate lending by adding to bank reserves. It failed largely because the government simultaneously seized private gold hoards, thus taking the profit from devaluation out of the consumer's hands. See Galbraith, *Money*, 210–13.

41. Franklin D. Roosevelt, *Public Papers and Addresses of Franklin D. Roosevelt* (New York, 1938), 5:617–18.

42. Johnson, *The Treasury and Monetary Policy*, 133–53.

43. See Timberlake, *Monetary Policy*, 295–99; Johnson, *Treasury and Monetary Policy*, chap. 5.

44. *New York Times*, January 27, 1933.

45. Roosevelt, "Some Notes for a Speech on Gold and other Monetary Manners," and the edited version of same, dated January 10, 1934, in "Selected Materials from the Papers of Franklin Delano Roosevelt Concerning Gold, 1933–1934," a microfilm reel in the Treasury Department Library, Washington, D.C. Hereafter abbreviated as "Selected Papers on Gold."

46. On FDR's general attitudes regarding race, see Greg Robinson, *By Order of the President: FDR and the Internment of the Japanese* (Cambridge, Mass., 2003).

47. Sitkoff, *New Deal for Blacks*, chap. 3.

48. Quotes from James Patterson, *Congressional Conservatism and the New Deal: The Growth of the Conservative Coalition in Congress, 1933–1939* (Lexington, Ky., 1967), 98, 257, 145, 195.

49. Roger Biles, *The South and the New Deal*, (Lexington, Ky., 2006) 140.

50. *New York Times*, February 2, 1936.

51. Chester M. Morgan, *Redneck Liberal: Theodore G. Bilbo and the New Deal* (Baton Rouge, La., 1988), 171.

52. *Time*, September 12, 1933, p. 10.

53. Morgan, *Redneck Liberal*, passim.

54. *Annual Report of the Director of the Mint*, 1936 (Washington, D.C., 1936), 6.

55. Freidman and Schwartz, *Monetary History of the United States*, 473.

56. William H. Harvey, *Coin's Financial School* (1895; reprint ed., Cambridge, Mass., 1963), 193; Galbraith, *Money*, 42–43.

57. See *Annual Report of the Director of the Mint* for 1933, 1934 and 1935. The Senate Committee on Military Affairs met to consider the transfer of land necessary to construct the vault, but the Treasury gives no reason for its request for transfer. See U.S. Congress, Senate, *Report No. 1169* (July 30, 1935).

58. The gold served in international exchange. If the Soviet Union needed to buy bauxite from Jamaica, employees of the Federal Reserve Bank in New York would carry gold bars from the USSR's cage in the vault to Jamaica's. The New York Fed merely stores the gold. Similar stores of gold exist in other places: Swit-

zerland, for example. Gold is still a valuable commodity: nations still own it and trade in it.

59. Bray Hammond, *Banks and Politics in America from the Revolution to the Civil War* (1958; reprint ed., Princeton, N.J., 1991), 70.

60. *New York Times*, August 8, 1936.

61. *Literary Digest*, January 16, 1937, p. 25.

62. "Guarding Your Gold," *Popular Mechanics* 71, no. 4 (April 1933): 573, 118A.

63. *Literary Digest*, May 23, 1935, p. 7.

64. Ibid., 8.

65. *Literary Digest*, August 29, 1936, p. 38.

66. *Congressional Record*, 76th Congress, 1st sess. (July 5, 1939), Appendix, p. 3033.

67. In *Fourteen Carrot Rabbit* (1952), duplicitous Klondike claim jumper Yosemite Sam lies repeatedly to fellow miners and violently tries to claim all gold for himself. Finally Bugs tricks Sam into chasing him across a map of the U.S. until they reach Kentucky. There Sam digs frantically, then finally emerges from the ground, stacking gold bars and shouting "I'm rich." He pauses to notice two military policeman, who haul him off to jail, while Bugs Bunny chortles "So long Sam! See you in twenty years!"

68. *Travel* 117–18 (September 1962): 50.

69. *New York Times*, April 18, 1952.

70. *New York Times*, March 28, 1951.

71. *New York Times*, January 7, 1953; January 11, 1953.

72. *New York Times*, January 31, 1953.

73. *New York Times*, February 12, 1953.

74. *The Washington Post*, March 30, 1939; *New York Times*, March 1, 1939; *The Christian Science Monitor*, February 24, 1939.

75. Scott Sandage, "A Marble House Divided: The Lincoln Memorial, the Civil Rights Movement, and the Politics of Memory, 1939–1963," *Journal of American History* 80 no. 1 (June 1993): 135–67.

76. Wanda Corn, *Grant Wood: The Regionalist Vision* (New Haven, Conn., 1983), 100.

77. *Time*, May 2, 1955, p. 23.

78. *Time*, May 5, 1961, p. 16.

79. *American Mercury* 79 (September 1954): 131–32; 86 (June 1958): 98–99.

80. *Life*, December 12, 1960, pp. 15–21.

81. The title essay in Walter Benn Michaels, *The Gold Standard and the Logic of Naturalism* (Berkeley and Los Angeles, 1987), points out that for many gold bugs the attraction to gold lay in imagining it never serving as money—imagining it as permanent and unchanging, stable and timeless.

82. *Newsweek*, December 21, 1964, pp. 72–73.

83. Searching the Internet in 2011 for the phrase "the Fort Knox of" produces nearly half a million results, including "the Fort Knox of uranium," "the Fort Knox of pet food," "the Fort Knox of external hard drives," and "the Fort Knox of prestige license plate covers."

Epilogue

1. Michael Lewis, *Liar's Poker: Rising Through the Wreckage on Wall Street* (New York 1989), 210.

2. *Wall Street*, DVD, directed by Oliver Stone (1987; Beverly Hills, Calif.: 20th Century Fox Home Entertainment, 2007).

3. The casting of the Sheens, who come from a Hispanic background but have assumed Irish names for their professional careers, reinforces the quasi-racial reading of the relation between money and character. Martin Sheen's other son, Emilio Estevez, is also an actor but uses his father's original last name. Stone obviously wanted to soften the film's anti-ethnic message by calling the characters "Fox," but when Gekko, riding with Fox in the back of his limo, derides the coldness and misanthropy of WASPs it seems clear that Fox is different, not a WASP.

4. *Wall Street* remains an iconic film. In the 2000 film *Boiler Room*, for example, the protagonists, a group of young Long Island ethnics on the rise, watch *Wall Street* repeatedly: they have memorized large chunks of the movie. *Boiler Room* has a remarkably similar plot—ethnic types rising quickly through unscrupulous practices, a father who stands for real and enduring values betrayed and then redeemed after the son is arrested and testifies for the prosecution against his former employer. The movie admires Carl Fox, Martin Sheen's character, but admires him because he knows his place.

5. *New York Times*, August 30, 1987.

6. *New York Times*, March 19, 1985.

7. It complicates the analysis to point out that Louis Stone was born Louis Silverstein, and changed his name to avoid anti-Semitism. He graduated from Yale and served as an aide to Dwight Eisenhower in World War II. See Lloyd Grove, "Oliver Stone's Mother Load," *Washington Post*, September 11, 1997.

8. Michael Lewis, *Liar's Poker*, 155.

9. Lewis, *Liar's Poker*, 36.

10. Ibid., 25.

11. The Latin comes from Tom Wolfe's *Bonfire of the Vanities* (New York, 1987), 60, which shares the same sadness at how "these sons of the great universities, these legatees of Jefferson, Emerson, Thoreau, William James, Frederick Jackson Turner, William Lyon Phelps, Samuel Flagg Bemis, and the other three-name giants of American scholarship—how these inheritors of the *lux* and the

veritas now flocked to Wall Street and the bond trading room." As an academic, I can share his sorrow at the failure of the liberal arts to restrain greed. But as a descendant of lowly Irish immigrants, I can't help but notice that it's a specific genetic legacy that he sees failing here—a bloodline, not a set of principles.

12. Ibid., 30.

13. Ibid., 48–49.

14. Ibid., 78.

15. Ibid., 68–69.

16. *Wall Street Journal*, September 1, 1971.

17. Friedman's statement appeared in *Time*, December 31, 1965. In the February 4, 1966 edition *Time* printed a letter from Friedman: "Sir: You quote me [Dec. 31] as saying: 'We are all Keynesians now.' The quotation is correct, but taken out of context. As best I can recall it, the context was: 'In one sense, we are all Keynesians now; in another, nobody is any longer a Keynesian.' The second half is at least as important as the first." For the Nixon quote see *New York Times*, January 10, 1971.

18. Milton Friedman and Anna Schwartz, *A Monetary History of the United States, 1867–1960* (Princeton, N.J., 1963).

19. Milton Friedman, *Capitalism and Freedom* (Chicago, 1962), 51.

20. Ibid., 15.

21. Friedman, *Capitalism and Freedom*, 111, 51. See also S. Herbert Frankel, *Money: Two Philosophies* (Oxford, 1977); George Macesich, *The Politics of Modernism* (Totowa, N.J., 1984); Gordon A. Fletcher, *The Keynesian Revolution and Its Critics: Issues of Theory and Policy for the Monetary Production Economy* (New York, 1986); Simon Clarke, *Keynesianism, Monetarism, and the Crisis of the State* (Brookfield, Vt., 1988); Charles P. Kindleberger, *Keynesianism vs. Monetarism and Other Essays in Financial History* (London, 1985).

22. Milton Friedman and Rose Freidman, *Two Lucky People: Memoirs* (Chicago, 1998), 208.

23. Milton Freidman, *Monetary Mischief: Episodes in Monetary Freedom* (New York, 1994), ix.

24. By "natural rate" Friedman meant something like the lowest level of unemployment that will not cause inflation. If unemployment drops close to zero, inflation results because when everyone is working, there is more money in the system, thus inflation. For monetarists, inflation is the main enemy. The "natural" rate of unemployment is the rate which prevents inflation. Friedman understood the grim implications of this phrase, that it makes unemployment a natural phenomenon like sunrise or the seasons, a structural inevitability and actually desirable. He wrote: "To avoid misunderstanding, let me emphasize that by using the term 'natural' rate of unemployment, I do not mean to suggest that it is immutable and unchangeable. On the contrary, many of the market characteristics that determine its level are man-made and policy-made. . . . I use the term

'natural' . . . to try to separate the *real forces* from the monetary forces." But the whole goal of monetarism is to make "monetary forces" operate like "real forces": that is, to make money be as much like natural law as possible. Friedman and Michael Bordo, "The Role of Monetary Policy," in *The Optimum Quantity of Money* (New Brunswick, N.J., 1969), 103; italics mine. Friedman distances himself from the determinist implications of the term, but persists in the argument that some economic forces are "real" and some are merely "monetary." In his Nobel Prize address, Friedman explicitly rejected the idea that "the social sciences . . . require fundamentally different methods of investigation than the biological sciences." "I myself have never accepted this view." But he went on to argue that in natural and human sciences "there is no 'certain' substantive knowledge," only the testing of hypotheses. Friedman was happy to use "natural" language for persuasive effect even while distancing himself from its implications.

25. *Newsweek*, February 19, 1973, p. 38.

26. Frederick Perry Powers, "A Financial Catechism," *Sound Currency* 2 (May 1895): 3.

27. "William Trenholm, "The People's Money," *Sound Currency* 2, issue 1 (December 1, 1894): 31.

28. Andrew Jackson, "Message Vetoing the Recharter of the Second United States Bank," July 10, 1832, reprinted in *Dearborn Independent*, June 26, 1926.

29. Ayn Rand, *The Fountainhead* (1943; reprint ed., New York, 2005), 727. My take here more or less follows Foucault's. It is not possible to imagine a self free from power relations: power relations are always the things out of which the self is made: the self cannot be free of power relations any more than bricks can be free of clay.

30. For an excellent overview see James Arnt Aune, *Selling the Free Market: The Rhetoric of Economic Correctness* (New York, 2002).

31. Murray N. Rothbard, "Origins of the Welfare State in America," *Mises Daily*, August 11, 2006; online at http://mises.org/daily/2225. Accessed August 7, 2010.

32. This quite extraordinary essay appeared originally in *The New Individualist Review* 3 (Summer 1963): 32–33; it appears online, with no apparent sense of irony, at "the Online Library of Liberty," a Project of Liberty Fund Inc., online at http://oll.libertyfund.org/?option=com_staticxt&staticfile=show.php%3F title=2136&chapter=195367&layout=html&Itemid=27.

33. The league states its goals at http://dixienet.org/New%20Site/whatthe southwants.shtml. The Southern Poverty Law Center offers a detailed account of the League at its website: http://www.splcenter.org/get-informed/intelligence-files/groups/league-of-the-south. In this view, slavery was not a manifestation of racism but a reflection of natural facts: *ending* slavery introduced racism.

34. Murray Rothbard, "Race! That Murray Book," in *The Irrepressible Roth-*

bard: The Rothbard-Rockwell Essays of Murray N. Rothbard (Burlingame, Calif., 2000), 390–91.

35. Murray N. Rothbard, *Egalitarianism as a Revolt against Nature and other Essays* (1974; reprint ed., Auburn, Ala., 2000), chap. 1.

36. For examples see Jason Kuznicki, "Never a Neutral State: American Race Relations and Government Power," *Cato Journal* 30, no. 3 (Fall 2009) 417–453; and Julian Sanchez, "Why Rand Paul Is Right . . . and Wrong," *Newsweek*, May 21, 2010.

37. Ludwig von Mises Institute, "Money Banking and the Federal Reserve," http://www.ronpaul.com/on-the-issues/fiat-money-inflation-federal-reserve/. Accessed August 4, 2010.

38. Ibid. Accessed August 8, 2010.

39. James Kirchick, "Angry White Man," *The New Republic*, January 30, 2008, p. 21. Paul claimed not to have written these passages and not to have known who wrote them: suspicion fell on Lew Rockwell, currently head of the von Mises Institute and formerly Paul's chief of staff, but he denied it and also claimed not to know. Rockwell and Rothbard seem the most likely suspects. See Julian Sanchez and David Weigel, "Who Wrote Ron Paul's Newsletters," *Reason*, January 16, 2008; online at http://reason.com/archives/2008/01/16/who-wrote-ron-pauls-newsletter. See also CNN's Politics.com at this link: http://www.cnn.com/2008/POLITICS/01/10/paul.newsletters/#cnnSTCOther1.

40. See Annie Lowery, "End the Fed? Actually, Maybe Not," at http://www.slate.com/id/2284503/.

41. Southern Poverty Law Center, *Intelligence Report*, no. 94 (Spring 1999).

42. *Washington Post*, November 17, 2007.

43. *United States vs. 3039.375 pounds of copper coins* (2009 U.S. Dist. LEXIS 69274).

44. *Washington Post*, November 17, 2007.

45. The Department of Justice press release announcing the conviction appears here: http://www.justice.gov/usao/ncw/press/nothaus.html. The U.S. Mint describes the case against "Liberty Dollars" here: http://www.usmint.gov/consumer/?action=archives#NORFED See also Eric Lach, "Feds Seeking $7M Worth of Privately Minted 'Liberty Dollars,'" at http://tpmmuckraker.talkingpointsmemo.com/2011/04/feds_seeking_7m_worth_of_privately-minted_liberty.php?ref=fpb. Accessed 4/4/2011.

46. David Frum, "Does Rand Paul Understand His Own Conspiracy Theories?" http://theweek.com/bullpen/column/203381/does-rand-paul-understand-his-own-conspiracy-theories.

47. http://www.youtube.com/watch?v=KL1O01FccaA. Accessed August 12, 2010.

48. http://www.marketwatch.com/story/do-we-need-a-north-american-currency?dist=TNMostRead. Accessed August 15, 2010.

49. Douglas Burns, "King sees some truth in far-fetched North American Union conspiracy, " in *Iowa Independent*, September 22, 2008

50. http://bachmann.house.gov/News/DocumentSingle.aspx?DocumentID=116036.

51. Stephanie Mencimer "Glenn Beck's Golden Fleece," *Mother Jones*, July/August 2010; online at http://motherjones.com/special-reports/2010/05/glenn-becks-golden-fleece.

52. Mencimer describes it thusly: "Twenty-franc Swiss coins are a little smaller than a nickel and contain a little less than two-tenths of an ounce of gold. The coins are about 60 to 110 years old and not especially hard to find (though Goldline describes them as 'rare'). They are not fully considered collectors' items nor commodities, making their value more subjective than bullion's. Goldline sets a 30 to 35 percent 'spread' on the coins, meaning that it will pay $375 to buy back coins it's currently selling for $500. At that rate, gold prices would have to jump by a third just for customers to recoup their investment, never mind making a profit. Investing in Goldline's 20 francs would be like buying a blue chip stock that lost a third of its value the minute it's purchased. It's difficult to think of any other investment that loses so much value almost instantly. So what persuades people to buy anyway?" http://www.stumbleupon.com/su/8RSkpl/motherjones.com/politics/2010/05/glenn-beck-goldline-weiner. Accessed August 4, 2010.

53. Wes Vernon, "21st Century Dark Ages Ahead?" at http://www.renewamerica.com/columns/vernon/101122. See also Jeff Neilson, "The Second Bubble Bursts," at http://www.gold-eagle.com/editorials_08/nielson062510.html; and Marc Faber, "Gloom and Doom report. Economic Collapse," at http://www.youtube.com/watch?v=Cr2AEYd_1d8. All accessed March 16, 2011.

54. Craig R. Smith and David Bradshaw, "Morally-Correct Money for the 21st Century" (September 4, 2009); online at http://www.swissamerica.com/article.php?art=09-2009/200909041235f.txt. Accessed August 5, 2010.

55. Smith quoted at "Kamikaze President: Expert Outlines how Obama's Crashing the Dollar," at http://specialguests.com/guests/viewnews.cgi?id=EkIZVuFyyVJvRCMpOm&style=Full%20Article, a site designed to serve conservative talk show hosts. Accessed March 16, 2011.

56. http://www.roslandcapital.com/testimonials/. Accessed August 6, 2010.

57. http://www.learcapital.com/marketcommentary/7028.html. Accessed August 5, 2010.

58. "Should We Brace for Deflation Now?" *New York Times*, August 12, 2010; online at http://www.nytimes.com/roomfordebate/2010/8/11/should-we-brace-for-deflation-now/make-inflation-happen. As of this writing, March 16, 2011, what inflation the economy is experiencing is related to the political crisis in the Middle East, and the earthquake/nuclear catastrophe in Japan, raising oil prices.

59. Eric Lach, "Fox News Discusses Return of Gold as Everyday Currency,"

at http://tpmmuckraker.talkingpointsmemo.com/2010/11/fox_news_discusses_
return_of_gold_as_everyday_curr.php?ref=fpblg. Accessed March 16, 2011.

60. The gold vending machines are described to customers at http://www
.gold-to-go.com/en/the-gold-vending-machine/the-gold-vending-machine/. On
the Miami gold vending machine see Kelli Kennedy, "Fancy ATM skips the
folding cash, spits out gold," (December 17, 2010) at http://www.miamiherald
.com/2010/12/18/1978875/fancy-atm-skips-the-folding-cash.html.

61. On Georgia, see Ian Millhiser, "Georgia Bill Would Force State Taxpayers to Pay Only in Gold or Silver," at http://thinkprogress.org/2010/12/29/georgia
-gold/; on South Carolina, see Josh Marshall, "South Carolina May Adopt Own
Currency," at http://www.talkingpointsmemo.com/archives/2011/02/picking_up_
on_the_ancestral.php#more?ref=fpblg; on Utah, see http://www.foxnews.com/
politics/2011/03/04/utah-house-passes-recognizing-gold-silver-legal-tender/; on
Montana, see Drew Zahn, "State Considers Return to Gold, Silver dollars" at
http://www.wnd.com/?pageId=92000. All accessed March 10, 2011.

Index

Lightning Source UK Ltd.
Milton Keynes UK
UKOW06n2107110617
303079UK00008B/57/P